1-2002

Angela
&
GEMMA — Can!
Yes you Can!

[signature]

GET OFF YOUR YO-YO!

ACHIEVE BALANCE IN YOUR DAILY LIFE!

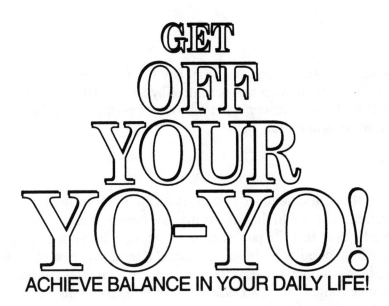

DR. ZONNYA

This publication is designed to provide accurate and authoritative information in regard to the subject matter covered. It is sold with the understanding that the publisher is not engaged in rendering legal, accounting, or other professional service. If legal advice or other assistance is required, the services of a competent professional person should be sought. *From A Declaration of Principles jointly adopted by a Committee of the American Bar Association and a Committee of Publishers.*

Library of Congress Cataloging-in Publication Data
Zonnya, Dr., 1949-
    Get off your yo-yo! : achieve balance in your daily life / by Dr. Zonnya
        p. cm.
    Includes index.
    ISBN 0-8119-0807-0 : $19.95
    1. Self-actualization (Psychology)   I. Title.
BF637.S4Z66   1995
158--dc20   95-3387
                               CIP

Manufactured in the United States of America

1 2 3 4 5 6 7 8 9 0

Dedication

This book is dedicated with my deepest love and appreciation to my husband, Bob. His love, belief in me, and faith in my ability to touch lives, encourages me to be **more, better, greater** in every area of my life. We have shared the best and worst times and I am grateful that we have travelled our life-journey together.

Acknowledgments

There are so many people who are a part of this project. Without them and their unique contribution, I would have been unable to reach my goal of writing this material. They have touched my life and I want to give recognition, appreciation and praise to each.

Jeanne Bader
Dr. Steve Beke
Sheila M. Burney
John Butler
Renée Butler
Lynn Caldwell
Rita Carney
Ron Chase
Harriet Coren
Casey Corwin
Dr. Harry Covert
Don Cox
Dr. Mark Davis
Alice and Mike DeLorenzio
Tracy Dyer
Syd Entel
Brian Feinblum
Don Frankenberg
Becky Hale
Rev. Ludie Harrington
Rev. Robert Harrington
Vicki Heil
Patricia Henning
Carolyn and Jim Hunter
Marianne Goebel Kamon

Dr. Timothy Kelley
Jean Kingsbury
J.L. LaFerney
Dr. Kurt Lotspeich
Andrea Mansur
Dr. Mary McCormick
J. Patrick McElroy
John Parker
Chris Pearl
Cheryl M. Persall
Pam Phillips
Debbie Pirkle
Jeff and Lu Prince
Debra Reiter
Ginny and Ed Rickles
Marc Rose
Larry Russell
Dennis Schulman
Lisa Seward
Bertie Smith
Shirrell Walter Smith, Jr.
Rev. Allan Stuart
Robert Tissot
Karen L. Valentine
Rev. Jim Willowby
King Z and Prince B

"Most of us will have so little respect for life that we will reach the point of death without ever having lived at all."
— Henry David Thoreau

Table of Contents

Introduction

*Playing with a yo-yo can be fun;
living life like a yo-yo will make you dizzy.*

Up - down, happy - sad, in love - out of love, losing weight - gaining weight, thinking positive - thinking negative, getting married - getting un-married, attending church - not attending church, excited - depressed. Are you dizzy yet? I know I am.

You may very well understand what living life on a yo-yo is like. While you may be smiling at the thoughts of living life like a yo-yo, it is clear that many times in your life you find yourself going up and down, up and down and really not getting anywhere. If you are going to live life productively and enjoyably, then you must **GET OFF YOUR YO-YO!**.

This experience called life is part of a journey we are on, one that I term the "life-journey". It has a beginning called birth. It has a middle called life. It has an end called death. I am convinced that the philosopher, Henry David Thoreau, only too well, understood that most people would reach death, the end of their journey, without ever having experienced life.

On our journey, we will travel many different roads. We will travel physical roads, health and sickness roads. There will be relationship roads with family, mates, children and friends. A few very important roads will be those of career, business, finances and money. From the beginning of our journey until the end, we will be faced with roads that will require many choices and decisions. Although each of our roads will be different, just as we are individually different, I believe there are some commonalities of the journey.

On our journey and on the roads we travel, there are directions we can follow to help us travel our roads with all of those positive qualities and characteristics we want to enjoy on this life-journey: good health, a clear mind, fulfilling relationships, job productivity, happiness and peace. I have termed these directions that we can follow as: "SignPosts". The purpose of SignPosts is to alert, direct, encourage, guide, instruct and warn us of what is ahead on the road. There are many SignPosts to follow that will help you **GET OFF YOUR YO-YO!**.

This Is It

This thing called life; this thing called today: "This Is It!" This is not rehearsal; there is no stop action for retakes; there is no repeat; this is not practice, and there is no summer re-run. "This Is It!"

Yet, far too often we never learn to live before we die. Life is a precious gift given to us at birth. Life will always be our most real and valued possession. Yet as Thoreau noted in *WALDEN*, "Most of us will have so little respect for life that we will reach the point of death without ever having lived at all". Often, we get so concerned about life after death that we forget about life after birth.

Generally speaking, all of us are concerned about our lives and usually we have high expectations of the kind of life we want to experience. However, we really are not taught, except by trial and error, how to go about achieving the kind of life we desire. Except for some rather vague and broad instructions, none of us is ever taught how to live. There is no school for living. There are few teachers of instruction. There are "scarce" models for examples. So, the questions become: Where and how do we learn what living life to the fullest really means?

Education alone does not give us the answers. Religion, alone, does not provide solutions. Government falls short in many areas. Family is limited because of the human liabilities that comprise it. News media only serves to point out the worst. So where do we go for the answers?

It is no wonder that many people live life on a yo-yo. How do we want to live life? Up? Down? Flat-lined? No, we want to live life with some sense of balance. Could balanced living be the answer to yo-yo living?

Balanced living offers alternatives to the many perplexing challenges that arise in your life on a daily basis. The questions and problems you face can be used to your constructive advantage if you know how to address them. It is productive to have questions, problems and challenges if you have answers, solutions and alternatives. What is not productive as you travel your roads is to have few or no answers, solutions and alternatives.

You will greatly benefit from the balanced living system. When you know and apply the answers, solutions and alternatives, you can experience productivity and enjoyment on every road of your life-journey. To achieve this, you must become a self-motivated student. You must be willing to take risks, look inside yourself, succeed and fail, and most of all, to grow regardless of the pain! You must fully understand and accept that with "gain," there can be "pain!"

Also, it is important to note that living life in balance does not mean "perfect" living. Achieving more balance in your life will not mean that you won't have to deal with "real life stuff." A lot of things and situations comprise the "real life stuff" we must deal with on a daily basis; i.e.: sickness, death, work, traffic, taxes, children, teenagers, mates, hurry, worry, stress, and the list is endless. The only term that I know that covers all of it is "real life stuff" and it is a part of the journey. What the balanced living system will do is help you address the "real life stuff" and enjoy the journey more.

The task of learning to live life to the fullest will be mainly left up to you as an individual. You will largely be your own teacher. Of course, there will be those from whom you can learn. Others can share ideas and thoughts. But when it comes down to the practical adaptation and actualization, the responsibility will be up to you, individually. As United States President, Harry Truman, from the great state of Missouri said, "The buck stops here."

For many, that responsibility will be too great a price to pay. But for a few, the rewards and benefits will be worth the effort and pain which translates into a life-journey worth taking.

Since we are all different, there will be no one way to experience this life-journey. There will be many different roads to choose and many SignPosts from which to choose. The choices will be yours to make. Your lifestyle will be individually different and unique.

The uniqueness of you is of utmost value. The inherent differences in you are sacred and should be protected at all costs. You are not a robot with a hairdo. You are not a yo-yo with a divine umbilical cord connected to the Creator of the universe. You are created in the greatest image of all. You are created by the greatest nobility and have been given the greatest ability and that is to experience the life-journey as you choose to travel it. It is through your choices and your individual uniqueness that you can make things happen on the roads of your life-journey.

Begin and begin now! Today is the day! Now is the time! This Is It! You must accept the reality that there is very little, if anything at all, you can do about yesterday. Yesterday is gone; tomorrow is not here. When tomorrow gets here, it will be today. So this is where your major emphasis must be. Certainly, you must set goals. The purpose of goal-setting is to make the present day fulfilling. Dedicate yourself, today, to learning to live before you die.

Throughout this book, I want to share with you questions, along with some answers; problems, along with some solutions; challenges, along with some alternatives to the experiences that the life-journey presents. The insights and SignPosts presented here are dedicated to offering you ideas, methods, and systems that are practical and adaptable to living in today's world.

All of us have read self-improvement books, listened to audio cassettes, watched video training cassettes, and attended seminars and meetings on how to be a better person, how to get motivated, how to get rich and a host of other "how to's". However, in most cases, what we got from the initial exposure was a "feeling" and then in a few days, the "feeling" left and we were back in the same old rut or even in a deeper rut.

We want to believe that there is a system that will work for us in our lives, and then, there are times when we are sure that it is all Pollyanna and none of it will work. All of us have experienced hearing or reading something that sounded good, but we just could not put it into practice. If you have experienced just one of these kinds of situations, this book is for you. I am diligently committed to presenting simple, practical, adaptable, usable, and workable systems, not lofty, pie-in-the sky ideas. These systems, when applied properly, will change the course of your life-journey.

Once, when I was conducting a seminar in Kansas City, after having presented part one, I gave the audience a break. One of the men attending walked up to me and asked to speak with me privately. He said: "Dr. Zonnya, I have attended seminars like this before, I've read books, listened to tapes, watched videos, and Dr. Zonnya, this stuff doesn't work." I gently, but firmly replied: "You're right. The stuff doesn't work; you have to work the stuff." I guarantee that if you work the systems and follow the SignPosts that I share in these pages, you will experience your life-journey with more pleasure and less pain.

If you want "more" of the good life, within these pages you will find ideas to help you achieve it! Don't be afraid of or shy away from, the word "more." Many philosophies and even religious teachings will insist that to want "more" is wrong. This teaching is a misleading SignPost. Do not be confused or side-tracked by these unrealistic opinions and misleading SignPosts. Whatever you have in life, you can have "more!" Wherever you are in life, you can be "more".

Does this mean that you can never settle for what you are? Yes, I am saying that you cannot settle for what you are, when you can become so much "more, better, greater". When you were created, you were given 100% of creative potential. Research shows, that on your best day, you are using only 8% - 10% of your potential. I don't know about you, but I think this should be against the law! What happens to the other 92% or 90%? It's not being used. While I will be the first to agree that in the complete experience of your life-journey, you most probably will never use 100%, I believe that you, and I am included here too, can increase the use of our mind, our creativity, our productiveness and our enjoyment of our life-journey.

You are healthy and you would like to be "more" healthy. You are happy and you would like to be "more" happy. You are wealthy and you would like to be "more" wealthy. You have good relationships and you would like to have "more" and even better relationships. You have a good lifestyle and you would like an even "more" beautiful lifestyle. Wouldn't you? Of course, you would. This is just the material that can help you achieve "more" of whatever it is that you desire and put an end to yo-yo living.

Abraham Maslow did much scientific study regarding the "special inner life" of the human being. Throughout his life, he continued to puzzle about why some of us were able to make something of ourselves and why others did not seem to "make it." He stated:

"Only a small portion of the human population get to the point of identity, or of self-hood, full humanness, self-actualization, etc., even in a society like ours which is relatively one of the most fortunate on the face of the earth. This is the great paradox. We have the impulse toward full development, then why is it that it doesn't happen more often?"

Maslow's point is well taken in today's world. We seem to want to improve, yet so many of us never seem to find the way to actually do it. We want to experience the "more" and better of life, but often, we don't know where to start. The problems seem to get so much of our attention, that we never get around to finding the solutions.

I personally related to Maslow's impulse toward wanting full development, but in reality, I took very little action. I, just like you, had many problems with few solutions. I had potential that was untapped. I had abilities that were dying. I had questions with few answers. I felt and experienced feelings of failure and frustration.

The answers, solutions and alternatives began to surface once I became fully committed to finding them. They are not "easy," but I have found they are "simple." "Easy" and "simple" are not synonymous; they definitely do not mean the same. For me, the art of living life in balance consists of a simple daily system to approaching this life-journey. As I present my message, I strive to share information, inspiration, motivation and a little humor with you as you travel your life-journey. If you gain just one new idea, if you incorporate just one new system from what you will read in the pages ahead, then I will have been fulfilled and you will have benefitted tremendously.

From time to time as together we explore this system of balanced living, I will ask you to take an inventory of the different areas of your life. Throughout, you will want to involve yourself in self-actualization, self-realization and self-introspection. As we travel this journey, I will provide specific exercises and ask you to participate. Different affirmations, meditations and plans for action will be offered for your consideration. Every system is presented for you to use as it applies to you individually. Neither guilt nor fear will be presented, thereby, creating for you an environment that will be conducive to both your personal and professional growth.

As we begin this unique experience of learning to approach life from a balanced perspective, I ask you to open your mind, your heart, your emotions, your rationale, and absorb what you can use to improve your life and enjoy an even more beautiful lifestyle. When I was a young woman, my daddy gave me a SignPost to follow:

Your Mind Is Like A Parachute;
It Has To Be Open To Work

Don't you know people who have a closed mind? If you review the quality of their life, you will find it to be substandard. You will find that they have only one way of seeing things.

You Can't Do Things Differently Until
You First See Things Differently

To see things differently, you must have an open mind to different ways of looking at things. I sincerely hope as you read these pages you will have an open mind and that some of the ideas shared will help you see things differently. It will be then, and only then, that you will do things differently.

Never let slip from your mind or from your perspective that you have only one lifetime to travel these roads of life. Each step moves you closer to the journey's end. You will choose the roads that you will travel; you will continue to change course and direction. You will always be reminded that you can never retrace a road that you have already experienced. What you can do is relentlessly dedicate and commit yourself to experiencing all the "more" of the best that you will make happen. In so doing, the purpose for your life becomes known and provides you with everlasting meaning in your own life and in the lives you touch.

Where do you start in order to get off your yo-yo? You start right where you are on the roads of your journey.

When do you start? You start now - at this very present moment.

With whom do you start? You start with yourself.

How do you start? You have taken the first step by making this material a part of your life-journey. You have my promise that there are many systems and SignPosts within these pages that will be just what you have been looking for and just what the doctor ordered to get you off your yo-yo and get you on the road of living life in balance.

Remember the SignPost: This Is It

A Personal Note
From Dr. Zonnya

I want to thank you for allowing me to be a part of your life-journey. You are to be applauded for choosing to be a student of life and of personal and professional growth. There is much to learn about this experience called "living" and it is an honor for me to share my ideas with you.

There are hundreds of books written on the subjects of self-help, motivation, how to's, etc. Each of them have something of value between their covers. So you may ask: "What makes this book different from all the others?"

In order to succinctly answer this very valid question, I will answer it in two parts. First, I bring to your table my life-world, intrinsically different from any other author you will ever read. Second, the systems I present are simple, practical, adaptable, usable and workable. I guarantee you "Immediate Success" when you understand and apply the systems shared between the covers of **GET OFF YOUR YO-YO!**

You are on a journey, and you will travel many roads before you reach the end of your journey. Many people will touch your life and you will touch the lives of many others. I deeply appreciate the opportunity to touch your life with positive powerful systems that will change the way you travel your journey. Equally important, thank you for touching my life. We both will be better for having encountered each other on our life-journey.

Part I — Part II

Because of the nature of this material and the way it is outlined, I have chosen to divide the book into two parts. Hopefully, it will offer you an opportunity to gain an effective perspective of the material presented. I want you to feel a sense of continuity without belaboring either the basic foundations of balance or the systems for applications. This entire work is written with ideas, concepts and systems for your use. Each chapter offers you answers, solutions and alternatives for getting off your yo-yo.

PART I: BALANCED LIVING BASICS AND FOUNDATIONS

In Part I, you will learn the basics and the foundations on which balanced living is built. The basics will serve to alert you to the systems and how you can apply them in Part II.

In Part I, you will receive great benefits from:

Chapter 1: Out-of-Balance Is No Fun

Chapter 2: Balanced Living For A More Beautiful Lifestyle

Chapter 3: Get Back to the Basics

Chapter 4: Balanced Self-Love

Chapter 5: Build Your Balanced Self-Love

At the end of each chapter, there will be a "Recap" of the chapter highlights. I will ask you to take a "Personal Self Inventory." This is vital to you if you are honest and sincere about your progress toward getting off your yo-yo. I will, also, share with you "Dr. Zonnya's First Aid" (things you can do to move you forward on the road to balance). Also, "Affirmations" will be presented for your use in maintaining balance in your life on a daily basis.

PART II: SYSTEMS FOR BALANCED LIVING

In Part II, we will examine, one by one, each area that composes your life-journey. Just as a car runs on four wheels, your life runs on six wheels. Just as a car will ride rough when one of the wheels is out of balance, so will your life-journey be rough when one of your six areas is out of balance. One of the goals, as we share these systems, is to identify where you are out of balance and then implement the systems that will put you back in balance and off the yo-yo.

We will apply each of the following three basics to each area of your life:

1. Awareness
2. Importance
3. Responsibility

Each area of your life will be discussed individually.

In Part II, we will discuss:

Chapter 6:   Physical Balance

Chapter 7:   Mental Balance

Chapter 8:   Spiritual Balance

Chapter 9:   Social Balance

Chapter 10: Financial Balance

Chapter 11: Family Balance

In each chapter, we will look at what keeps us out-of-balance, as well as the questions, problems and challenges that confront us daily and throughout our lives. In turn, you are offered simple, practical, usable and workable answers, solutions and alternatives. My promise to you is that I will not present a problem without presenting a viable solution.

As in Part I, Part II will offer you:

1. A Chapter Recap
2. Personal Self Inventory
3. Dr. Zonnya's First Aid
4. Affirmations

Part I presents the basics and foundations.
Part II presents the areas and systems for each of the six areas.

As we begin this journey together, I want to make just one request of you. Please adapt each idea, each system, each SignPost to yourself. Take your valuable and precious time and devote it to living life each moment to the fullest. Read each word, each line, each page and know without doubt that I want to share at least one idea that will benefit you. If you find something that you question - research it! If you find something that you don't like - "flush it"! Focus on what can be of help to YOU!

It is obvious that you are a student of self-improvement. You want to get off the yo-yo; you want to achieve a sense of balance on your life-journey. I thank you for allowing me to be a part of your personal and professional growth!

Remember the SignPost: This Is It

"Having more of life and less of death is what it's all about!"
— Henry David Thoreau

PART I

BALANCED LIVING BASICS AND FOUNDATIONS

Every system must have basics and foundations upon which it is developed and built. The balanced living system for your life-journey, also has basics and foundations. Once you know the basics, you can choose to implement them in your life. When you get away from the basics, you can always choose to get back to them.

You are on a journey and you have taken the first step toward getting off your yo-yo.

Chapter 1

OUT-OF-BALANCE IS NO FUN

"You do not have to suffer continual
chaos in order to grow."
—John Lilly, English Dramatist

Remember earlier, I said: "Playing with a yo-yo can be fun; living life like a yo-yo will make you dizzy." To that I add: "Out-Of-Balance Is No Fun."

There is one word that sums up the out-of-balance condition and that word is "problems."

PROBLEMS! PROBLEMS! PROBLEMS!

Everybody has PROBLEMS!

Everywhere you look, there are problems. Everyone you know has problems. Everything you hear is about problems. How did we arrive on the "problems" road of our life-journey? What can we do to solve our problems? "How?" and "What?" are the two proverbial questions that have seemed to linger through generation after generation.

I think we can agree that before we can solve a problem, we must first know what it is. But, there may be one more step that we need to take before we can solve the problem. It may be necessary to understand "how" the problem evolved. I use the term "how" as opposed to "why" for a specific reason. I have learned over many years of experience in dealing with people and life situations that there is not always an answer to "why". Many people will beat themselves up asking: Why did this happen to me or my family? Why me?

When in reality, there may or may not be an answer to "why?" However, 99% of the time, there is an answer to "how?" An interesting thought about asking the question "why?": If you knew "why?," would it change the facts or the reality? 99% of the time, it would not. So in lieu of this insight, I find it more productive to ask "how?" and in so doing, learn more about the problem itself.

I propose there are three questions you must ask yourself when you find yourself dealing with a problem, question or challenge.

- ☑ What Is The Problem?
- ☑ How Did The Problem Evolve?
- ☑ What Can I Do To Solve The Problem?

These are the three major questions that I asked myself when I first began to notice my life was out-of-balance. I will ask you to carefully consider these three questions and your personal answers. Often, the answers to many of your problems will originate from within you once you have cleared your thought road of debris and garbage.

After my own soul-searching, asking questions, and self-introspection, I recognized that the problems on my life-journey originated from being out-of-balance. I literally lived the dizzy yo-yo life on a daily basis. After some time, I realized what I was choosing to do with my life. I asked myself the same three questions that you will need to ask yourself, and then I made a decision that my journey was too short to live it the way I was experiencing it. From this decision, many of the systems and SignPosts presented here were developed.

Having problems without solutions is no fun. Having questions without answers is no fun. Having challenges without alternatives is no fun. Being out-of-balance is no fun, either.

You can add one more "no-fun" factor to yo-yo living. We generally do not like ourselves very much when we are burdened down with problems. Our self-value, self-worth, self-confidence are intensely affected when we go up and down. While we seem to know the effects of yo-yo living, often we do not take the measures to prevent ourselves from experiencing it, nor do we exert the effort to solve the problems.

Let us discuss some of the problems or shall we call them out-of-balance conditions that you do, or can, experience. You may have experienced, are experiencing, or will experience such conditions.

Overweight, loneliness, stress, burn-out, divorce, nervous break-down, worry, guilt, depression, debt, bankruptcy, failure, alcoholism, drug abuse, thoughts of suicide...the list of out-of-balance conditions is endless. Doesn't the list sound like I've just read the morning paper or have been listening in on someone's telephone conversation? In our society, in our families, and in our own individual lives, we experience far too many of the out-of-balance conditions on a daily basis.

Would it surprise you to know that most people experience being out-of-balance and are convinced that it is part of the scheme of life? In my research, in my daily work, and in my own daily life, I have arrived at some rude awakenings. Most people are out-of-balance and expect to be so during the entire course of their lifetime. Most people are not happy, or productive, or successful, and do not expect to be. Most people are sick, sad, sarcastic, and suffer through what should be a joyous celebration of challenge and reward on the life-journey.

Mental health statistics continue to show an increase in patients being treated both in institutions and in out-patient clinics. The rise in emotionally disturbed children is frightening. The use of prescription drugs to control a countless number of conditions prevails. Thousands of men, women, and now boys and girls, commit suicide every year. Much to our chagrin, the numbers are alarming and growing.

Divorce rates remain high. Men and women continue to treat the out-of-balance marriage by choosing to terminate it, rather than repair it by putting it into balance. Spouse and child abuse has become almost epidemic. Shelters and homes for the battered are now a priority in most communities. The rate of runaways has so increased that neither legal nor social nor religious institutions can begin to serve their needs.

Death from cancer caused by cigarette smoking has increased every year in spite of the knowledge we have concerning its effects. Early heart attacks, strokes and vital organ diseases continue to increase even with the warnings medical science offers us. It seems the capability we have to prevent problems is not what we prefer to do. Most of us seem to prefer the extensive and costly treatment that the problems require once they are identified.

Alcohol and drug abuse have never been as prevalent as they are today. Not only do the alcoholics and drug abusers create severe out-of-balance problems for themselves, but they bring devastating problems to family, friends and innocent victims.

We all seem to be familiar with many of these situations. We have experienced many of these problems personally. Many have been experienced by people we love. You may be thinking by now that Dr. Zonnya is very negative and a bearer of doomsday news. Please understand this is not the reason I want to clearly paint the out-of-balance picture. I remain convinced that we must know what the problem is, identify how the problem evolved, and then proceed to find the solution. It is my choice to prevent rather than treat when possible. Of course, there will always be a need for treatment. I only want to make the point that many of our problems could be prevented if we use productive systems and follow guiding SignPosts.

Treat or Prevent? That Is The Question

Down through history, it seems as though our society has always preferred to treat rather than prevent the problems that exist on our life-journey. We are a treatment-oriented society as opposed to a prevention-oriented society. We tend to wait until we have a problem and then desperately search for a treatment. Fortunately, we do have an alternative to this kind of lifestyle choice. We can choose to prevent many of our problems. In preventing rather than treating, we often are able to reduce the problems encountered, to diminish the cost that our problems present, and to lessen the emotional and psychological effects that most problems carry with them.

Personally speaking, I have experienced out-of-balance living. It is important that we remember that in the bigger picture, we are not taught how to live in balance. We grow up with people who are out-of-balance and therefore, we learn by example what out-of-balance living is. Because we tend to be highly affected by our environment, we learn to treat instead of prevent. We are programmed to see the world and our lives, in particular, from an out-of-balance viewpoint. Once we become adults, we are primed and ready to begin our own out-of-balance journey.

It must be noted that we cannot march to the beat of today's drum while harboring within us the crutches of our past teachings.

We are not prisoners of the past. We can begin where we are. As we will discover, there can be no blame if we are to enjoy the journey of balanced living. However, I do feel it is necessary to recognize and deal with the fact that every person and every event that we experience does play a part in the kind of life we ultimately lead.

From our past and present experiences, we can choose to become self-motivated students dedicated to the study and discovery of our individual selves. Becoming that student will be in and of itself one of the greatest challenges. It will be fun, frustrating and frightening. It may totally surprise you that many of the people you know, your family, friends and peers, will not want to accept this challenge for themselves and will not want you to accept this challenge, either.

This is when your commitment to living must be like a fortress. You will be required to struggle with those who wish you to remain the same. You will need to understand the reasons those you know and love may be your greatest obstacles. Always remember:

Little People Don't Like
To Be Around Big Thinkers

As a matter of fact, little thinkers become big stinkers to anyone who is wanting more out of life.

Watch out for the little squirts. They will drip on you and get you so warped that you will forget where you are going. Hang around people like yourself who are choosing to turn yo-yo living into balanced living. Dedication and commitment to being a self-motivated student is essential. There can be no substitute for what these two learned qualities can bring to getting off the yo-yo and achieving balance in your life. Dedicate yourself to making the choices that lead you to happiness, health, love, success, wealth, etc. Commit to self-inventory, honesty, and plans for action that will help you realize your dreams.

Everything Is A Matter Of Choice;
Choice Equals Results

I feel it is important to share further insights with you regarding the "choice" SignPost because it is indeed, the foundation for your life-journey. Choice is the primary element for every action, reaction and response. We understand what an "action" is, but let me make a distinction between "reaction" and "response". A reaction is an automatic impulse to an action. A response is a thought process that leads to a choice for action. A simple example that will make this clear is that of touching a hot stove (action), and without thinking, you pull your hand back (reaction). On the other hand, you quickly engage in a thought process and choose to put ice or aloe or some other medication on the blister (response). When you realize the difference in these two terms, you can: (1) internalize them; (2) actualize a crystal clear focus of your choices; (3) know who is in charge of making your choices; and (4) choose how you will respond to situations that you do not choose.

Everything is a matter of choice. From the time you are born, the process of choice-making begins. As you grow from infancy into childhood, you began to make more choices, although many choices will be made for you at this juncture of the life-journey. As you become a teenager and finally an adult, everything will be a matter of choice and choice equals results.

If you live a yo-yo life, it is because you choose to, and from this choice, you will receive yo-yo results. If you live a balanced life, it will be because of your choice and you will receive the results of that choice. Whatever results you are experiencing in your life right now is because of the choices you have made or are making. If you are happy with the results, then keep making the same choices. If you are not happy with the results, then you can choose to change your choices.

While I think it is simple to understand that your choices equal your results, there is one area of choice-making that is more demanding to comprehend. However, once you fully understand the concept, it will change the way you look at what happens to you on your life-journey. Have you ever had something happen to you that you absolutely had no control over? You did not choose it, and yet it may have dramatically affected your life. I have, and I am sure you have, too. How does the "choice" SignPost apply to this scenario? Let me answer that question with another SignPost.

What Happens To You In Your Life Is
Not As Important As How You Choose To
Respond To What Happens To You

Once again, it comes back to choice. Let me share with you some real life situations that will give you total clarity as to how you can apply this SignPost to your own life.

I have a good friend in Ohio who was in a motorcycle accident that left him paralyzed from the neck down. His initial reaction was one of anger, denial and seclusion. After much time with the help of family and friends, he thought about his choice, and he changed his reaction to a response. He chose to respond to something that he did not choose to happen to him. He decided to put together a program on playground safety for middle school children. Because of his need for assistance in moving himself around, he added a big furry friend to his life, Champ. Champ is a big dog who just loves children. After his presentation to the children, they all gather around and play with Champ. My friend is making a difference in the lives of the children because he knows and follows the SignPost.

What Happens To You In Your Life
Is Not As Important As
How You Choose To Respond
To What Happens To You

You are probably familiar with the scenario of one mate choosing to end a relationship, while the other mate does not want the relationship to end. Once one mate has made the choice to leave, the second mate now has choices to make. Although the second mate did not choose what initially happened, the second mate will choose a response to what happened.

A teenager makes a choice that affects the parents. While the parents had no control over the choice the teenager made, the parents will choose to respond.

Everything Is A Matter Of Choice;
Choice Equals Results

Now, you've come to the point on your life-journey where you will choose to exist or live.

Existing or Living?

The statistics, unfortunately, indicate that most people are satisfied to stay just the way they are. They dislike themselves and where they are. They would choose, if they could, to be someone else and somewhere else. Yet, they remain the same. Those same people are the ones who are suspicious of those who grow and change. Those same people are restrained by fear, overcome by guilt, and conquered by self-defeating thoughts and actions. They refuse to become self-motivated students of life. They ignore the fact that they have only one trip on the life-journey. They have little concern for their lifestyles or personal growth.

They are what I call "Existing", which is defined as settling for **less** in life. "Living" is defined as experiencing **more** in life. Thousands upon thousands of people choose to go through life merely existing. Obviously, you have chosen to be among the few who want to go through life living. You've made your choice to change and grow.

Out-of-balance living begins when one refuses to change and grow. The idea that we make our own life is not new, but most of us resist it because if we do in fact accept it, we will be forced to change, grow, make different choices, and be individually responsible for the successes and failures that we make happen. If we accept this responsibility, we will have to stop blaming others. As we all know, it is much easier not to accept the idea that we make our own life. But, we must also know that the rewards and benefits are not the same when we refuse to make our own choices and be responsible for our own lives.

If we make choices that create the existing way of life, we will settle for **less**. On the other hand, we can make choices that create the living way of life and experience **more** as we travel our life-journey. To know if you are existing or living, you will want to take a self-inventory. Let me share with you my experience with a very revealing "self-inventory."

Dr. Zonnya's Personal Self-Inventory

One morning nearly twenty years ago, sitting at our kitchen table, racked with problems on every side, I began a self-inventory. In order for me to be productive, I asked my husband to also participate. The inventory was essential for me and it is essential for you as you begin this balancing process. As we began to communicate with each other, we verbalized what we both had known for quite some time. The problems were too big. They were too much to handle. Something had to be done. One of the phrases that came out of my mouth that morning was: "I am sick and tired of being sick and tired." From the looks of the statistics, many people at some time in their life experience these same feelings.

I had been blaming my past, my parents, my religion, God, my husband, the economy. I blamed everybody and everything. I was caught in the self-imposed trap of blaming everybody else for the situations in which I found myself. I was wallowing in self-pity, doubt, fear, anger and depression. I was convinced that I was helpless to change things. There was no question in my mind that I was a puppet caught in all the circumstances around me, with no possible way out! Out-of-balance living was in control of my life. It is sad to say, but I find so many people in all walks of life who have similar impressions of their lives. Because I deal, both personally and professionally, with men and women who are literally living the same kind of life I was living, I feel the need to share my own story along with the circumstances and events that led me to a new-found freedom, as I travel the roads of my life-journey.

To begin my personal process of getting off the yo-yo, I had to ask myself the three very important questions that I mentioned earlier.

What Is The Problem?

As I reflect on the early days of developing this system for balanced living, I remember the hard cold facts of my life. I was 40 pounds overweight. I had developed negative attitudes (I certainly was not born with them). My husband, Bob, is a minister, known internationally as the "Chaplain of Bourbon Street." I perceived him

so overly spiritual that nothing else or no one else was quite as important as his ministry. I was critical, judgmental and condemning. The
number of close friends I had could be counted on one hand. The
proverbial "idiot box" had become my primary line of communication with the world.

I had become distrusting of myself, my husband and of those
around me. I had become so involved in my work and in making
money, I had forgotten that there were other things important in life.
From a previous marriage, Bob had two daughters with whom I had
little communication.

Between my husband and me, I had allowed anger, suspicion,
doubt and resentment to develop. We were on our way to becoming
another marital statistic. So it would, in all fairness, be appropriate to
say that I was out-of-balance.

From my self-inventory, I was confident that I had identified the
problems. Let me put some special emphasis on the intensity of that
moment of self-inventory. It was one of the most difficult times in
my life. It was painful, exasperating, frustrating and embarrassing.
At times, I wanted to just quit. But before I began to examine my life,
I made a commitment to do whatever I had to do to change the kind
of life I was living. I made the decision that nothing could be worse
than the hell and torment that I was experiencing living life on a yo-
yo. My commitment was to define, understand and solve my out-of-
balance situations. Whatever the price, no matter what the sacrifice,
I wanted answers and solutions.

Next, I needed to address the second question.

How Did The Problems Evolve?

First, I asked: "What is the problem?" Now that I knew what the
problems were, the second question needed to be addressed: "How
did the problems evolve?"

It is important to define how problems evolve. I identified four
explanations. Not only did they apply to my problems, but I believe
they have universal application.

First, neglect. I neglected my body. I neglected my mind. I neglected my soul. I neglected my friends. I neglected my marriage and
the family. Guess what? I ended up with a lot of problems.

Second, a low self-image. This is without question the basic underlying factor that will interfere with, sometimes even prevent, a person from getting off the yo-yo and enjoying the life-journey. A low self-image will retard growth and change, and will create self-sabotage. My challenge was to overcome this debilitating liability.

Third, setting unrealistic priorities. Most of us during some point in our lives get our priorities out-of-order or confused. Because of the fast pace that we live, we get caught up in our work, our careers, our money-making endeavors, and forget to remember that there is so much more to life! We often are so involved in our children, that we forget about our spouses. Sometimes, we are so preoccupied with our spiritual commitments that we dismiss other aspects of our lives that demand attention. Out-of-balance living is usually a product of our own misjudgments and our self-declared priorities.

Fourth, unrealistic expectations of people and situations. I had to realistically evaluate what I was expecting of myself, as well as of the people and places around me. It is a common factor among people to have unrealistic expectations regarding career, spouse, children, money, happiness, love, performance, etc. Once I defined some realistic expectations for myself, I began to accept realistic expectations for my family, friends, and situations in my life.

When I reached the point of having a firm grip on "What is the problem?" and "How did the problem evolve?," I was ready to go to question number three. This became a pursuing challenge for me.

What Can I Do to Solve the Problem?

I was somewhat surprised to learn that I did, in fact, have answers, solutions and alternatives. When you take your personal inventory, do not be overwhelmed by all of the problems that you identify. Be encouraged by this SignPost:

SignPost:

*You Do Not Have As Many Problems To Solve
As You Have Decisions To Make*

I came face to face with many decisions that had to be made. It was almost unbelievable that once I began making some definite decisions, many of my problems automatically found solutions.

This third major question: "What Can I Do To Solve The Problem?" will be addressed in detail in each of the following chapters. Please feel assured that I will not propose an out-of-balance situation without at least giving alternatives for its resolution.

At this point, I know we agree: out-of-balance is no fun. The problems we experience can serve as a catalyst to help us reach a fully functioning life if we dedicate ourselves to the solutions. Out-of-balance situations should serve to lead us to the major questions of "What?" and "How?". From our inventory, we can learn honestly and openly about our own liabilities, as well as our own assets.

Realizing and accepting ourselves as being out-of-balance is the first step toward getting off the yo-yo. As we continue to progress through the next chapters, you will learn more about the basic foundations for living life in balance and you will gain great insights as to systems and applications for achieving it.

Remember: This Is It! Out-Of-Balance Is No Fun!

RECAP FOR "OUT-OF-BALANCE IS NO FUN"

Three major questions to ask in problem-solving and choice-making.

   1. What is the problem?
   2. How did the problem evolve?
   3. What can I do to solve the problem?

Existing or Living? That is the question.

   Existing is settling for "less" on your life-journey.
   Living is experiencing "more" on your life-journey.

Reasons for out-of-balance situations:

   1. Neglect
   2. Low self-image
   3. Unrealistic priorities
   4. Unrealistic expectations

SignPosts For Your Life-Journey:

1. Everything Is A Matter Of Choice;
    Choice Equals Results

2. What Happens To You In Your Life Is Not
    As Important As How You Choose To Respond
    To What Happens To You

3. You Don't Have As Many Problems To Solve
    As You Have Decisions To Make

4. Little People Don't Like To Be Around Big Thinkers

PERSONAL SELF-INVENTORY

1. List three problems or situations that I am experiencing: Ask: "What is the problem?"

   1. _____

   2. _____

   3. _____

2. Next, ask: "How did the problem evolve?"

   1. _____

   2. _____

   3. _____

3. List three alternatives to the problem:

   1. _____

   2. _____

   3. _____

4. How do I see myself? _____

   _____

5. In what ways do I occasionally express a low self-image? _____

   _____

   _____

6. List my priorities for living life in balance:
   1. _____

   2. _____

   3. _____

7. List two unrealistic expectations that I have of myself:
   1. _____

   2. _____

8. List two unrealistic expectations that I have of someone I love:
   1. _____

   2. _____

9. List two realistic expectations that I have of myself:
   1. _____

   2. _____

10. List two realistic expectations that I have of someone I love:
    1. _____

    2. _____

DR. ZONNYA'S FIRST AID

1. Review one problem that you have experienced in the past.
   Dissect it!
   1. What was the problem?
   2. How did the problem evolve?
   3. What did you do about the problem?

2. Dissect one problem that you are experiencing now by using the three-question technique.
   1. What is the problem?
   2. How did the problem evolve?
   3. What can I do to solve the problem?
   Use the three question technique with each situation or problem that you experience.

3. Take a self-inventory frequently, to keep you in touch with your reality. When you take the self-inventory, it will be simple to recognize yo-yo living.

4. Give more attention to the answers, solutions and alternatives than you give to the questions, problems and challenges.

5. Make a commitment to yourself to experience "more" and not to settle for less - today and every day!

6. Do one thing each day that leads you to personal change and growth.

AFFIRMATIONS

An affirmation is a positive statement that expresses a specific belief concerning you and the state of the affairs of your life. It begins with "I" or "My" and always will serve to reinforce all that is unique, special and distinctive about you. Use it often throughout the day. It will inspire, encourage and motivate you as you commit yourself to living life in balance.

I, _____, accept my

(name)

right to a more beautiful lifestyle.

I, _____, am willing to

(name)

solve my problems by finding balanced solutions.

I,_____, know that I

(name)

can overcome my yo-yo way of living.

> *"You were born with wings;*
> *why prefer to crawl through life?"*
> —Rumi, Persian Poet

Chapter 2

BALANCED LIVING FOR A MORE BEAUTIFUL LIFESTYLE

*"You cannot really cope with your existence
till you are a whole person."*
—Fritz Perls

Everybody wants a **more** beautiful lifestyle. Everyone wishes for "more" of the good life. But we do not get it by wishing. In order to enjoy the benefits of a **more** beautiful lifestyle, we must make certain choices and take certain actions in a systematic way that will bring about the desired results, as we travel our life-journey.

We agree that a life filled with problems is **not** conducive to a beautiful lifestyle. For too long in our main-stream society, we have been more problem-conscious than solution-oriented. A reversal in our sense of priorities is necessary if we are to improve our non-fated lives. It is not comprehendible to me that we are fated to have problems. I suggest that most of our so-called problems are results of the choices we make. Nevertheless, we must assume the position which puts the primary focus on the solution, instead of the problem.

Balanced living is a system approach for re-structuring our priorities. Balanced living is not perfect living. It does not remove all those troublesome situations in which we often find ourselves. Rather, it offers an opportunity to re-think the answers to the questions, the solutions to the problems, and the alternatives to the challenges.

21

Balanced living has been developed on several basic premises. One, it is not a religion, or a doctrine, or a dogma. It is rather, a lifestyle. Two, balanced living offers a solution to every problem. Three, its main focus is on "preventing" as opposed to "treating." Preventing the problem, instead of treating it, can stop yo-yo living. Fourth, creating the solution should be a thrilling, exciting and fun process.

In order for you to further understand how this lifestyle was born and developed, let me share with you just a brief background history.

The Development of Balanced Living

One morning, as I sat with my husband, Bob, discussing the obvious problems that were such a major part of our lives, I slowly began to see my first glimmer of hope toward what I could do. I took a piece of paper, drew a circle on it, and divided it into pieces, sort of like cutting a pie into pieces. I was just rambling that morning as I was verbally searching for answers, for solutions, for alternatives.

I had to begin somewhere, so the first thing I thought was that I had a body which I defined as Physical. I wrote "Physical" in one of the pieces of the circle on the paper that was laying there on the table. At the time, I had no idea how valuable this piece of paper would become to my life-journey. I had no clue that the circle I had drawn on the piece of paper would ultimately help me focus on the roads I would choose to travel.

Continuing the search, I identified another part of my life: my mind. The mind is the center of learning, the center of attitudes, emotions and feelings. It is also the center of choice-making. The choices I had been making had created my yo-yo, my out-of-balance. So, in the second piece of the circle, I wrote: "Mental."

Since I grew-up with a highly intense fundamental religious background, I automatically knew that I could not overlook an area called "Spiritual". This filled the third piece of the circle.

I had been convinced for years, that many of the things I had been taught growing-up were misleading SignPosts when it came to spiritual matters. I was searching for SignPosts that could guide me on the roads of my spiritual journey. I was not fully aware of just how far my examination would take me. As I continued, I discovered many discrepancies in what I had been taught about spirituality. I found that many out-of-balance people and conditions exist in our religious institutions and religious philosophies.

As I reviewed my circle, I saw that I had filled in the following pieces: Physical, Mental, Spiritual. All three operate in our lives individually, as none of us have the same body, mind, or spirit. Each is separate and unique in every one of us. At this point, I felt like I was at least on the road that would lead me to define life, its areas, its meanings, its purposes. However, I knew there were other pieces of the circle that needed identifying. My circle required I give it more attention. I was not satisfied that my life was just Physical, Mental, Spiritual. So I dug deeper.

As I sat looking at my husband, I realized I had not identified him in my life. So there, "Family," went in the circle as the fourth area. Family is comprised of the centrifugal family, the extended family and anyone whom the family invites to be a part.

About that time, the phone rang, and it was one of our very good friends who was in a crisis. I listened. I empathized. I responded. I invited him over to talk. After the ten minute conversation, I returned to my table with that same piece of paper staring me in the face. At this point, I was getting somewhat frustrated, because I wanted instant answers, instant solutions, instant alternatives. I did not know this Signpost:

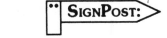

You Don't Get Messed-up Over Night;
You Don't Get Fixed-up Overnight

Anyway, after the call, there I was back at the table. I briefly told my husband what the conversation was regarding our friend, and that I had invited him over. Then I said: "That's what friends are for." Immediately, I knew I had anther piece to fill-in the circle. The fifth piece became: "Social."

We continued to talk and finally, we got around to talking about the subject that is at the crux of over 50 % of all problems: **money.** I had my views about career, job, money, income, savings, etc., and I was more than aware that this area occupies a great deal of our waking hours, and sleeping hours for that matter. I knew people who had no money and they were definitely out-of-balance. I knew people who had lots of money and they seemed to have as many problems in the areas of life as people with no money. I also knew hundreds of people, like me, who made "good" money, but were un-happy with life in general. It occurred to me if this area gets so much attention from every strata of life, it most certainly needed to be included in my circle. The sixth piece of the circle became: "Financial."

As I reviewed my circle, I had identified:

Physical
Mental
Spiritual
Social
Financial
Family

At last, I felt I had a clear, concise, understandable picture of what composed the roads of my life-journey.

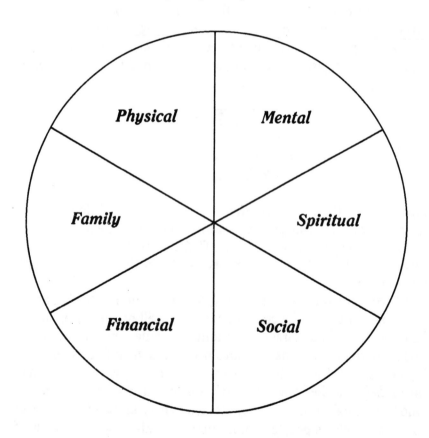

Balanced Living Areas

At birth, you begin the life-journey with these six areas operating in your life on a daily basis. Each area carries with it certain potential problems that are based on your choices and the choices of others. Personally, I prefer to convert the word "problems" to "opportunities." No one ever looks forward to problems; yet most us can accept opportunities with possible positive expectations. Why not invert negative problems into positive expectations? Why not turn yo-yo living into balanced living?

From that morning of my first real self-inventory, I realized I had negative problems existing in all six areas. It also was on that morning that I realized I could change my reality. As you think about your own six areas, does an out-of-balance problem or situation come to your mind? Sure it does! All of us, during some period of our lives, will encounter situations that create unpleasant and unproductive results. Our goal should be to prevent as many of these situations as possible and to quickly treat those that do arise.

At the same time that you are identifying your negative problems, also be in-tune with your positive situations. I believe that many of us experience many of the aspects of balanced living. Many of us are happy and healthy, have good marriages, enjoy a productive job, etc. But there are three key words which can help you even improve positive situations. They are:

More
Better
Greater

Let's look specifically at what I mean when I use these terms.

To our own degree, all of us enjoy happiness - but do we want to experience more happiness?

From our own definition, all of us are successful - but do we want to be more successful?

All of us have friends - but do we want more and greater friendships?

We have good marriages - but can we have greater and more fulfilling marriages?

We engage in good jobs and careers - but could we be more productive, thereby achieving better results in our jobs and careers?

My research indicates that most of us experience some good in all six areas of life. But by practicing the systems that balanced living presents, we can increase the "good" to "more - better - greater" in all six areas.

If you are not experiencing the good that you desire, balanced living can be just the system that you can use to help you get off your yo-yo and begin to enjoy a more beautiful lifestyle. With the practice of balanced living, you can introduce the good into your life and then proceed further into the "more - better - greater" of life.

Balanced Living Empowers You To:

1. Enjoy a good and pleasant appearance.

2. Expand your mind, feelings, emotions and ability to learn.

3. Elevate your spiritual communication and commitment.

4. Enhance friendships and community involvements.

5. Extend career and job opportunities toward financial independence and fulfillment.

6. Establish positive support systems that make a family unit effective.

Balanced Living Fundamentals

Balanced living slices the pie of life into six areas:

> Physical
> Mental
> Spiritual
> Social
> Financial
> Family

As this system began to develop and evolve, I realized there were two concepts that seemed to repeat themselves in each of the six areas. The concept of "Individual" and the concept of "Daily."

Every person has an <u>individual</u> physical area functioning on a <u>daily</u> basis. The same is true of each of the other five areas. Each area applies to each person on an <u>individual</u> basis and on a <u>daily</u> basis. From this reality, I begin to build my own individual balance on a daily basis in each area.

We agree that no two people are alike. We agree that we are each unique and different. Because of our individuality, our balance is an individual process. We cannot force our balance on someone else. You cannot expect your balance to be the same as mine, nor can I expect mine to be the same as yours. What we can expect from each other is the individual pursuit to establish our own individual balance, as we travel different roads on our life-journey.

In addition to individual balance, I realized it is also a <u>daily</u> process. You cannot post-date or pre-date your balance in the six areas of life. It is impossible to change the out-of-balance or balanced conditions of yesterday. Yesterday is dead and gone. It is equally impractical to look ahead into your tomorrow and determine the quality of balance that you may experience. Tomorrow is not here, and when it gets here, it will be today. The only time you have to get off your yo-yo is today, on a daily basis.

As a child, in Sunday School at our church, I was taught the lesson of the "Lord's Prayer." One line is quoted as: "Give us this day our <u>daily</u> bread." Bread is anything that brings you life, that sustains you, that maintains you. Balanced living is bread for your life, and it is only good when you apply it on a daily basis. Each area of life will ask something of you on a daily basis. You must be prepared to recognize and address each area if you are to enjoy a **more** beautiful lifestyle.

Many times, I am asked: "How do you find time for each area on a daily basis?" There are several perspectives that one can take in answering this seemingly complex question.

First, let's look at the alternative of not taking time. The way I see it, you will either give individual daily emphasis to each area and thereby prevent many of the problems that could possibly arise, or you will be forced by the problems that occur to give individual daily treatment.

Many examples are available. One that we can easily relate to would be the person who abuses the body with over-eating, over-drinking, smoking, little or no exercise, etc. These can be causes that lead to an effect called: "heart attack."

The statistics show that far too many heart attacks are caused by being physically out-of-balance. In many cases, individual daily emphasis on the physical area could prevent what becomes a long stay in the hospital, surgery, or death! In my way of thinking, taking time for individual daily attention to the physical area is a much more viable and productive alternative.

This same principle applies, not only to the physical area of life, but to each of the other five areas of life. Each area needs individual daily attention and each area will get your attention one way or the other.

You probably are thinking that there is no way on earth to give time and attention to each area on a daily basis. You are probably saying: "I'm too busy." Certainly, you are busy. Do you know anyone who is living life who isn't busy? Of course not. Therefore, the two questions to ask are: "What are your priorities in life?" and "What do you choose to do to give each area individual daily attention?"

To the first question: "What are your priorities in life?" Every person will have a different set of priorities by which his/her life is guided. Your priorities will be different from mine and mine different from yours.

Simply defined, your priorities will be those people and/or things to which you assign the most value. Think of your life in terms of the circle. Assign a number, from one through six to each area with #1 being the **most** important or most valued. You may choose family #1 as the most important and valued and social #6, as important and valued, but least of your priorities. Typically, the structure of your life will depend upon who and what you value most and where each area falls on your most-to-least valued list. Balanced living emphasizes there is a connection between each of the six areas and the kind of lifestyle you experience. Once you're convinced **logically** and **emotionally** that each area needs individual daily attention, you will choose both the time and the system to meet those needs effectively. Please let me emphasize that "you must be convinced both **logically** and **emotionally**." These two factors are critical to employ if you are to capitalize on their power.

Often, you logically can understand something, but do not accept it emotionally as how it applies to you individually. Then on the other hand, you sometimes accept something emotionally that you do not understand logically. As you continue to explore the balanced living lifestyle, you will find it is a concept delicately balanced between logic and emotion. It takes a substantial amount of both in order to develop and continue this lifestyle for the entire life-journey.

To the second question: "What do you choose to do to give each area individual daily attention?" The more systems you know, the more you will have to work with, as you address each area daily. What I find with most people is that they use the worn out whine: "I don't have time." So let's address this time issue. Time is about **choosing**, not about **having**.

SIGNPOST:

*You Have Time To Do Exactly
What You Choose To Do*

You do not have time to do what you want to do. You do not have time to do what you should do. You do not have time to do what you ought to do or better do. But you **always** have time to do what you **choose** to do. By the very nature that you are doing it, you are choosing to do it. If you do not choose to do it, you do not do it.

This SignPost changed the way I travelled the roads of my life-journey. I can remember that worn out whine coming out of my very own mouth: "I don't have time to exercise. I don't have time to go to church. I don't have time for myself. I don't have time to read or listen to materials that can help me improve who I am. I just don't have time." But it was amazing that I had time to sit and have coffee, go to the movies, moan, groan and complain. In other words, I had time to do what I chose to do. When I am faced with something that has to do with me and time, I understand that time is not about **having**; it is about **choosing.**

Take your own personal inventory regarding you and time. What are you **choosing** to do with your time? You need never use the worn out whine again. I promise this system, alone, will help you get off your yo-yo.

The second perspective from which to address the question: "How do you find time for balance?" is found by reviewing the benefits of choosing time.

On our life-journey, we will make certain choices depending on the benefits of those choices. From my many years in sales, I learned that to close a sale effectively, you must sell the benefits. I believe that a lifestyle system should, like a sale, offer dramatic benefits to the person who buys. There are many benefits when you know and use the systems for a balanced living lifestyle. The benefits are numerous and endless. They will be with you for your whole life and they become obvious in all six areas as you travel the many roads of your life-journey.

Just think of such benefits as: good health, positive attitudes, friendships, love, happiness, prosperity, peace, joy, faith and a sense of inner fulfillment. If you are convinced that these benefits (just to name a few) are important to you and that their presence can make a remarkable difference in your lifestyle, then you are on the right road and the SignPosts on this road will guide you through your life-journey.

It is vitally important for you to fully perceive the benefits and rewards that are available to you once you begin to give individual daily attention to each area of your life. When you picture the benefits, they will give you the inspiration you need to motivate you toward the individual emphasis on each area. Make a commitment to begin now.

The Results Start The Minute You Do

In Part II, I will address each of the six areas individually. I will offer simple, practical, adaptable, usable, and workable systems that will bring you immediate results when you apply them to your life-journey on a daily basis, beginning now. Balanced living is the system for getting off your yo-yo and enjoying a more beautiful lifestyle.

RECAP FOR "BALANCED LIVING FOR A MORE BEAUTIFUL LIFESTYLE"

Balanced Living Is A Lifestyle.

1. It is not a religion, doctrine, or dogma.
2. It offers a solution to every problem.
3. Its main focus is on preventing, instead of treating. Preventing the problem, instead of treating it, can stop yo-yo living.
4. Creating the solutions to your problems should be a thrilling, exciting and fun process.

Balanced Living Defines Life Into Six Areas:

Physical

Mental

Spiritual

Social

Financial

Family

Balanced Living Empowers You To Experience:

More

Better

Greater

Whatever you are experiencing in life, your lifestyle can be enhanced by accepting and realizing "more, better, greater" in each area of your life.

Balanced Living Empowers You To:

1. Enjoy a good and pleasant appearance.

2. Expand your mind, feelings, emotions, and ability to learn.

3. Elevate your spiritual communication and commitment.

4. Enhance friendships and community involvements.

5. Extend career and job opportunities toward financial independence and fulfillment.

6. Establish positive support systems that make a family unit effective.

Two Key Words Essential To Balanced Living:

1. Individual
2. Daily

Balanced living is an individual daily experience.

SignPosts For Your Life-Journey:

1. You Don't Get Messed-up Over Night;
   You Don't Get Fixed-up Over Night

2. You Have Time To Do Exactly What You Choose To Do

3. The Results Start The Minute You Do

PERSONAL SELF-INVENTORY

1. Can I enjoy a **MORE** beautiful lifestyle?_____

2. Do I believe that wanting "more, better, greater" of the productive things in life will improve my lifestyle? _____

3. Will my lifestyle improve by me giving individual daily attention to each area? _____

4. Through more of my individual daily attention, I can enjoy balanced living. What steps will I choose to take in each area?

PHYSICAL: _____

_____

MENTAL: _____

_____

SPIRITUAL: _____

_____

SOCIAL: _____

_____

FINANCIAL: _____

_____

FAMILY: _____

_____

DR. ZONNYA'S FIRST AID

1. Make an agreement and sign a contract with yourself that you want to experience "more, better, greater" in all areas of your life.

2. Set aside a short period of time in the early morning to begin your day on a positive note.

3. Read one chapter in a challenging book or listen to a segment of a challenging audio cassette or view a motivating video.

4. Repeat your affirmations to root out any negatives in your thinking.

5. Set aside a short period of time in the evening to prepare for your following day. Use the six areas as a guide on your life-journey. Outline just one action that you can take in each area to maintain a sense of balance.

6. Assign priorities to your needs and desires.

7. Commit yourself to a **daily** approach to life.

AFFIRMATIONS

An affirmation is a positive assertion that expresses a specific belief concerning you and the state of the affairs of your life. It begins with "I" or "My" and always will serve to reinforce all that is unique, special, and distinctive about you. Use it often throughout the day. It will inspire, encourage and motivate you as you commit yourself to balanced living for a **more** beautiful lifestyle.

I, _____, accept that

balanced living is a productive way to live.

I, _____, know that

by giving individual daily attention to each area of my life, I can enjoy

a **more** beautiful lifestyle.

I, _____, choose to

receive "more, better, greater" of all the abundance in life.

*"Place yourself in the middle of the
stream of power and wisdom which flows into
you as life; place yourself in the full
center of that flood. Then you are without
effort impelled to truth, to right,
and a perfect contentment."*
—Ralph Waldo Emerson

Chapter 3

GET BACK TO THE BASICS

"If we work marble, it will perish; if we work brass,
time will efface it; if we rear temples, they will crumble
into dust; but if we work upon immortal
minds and instill in them just principles
we are then engraving upon them tablets which
no time will efface, but will
brighten and brighten to all eternity."
—Daniel Webster, American Statesman

One of the greatest football coaches of all time was the great Vince Lombardi of the Green Bay Packers. In his biography, he told of a happening from which I learned an immense lesson. Vince was a tower of a man and his players were totally dedicated to the principles he taught. He believed in winning. However after several seasons of winning, he and his great team began to encounter some losses. The first loss was bad enough, but then it continued into several losses. Lombardi was confused and frustrated (as we can get when we encounter losses). He went over the plays, counseled with his players individually, and did all he thought he knew to do. With all this, the losses still continued.

Then early one morning, it dawned on Lombardi. The basics. They had left the basics. They had to get back to the basics. So he called the team together in the locker room. Gathered there were his fine, intelligent, rough-tough players. The team did not know exactly what to expect, but they knew one thing for certain. Vince Lombardi meant business.

As he began, Vince made an astounding, astonishing comment. He picked up the football in his hand that he and his team had handled game after game after game and he said: "Boys, this is a football." A gasp could be heard in the quietude of those "Absorbine Junior smelling" quarters. A look of exasperation struck the face of each player who was deemed a "pro" of this game. But Lombardi was not through. He motioned for them to follow him. Out of the closeness of the locker room they stalked. Once they entered the openness of the clear blue skies, toward the field they marched. Vince suddenly stopped. Pointing to the field, he said, "Boys, this is a football field." He pointed at the uprights and yelled, "Boys, that is a goal post. We seemed to have forgotten the basics!" Vince Lombardi made his point to those "pros."

We never become so "pro" that we can forget the fundamental principles that guide us on our life-journey. In order to further understand how this system can get you off your yo-yo and lead you to a more beautiful lifestyle, let's get down to some basic foundations for building balanced living.

Let me divert back to football for a brief look at what we can learn from this game and apply to our daily lives. Even if you are not a football fan, you can still benefit from the principles. I happen to be a fan, and I enjoy the game, the sport, and what I have learned from it. I have learned much from the sports experience. Often, I have compared what happens in life to those things that happen during a game. If we compare the game of football to the game of life, we might find it is something like this.

1. In the game of football, there are people called "players"; they make the game possible. There are two teams made up of the same number of players. Each player has an assignment, a position to play, and goals to reach. In the game of life, you and I are the players. We play on many different teams, have specific positions to play, and goals to reach.
2. There are "rules" in the game of football for the players to observe. The rules insure that every player has a fair and equal op-

portunity. The rules protect the players. In life, we call the rules - "laws". We know there are three basic laws that exist:

1. Laws of God
2. Laws of Nature
3. Laws of Humankind

In life, we have laws to protect us and to direct us on the roads of our life-journey.

3. Football has an objective: To play the game at the highest level of performance and score the most points. So it is with our lives. We have an objective. We want to live life to the fullest, experience the highest level in each area, and score with a beautiful lifestyle that is rewarding and fulfilling. In both cases, the objective is to reach the goal. Do you clearly know what your goals are?

4. The obstacles in football are called blocking, tackling, sacking, etc. We call the obstacles in life worry, financial problems, sickness, and any self-defeating thoughts and actions. As players, all of us have been blocked, tackled, and sacked. These obstacles should only serve to slow us down, not keep us down.

5. The football game is played by individuals who make up a team. Each player has a specific assignment, but when all of the assignments are combined, the team plays as a unit. In life, each of us is an individual, but we make up many different teams, i.e.: family team, work team, the team of friends, the team of church, community, government, etc. We are not islands. The word master English Poet John Donne said: "No man is an island." We need each other to help us reach our individual goals and to reach the ultimate goal: a better world.

6. The penalties in the football game serve to remind the players that infringements of the rules are not allowed. A player is penalized; a play is forfeited; the reaching of the goal is delayed. The players learn to abide by the rules for the maximum level of productivity. When we, as players in the game of life, infringe upon the laws, we are penalized. We are often delayed in reaching our goals.

7. The extra point or two-point conversion in the football game gives the scoring team an opportunity to capitalize further on their

success. After the touchdown has been accomplished, this is another way of gaining more points. With the right play, the right player, a definite target and strategy, an extra point or points can be scored. So it is with us as players in life. Once we have reached our initial goal, we then have the opportunity to capitalize further on our momentum. With specific purpose and a definite strategy, we are often able to experience what could be called "lagniappe" or the cherry on top of the already delicious cake!

8. One key ingredient to both of these games, football and life, is extra effort. To get to the goal, to overcome the obstacles, to seize the extra success available, we must put forth every ounce of extra effort. When it seems too tough, when we get hurt, when we get penalized, or when we want to quit, we must incite within us the extra effort that can propel us to the desired end.

9. Football and life are games of winning and losing. They are made up of winners and losers. A game teaches us how to be good winners, good losers and how to play the game to the best of our ability. It has been said, "It's not whether you win or lose, but how you play the game!" There is something intrinsically good and bad about this statement. It *is* important how you play and it *is* important whether you win or lose. What you want to do is learn to play the game to the highest extent of your ability and to maximize your efficiency. When you win, you celebrate; when you lose, you re-evaluate. The re-evaluation will help you in the next game.

10. Last, but not least, the highest honor paid in the game of football is to play in the Super Bowl. The winner of that Super Bowl game is recognized as the world's champion. In life, the greatest honor is getting off the yo-yo and living life in balance. When you win at balanced living, you are the champion of the greatest game of all: Life.

While life and football have some interesting comparisons, always remember one thing:

Life Is Like A Game,
But It's Not A Spectator Sport

With the game of life, you cannot sit on the sidelines. You have to jump right in and play your hardest and best if you are going to enjoy the trip on your life-journey. As you travel your many roads, it will be imperative that you remember the basics, so let's get back to them.

THE BASICS FOR BALANCED LIVING

Remember, the first basic is that balanced living defines six areas:

Physical
Mental
Spiritual
Social
Financial
Family

Second basic: Each area operates individually on a daily basis. Now, let me share with you further fundamental principles that will give you even brighter clarity of this powerful, life-changing system. Every system has a foundation and the foundation for balanced living are its three pillars.

Balanced Living Pillars

There are three basic foundations upon which the system is built. These three principles are the underlying force and power for getting you off your yo-yo. The pillars of strength for balanced living are:

1. Individual Awareness Daily
2. Individual Importance Daily
3. Individual Responsibility Daily

For the remaining part of this chapter, I will focus on the application, understanding and adaptability of these three.

In my speaking and in my writing, I use the technique of acronyms. Acronym speaking is taking a word and assigning a word to each letter. I mention this to you because I will be using many acronyms as we continue.

If I were to ask you what three letter word describes what keeps us alive, you might respond "air." You would be right. If I were to ask you what three-letter word describes the basis for balanced living, you would be right again, if you answered "air." It looks something like this:

A - Awareness
I - Importance
R - Responsibility

These three systems, when applied to each of the six areas of life, will lead you to the road of balanced living.

A - Awareness

Individual Awareness Daily

"Awareness" is a key SignPost as you begin the balanced living experience. Exactly what is awareness? Webster defines awareness as: "Having or showing realization, perception, or knowledge."

If you are to enjoy this lifestyle, you must realize, and be knowledgeable of, what each area is and of what each area needs. Before you can prevent a problem from arising in an area, you must be fully aware of the area. To be fully aware means that you must engage in honest self-inventory. From an honest, open and straight-forward inventory, you can clearly identify, either what the problem has been or is, and then choose to treat it or preferably prevent it.

It has been said that it is not so bad to have a problem. What is bad, is to not know what the problem is, or how the problem evolved. How many times do you find yourself unhappy, sick, depressed and non-productive, and not know how you got that way? You can never solve a problem until you know clearly what the problem is and how the problem evolved. All you can ever hope to do is treat your problems until your awareness is activated and upgraded.

How do you develop awareness? It comes from knowledge and experience. Your drive for getting off your yo-yo and building a balanced lifestyle starts with your desire to learn more about yourself, the roads you are choosing and the kind of life-journey you want to experience. Once you activate your awareness in your subconscious, you begin to experience more awareness. Your subconscious kicks-in and helps as you desire to pursue realization and perception.

When I first began focusing on my awareness, I realized how very little I knew about, not to mention practiced, the fine art of awareness. Awareness is not a born trait. It is learned and developed. As you become less and less satisfied with your lifestyle, you become more intrigued and challenged to learn and develop more of this essential principle.

When I survey each area of life, I find that awareness applies to each area on an individual basis. You must be aware of each individual area. I shared with you that when I started my self-inventory, I was out-of-balance in every area. One of the reasons was that I had put blinders on my awareness. I was overweight; not because I had a thyroid gland problem, but because I had an elbow gland problem. (There are many cases where overweight is caused by out-of-balance hormones or physical problems. Special attention, both medical and emotional, is recommended in these cases).

My problem was that I had stopped being aware of my physical condition. I treated my body like a garbage can with a hairy lid. I put things in and on my body that my dogs would run from. I was making choices, but because my awareness had ceased to function properly, I was making the wrong choices. I had depressed my awareness to the point that it was not able to serve me as a guide on my life-journey. I was headed for severe problems caused by being physically out-of-balance. I did nothing to improve my self-imposed plight until my awareness level or awareness consciousness was raised, and my eyes were opened.

SignPost:

*You Can't Do Things Differently Until
You First See Things Differently*

Awareness also means "knowing one's assets and liabilities; knowing one's efficiencies and deficiencies in each area of life." Once you know your assets and liabilities, you can more clearly define the opportunities open to you for development. Awareness is the first positive step to getting off your yo-yo and getting control of your life. Awareness includes knowing the negative points, the positive points and the realistic points of your life.

Once you become aware of the conditions that exist in each area, you can begin to look for the answers, solutions, and alternatives to those conditions. For example, in my physical area, I began to ask myself questions about my eating habits, my exercising habits, my personal hygiene habits. Each answer led me to another question which further opened-up more awareness. Awareness should create a desire for more awareness.

The more questions you ask, the more questions you find to ask. The more knowledge about yourself you acquire, the more knowledge about yourself you want to acquire. In other words, awareness begets awareness and that awareness leads you on roads of many discoveries. Each discovery leads you to answers, to solutions and to alternatives for getting off your yo-yo and enjoying balance in your life.

You are individually in charge of your perception, knowledge and enlightenment about yourself. As you continue to grow and change, you will need to maintain your awareness daily. The only constant in life is change, so inherently, you are changing. The key is to be aware of the changes that you are experiencing on a daily basis in every area. Many times, it is so easy to get caught up in the day-to-day activities of life, that you become somewhat numb to the changes that are consciously and subconsciously occurring within and around you.

To preclude this occurrence, dedicate yourself to individual awareness daily in each area. Once you commit yourself to daily awareness, you will approach your problems or opportunities, whether they are positive, negative, or realistic, with an attitude subject to creating solutions. There is no question that individual daily awareness, in each of the six areas of life, is essential to the process of balanced living.

There are basically two vital steps to increasing your awareness in each area of life.

1. Take an honest personal self inventory of each of the six areas of your life. As you frequently do this, you will find that you are more tuned-in to the real you with all your assets and liabilities.

2. Increase your knowledge about each area of your life. Continue to read, listen, and observe that which will guide you as your awareness continues to heighten. Not only do you want to learn more about each area, but you want to apply what you learn to the areas of your life.

When I was in college I remember a professor exalting the praises of getting an education. I can still hear his voice ring out: "Knowledge means power!" It was only after I entered the work force that I learned this was a misleading SignPost. More accurately stated:

Applied Knowledge Means Power

If you want to have more power over the areas of your life, then yes, you must learn about each of them and have knowledge. But the knowledge is not what will give you power. When you apply the knowledge, you then have the power to make changes that will revolutionize your life and end your yo-yo living forever.

In Part II, the basic need for awareness in each area will be further developed, as I address each of the six areas individually.

First Pillar For Balanced Living: Individual Awareness Daily.

I - Importance

Individual Importance Daily

This is the second pillar of your balanced living foundation. Within this second basic, there are two points of focus.

1. You, as an individual, are important.

2. Each of the six areas is individually important.

The whole is equal to the sum of its parts, and the whole will only be as complete as each of the six areas are complete in your life. No one area is more important than the other. They are all equally important if you are to travel the roads of your life-journey in balance.

This first point of focus in individual daily importance is significant for you to realize and internalize. You, as an individual, are important. Everything you will choose to do in your life will be from the vantage point of how you see and feel about yourself. Hundreds of books have been written on the subjects of self-value, self-worth, self-esteem. Even with all of the information available, hundreds of thousands of people continue to see themselves as having little or no value. It is important that regardless of how you have seen, or felt about, yourself in the past, now is the time to choose to follow SignPosts that will enhance how you see, and feel, about yourself. Ultimately, this will lead you to a happier, healthier, wealthier life.

Open your mind to see and feel differently about yourself. Once you see and feel who you are, you will make different choices as you travel your life roads. Would you like to know who you are? Are you ready? This is "you."

You are unique. You are special. There is no one else just like you. There never has been and there never will be another you. Nature never duplicates itself. You are a unique and individual expression of life. Life is expressing itself in and through you in a way that is a one-time-only creation.

You are the most important person in the world. This is not conceit, for every other person is also the most important person. You have a special place to fill on this journey called "life." No one can do what you do. No one can say what you say. No one can give and take what you give and take. No one can contribute to life what you can contribute to life.

Do you know just how vital, exceptional and incomparable you are? Do you accept your uniqueness, your extraordinary presence, your distinctive rarity?

Right now, experience the uniqueness that only you can experience. Come to value more your place in the scheme of things. Forever seek to discover the best that is within you, and never cease to express to the fullest, your creative ability in every area.

The Best You Do Will Always Be
A Far Cry From The Best You Can Do

Understand and accept that there is a limitless potential of ability that is always wanting to find its way into expression through you. Yes, I'm talking about you.

You are important! You make a difference in life. Your home would be different without you! Your relationships would be different without you! Your job, career, and work would be different without you! Your church, your community, your government and your world would be different if you were not a vital contributing part.

On a daily basis, you as an individual can create the greatest possible good or bad for yourself. In doing this, you accept your importance in the scheme of life. You know that only when you strive to bring a balance to your own life will you be able to reflect a sense of balance in your own life and will you be able to reflect a sense of balance into the world.

Everything you say and do in life is said and done from the way you see yourself. Once you see and feel your individual importance daily, you will choose to get off your yo-yo and create for yourself a lifestyle of wonderment. You will look at your life and want the best possible results. This bottom line will be a measuring stick for your definition of balanced living.

In chapters four and five, you will gain great insights into this powerful subject of how you see and feel about yourself. I passionately believe this is one of the more pressing problems people deal with for the entire trip of their life-journey. If you can come to positive powerful terms with how you see and feel about yourself, you will dramatically change the course of your journey.

The second point of focus, for "Individual Importance Daily", is equally vital to your overall view of your life. While life is made up of all the parts, the whole depends on each part being a fully alive and functioning part. If just one of the parts is not functioning at its optimum, then the whole is affected. Balanced living divides life into six parts to makeup the whole. However, no single area is any more important than the other. If you are going to get off your yo-yo, each area must receive individual daily attention. It will be from your own individual perspective that you will set your priorities on a daily basis.

Many people will argue that one area is more important than the other. Out-of-balance, overly religious people will debate that the soul is of the highest priority. Yet, without the body, the soul would have no place to live.

Others say the mind is most important, but without body and soul, the mind would have nothing to govern.

Others put the family as the most important. Many mothers give all their attention to their children and when they leave home, mother is left alone and feeling useless.

And let us not forget those who think that making money is the most important, thereby giving little attention to the other areas. They turn out to be **money making failures**.

It is critical you understand and accept as fact that each area is equally important on a daily basis.

The two points of focus for this second pillar are:

1. You, as an individual, are important.

2. Each area of life is individually important.

The third basic for balanced living completes the connection.

R - Responsibility

Individual Responsibility Daily

For many people, this third pillar is the crux that will determine the success of getting off your yo-yo and experiencing a balanced lifestyle. Responsibility has different meanings for different people. It will be important that we have, for this discussion, a workable definition that can be applied to our lives as we travel this life-journey.

Responsibility can mean:

1. Moral, legal, or mental accountability

2. Being the cause or explanation of something

3. Answering for one's conduct or obligation

4. Ability to choose to respond

You may think of responsibility in terms of being responsible to someone or something. You are responsible not to a person, not to a situation, nor to a duty, but rather, to yourself and all those laws and principles that you find good, natural, harmonious, and balanced for the process of ordering your life.

While all four definitions are applicable to the concept of responsibility, I particularly want to focus on the fourth definition: "Ability to choose to respond." I am convinced if you fully understand the specific focus of responsibility, it will change how you view your position and power in the big picture. Your responsibility is your ability to choose to respond. Inherently, you were created with the greatest power known to humankind, and that is the power of choice. You have the power to choose; you have the power to choose to respond. This is your responsibility. When you look at it from this point of view, you no longer need to look at responsibility as a burden to bear. It is a birthright, a privilege, and an honor to have the ability to choose to respond.

The concept of personal responsibility, at some point, got lost somewhere in our social, moral, and religious teachings. Instead of accepting our ability to choose to respond to our thoughts and actions, it seems to be acceptable to find someone to blame for our thoughts and actions. We give away our right to choose to respond when we play the blame-game.

No Blame Is Allowed

In your own life, think how many times in the past you found someone or something that you could blame your situation on? Maybe even now, you are still finding people, places, things that you can point to as the culprit of your problems. Over the years of helping people, I think I have heard all the blame-game noises and seen all the finger pointing. You are familiar with them too.

Who gets the blame? Parents, mates, children, race, religion and even God. Add to that list: the boss, the pastor, the doctor, the government, the school and you can take the list to infinitum.

When I started my journey toward a balanced living lifestyle, I had to come face-to-face with this issue of "who's to blame?" I, like most people I know, had travelled the roads of my life-journey pointing my finger in the wrong direction. One day as I was pointing out to the people and the problem, I saw what was coming toward me: three fingers pointing back to me where the problem originated and one finger going up where I could look for encouragement.

What I learned from my very intense self-inventory totally changed my life. I get very excited about sharing this system of balanced living because I know first hand what a positive and powerful difference it can make in the way life is experienced. I developed an affirmation that sums up the "individual responsibility daily" focus and it has become, for me, my #1 SignPost:

1 Am 1n Charge Of Me On A Daily Basis
Beginning Now With God's Help

When I look in the mirror, I see the person who is in charge of the way I think, the choices I make, the way I respond. No one else is in charge of me. This does not mean that I do not abide by the rules, law and regulations that are set forth by God, nature or humankind. I recognize the laws that govern, and within the government regulations, within the family standards, within the educational system, within the laws of God, nature, and humankind, I am in charge of me as I operate within these set forth principles. Just as I am in charge of me, you are in charge of you and "No Blame Is Allowed."

Accepting your own individual responsibility for how you act, react and respond is not always the easiest thing to do; nor is it the popular thing to do. If you are to enjoy the fulfilling and rewarding lifestyle that you desire, then you must activate your ability to choose to respond.

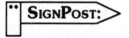

Take Charge Of Your Life On A Daily Basis

Being in charge is frightening for many people. Generally speaking, nowhere in the learning experience are you taught that what happens to you in your life depends on your ability to choose to respond. However, once you learn to accept your individual responsibility on a daily basis, you can begin to function personally at a higher level of accomplishment. You will then choose to get off your yo-yo because you have the ability to choose to respond. As you continue your journey in choosing to respond, you will begin to enjoy more balance in your life.

Individual daily responsibility has a two-fold significance. First, when you are responsible for your actions, reactions, and responses and are successful in an endeavor, you are entitled to the credit for your input and contribution. Even when you work together with another person or persons, you still like to take credit for what you contribute. Secondly, and conversely, when you assume responsibility for yourself individually and are not as successful as you would like to be, you also have the joy of knowing that you can change your choices to improve the actions, reactions, and responses that created the not-so-successful situation or failure.

Almost without saying, everybody wants to take credit for the successes. However, few want to accept the responsibility for the failure. Instead, the blame-game comes into play. Because we have been conditioned not to fail and that failure is a sign of weakness or disgrace, we look for someone or something to absorb the embarrassment of a failure. We are not taught that failure has its place in the scheme of life just like success. So consequently, we accept less and less responsibility for either our successes or our failures.

The balanced living system teaches that whether you experience the highest successes or lowest failures, the "I Am In Charge Of Me On A Daily Basis Beginning Now With God's Help" principle still applies. Regardless of the circumstances, the "No Blame Is Allowed" reigns supreme for individual daily responsibility.

How do you develop individual responsibility daily? The answer to this question is not easy, but there are some simple steps that you can take. As a matter of fact, there are no easy answers to any of the questions that will be asked as you travel your life-journey. What you are looking for is practical, adaptable, usable, and workable answers, solutions and alternatives.

To develop individual responsibility daily, you must first make a commitment to a new way of thinking. It will take time to replace the old unrealistic record that is playing around in your head. It is impossible to get rid of the old record. It must be replaced with a new exciting realistic record. You may find that you will get discouraged in your task. Do not be discouraged. Remember what it is you are wanting to achieve. Dedicate yourself to being a student of individual responsibility daily. You must first make the commitment before you can ever hope to achieve your goal of getting off your yo-yo.

Once you have made the commitment, secondly, stop blaming. To do this, listen to your conversations. You will be amazed at the number of times you will hear yourself indicating the cause for your behavior was "so-and-so." You may even find it amusing, once you fully tune into this process of discovery. You will be surprised to learn that everything from the dog, to the traffic light, to the weather, to a television show (news, soap operas, etc.), to the car, to the computer, will come up as objects of your blame. You will be in awe as you hear yourself turn to everyone from the mailman, to the children, to the spouse, to the pastor, to the boss to find someone to help you shoulder your responsibility. After using this system for a while, you will be immediately tuned in when you start the blame-game.

When I first began using this system, I was in shock the first few weeks. I blamed everyone and everything. At the time, it simply was not in my understanding that I was to blame: either good blame or bad blame. Let me encourage you. Do not be discouraged. I am fully aware that it is easy to say: "Don't be discouraged. Accept your responsibility." I am also fully aware that it is easier said than done. The good news is **you can do it!**

Remove the blaming phrases from your conversation. Stop making statements such as: "She makes me so mad." "If it weren't for...." "How could you do this to me?" Once you become more aware, you will find many of these blaming statements and questions a regular part of your communication. Not only do you need to remove these from your vocabulary, you must also stop thinking these kinds of self-defeating thoughts. You must continually work on the kinds of thoughts you choose inside your head. When a blaming thought begins, immediately stop and replace it with an accepting thought of you and your ability to choose to respond. It will take effort, time, and dedication for you to build a pattern of this kind. Please believe me when I reassure you that it will be worth all the effort that you exert. Just don't give up!

Next, after eliminating the blaming thoughts from your conversation and thinking, you must, thirdly, take action! Each day you are confronted with new situations, circumstances and events that require you to respond. The alternatives are: 1) you respond for yourself or 2) you allow someone else to respond for you. It is essential for you to respond to each situation as it occurs.

Action is a two-fold process. First, you must take action in your thinking. Every outside action is first preceded with an action in the thinking process. When a situation presents itself, you must choose in your mind that you will take an outside action. Action occurs inside, first, then outside.

Every Outside Action Is First An Inside Thought

Once the choice has been made inside the thinking process, it becomes a natural progression to outside manifestation. Action is the determining factor that signals to you that you are, in fact, accepting your individual responsibility daily.

For someone who is accustomed to giving up his/her responsibility, taking action will be a new experience. It will be challenging, frustrating at times, but highly rewarding. There will be mistakes made along the way. There will also be successes to celebrate. This too is important. Don't forget to reward yourself. Celebrate as you break the self-defeating habit of blaming others.

To begin the process of developing your individual responsibility daily, apply these three steps.

1. Commit yourself to a new way of thinking and acting.

2. Eliminate the blaming phrases from your thinking and conversation.

3. Take Action!

Apply these three steps to any situation that you are confronted with on a daily basis. Practice...Practice...Practice!

Practice Does Not Make Perfect;
Perfect Practice Makes Perfect

Balanced living is a simple, practical, adaptable, usable, workable system to guide you as you travel the roads of your life-journey. It is not lofty; it is not dreamy; it is not Pollyanna. Balanced living is real and it is yours for the choosing. It takes commitment, dedication and work to be aware and responsible for each important area of your life on a daily basis.

If Vince Lombardi could address us now, he just might say: "Get Back To The Basics."

RECAP FOR "GET BACK TO THE BASICS"

Three Laws That Govern Our Lives:

1. Laws of God
2. Laws of Nature
3. Laws of Humankind

Balanced Living Basics:

1. There are six areas in life:

   Physical
   Mental
   Spiritual
   Social
   Financial
   Family

2. Each area operates individually on a daily basis.

Balanced Living Pillars:

A - Individual Awareness Daily

I - Individual Importance Daily

R - Individual Responsibility Daily

Individual Awareness Daily:

Defined as:
Having or showing realization, perception, or knowledge.

To begin increasing your awareness:

1. Take your own personal self inventory in each of the six areas.

2. Increase your knowledge and information about each of the six areas.

Individual Importance Daily:

1. You, as an individual, are important.

2. Each area of life is individually important.

Individual Responsibility Daily:

Defined as:

1. Ability to choose to respond

To begin increasing your individual responsibility daily:

1. Commit yourself to a new way of thinking and acting.

2. Eliminate the blaming phrases from your thinking and conversation.

3. Take action!

Signposts For Your Life-Journey

1. Life Is Like A Game,
   But It's Not A Spectator Sport

2. You Can't Do Things Differently, Until
   You First See Things Differently

3. Applied Knowledge Means Power

4. The Best You Do Will Always Be
   A Far Cry From The Best You Can Do

5. No Blame Is Allowed

6. I Am In Charge Of Me On A Daily Basis
   Beginning Now With God's Help

7. Take Charge Of Your Life On A Daily Basis

8. Every Outside Action Is First An
   Inside Thought

9. Practice Does Not Make Perfect;
   Perfect Practice Makes Perfect

PERSONAL SELF-INVENTORY

1. Can I improve my awareness? _____

2. In what areas do I need to be more aware?

    _____

    _____

    _____

    _____

    _____

    _____

3. Do I accept myself as a valuable part of life? _____

    _____

4. Am I placing more importance on any one of the six areas?

    _____

    Which one? _____

5. Do I accept my own responsibility for what happens in my life?

    _____

6. Am I willing to dedicate, commit, and work toward more of my individual awareness, importance, and responsibility?

    _____

    _____

DR. ZONNYA'S FIRST AID

1. List three things you highly value. Apply your awareness, importance and responsibility to each of them.

2. Render one action each day to yourself and to one other person who displays your developing awareness.

3. Learn one new piece of information each day in each area.

4. Daily, add to your value as a person.

5. Replace blame with acceptance of your ability to choose to respond.

6. Before confronting a problem or making a choice, repeat: "I am in charge of me on a daily basis beginning now with God's help."

AFFIRMATIONS

An affirmation is a positive assertion that expresses a specific belief concerning you and the state of the affairs of your life. It begins with "I" or "My" and always will serve to reinforce all that is unique, special and distinctive about you. Use it often throughout the day. It will inspire, encourage and motivate you as you dedicate yourself to balanced living for a more beautiful lifestyle.

I, _____, know that

the basics of balanced living will help me to live a more fully function

ing life.

I, _____, accept myself
as a unique and valuable part of life.

I, _____, am willing

and able to expand my awareness, value my importance, and accept

my responsibility for each area of my life on a daily basis beginning

now.

*"Our doubts are traitors and
make us lose the good we oft
would win by fearing to attempt."*
—William Shakespeare

Chapter 4

BALANCED SELF-LOVE

"But where was I to start? The world is so vast,
I shall start with the country I know best,
my own. But my country is so very large, I had
better start with my town, but my town, too is large.
I had best start with my street. No: my home.
No: my family. Never mind, I shall start with myself."
—Elie Wiesel, "Souls On Fire"

There has been so much written and said about this subject that it would seem redundant to write or say anymore. However, the stark truth is even with all that's been written and said, most of us still wrestle with what self-love is and isn't. I want to add my thoughts, ideas and SignPosts to the existing volumes of material in hope that maybe from my viewpoint, one more person will be encouraged to address this issue from a positive and powerful perspective. I unequivocally feel that a healthy understanding of this principle is essential for you as you commit to getting off your yo-yo and develop a more beautiful lifestyle. For many years, the "experts" (doctors, philosophers, psychiatrists, psychologists, psychoanalysts, religious leaders, etc.) have debated the concept of "self." It has been presented from the positive perspective and also, from the negative perspective.

The goal here is to share simple, practical, adaptable, usable and workable systems on what "self" is and how to use this entity to your best advantage. I will define a few terms in order to put us on the same wave length. I will lay to rest some misleading SignPosts, and offer viable systems for maximizing your positive self and minimizing your negative self.

I am convinced that everything you do in life, everything you say, everything you feel, everything you are, comes from the way you see and feel about yourself. This is a primary determining factor of how you will travel the roads of your life-journey.

To begin our journey into the study of balanced self-love, let's start by understanding the negative aspects of this powerful force that operates within our beings.

Narcissism

It is interesting to know how this theory began. The word "narcissism" comes from the myth of the Greek god, Narcissus. He was an exceptionally beautiful sixteen-year-old boy who scorned the love of others. The nymph, Echo, fell in love with him. She approached him, but he shunned her. Then one day, tired from his work, he lay down beside a pool. Seeing his reflection, he was so smitten by his own beauty that he fell in love with it. Not knowing it was only a reflection of himself, he tried to kiss it, to hold on to it. But naturally, he was unable to do so. Frustrated and tormented by not being able to possess what he really loved, he grieved incessantly. Unable to eat or sleep, he gradually withered and died. When mourners came for him, even his body had disappeared.

The ancient Greeks developed the idea that the punishment for self-love was death. This is definitely a misleading SignPost. They also came to believe that too much love of self precluded love of anyone else, also a misleading SignPost. Although this is an ancient theory based on Greek mythology, it remains a factor in modern day thought of self-love. It is just one of the "negative" theories we shall address.

Next, we have what I call "modern narcissism," and it also has its negative aspect. This theory is based on the thought that individual people are committed to insuring their own individual survival regardless of what happens to anyone else. This period of history was dubbed the "Me Decade." It was identified by many experts as the most prevalent psychological disorder of modern Western culture. The "modern Narcissus" is someone who cannot relate to others and who sees the world beyond as a mirror that reflects alternating feelings of personal power on one hand and helplessness on the other.

The modern Narcissus neither falls in love with himself nor returns the love of others. The problem is not too much self-love, but too little. The fatal flaw is not an overdose of self-love, but rather a large measure of self-hate. Unhealthy narcissists are secretly filled with anger, frustration, loneliness and hopelessness. The absence, rather than the abundance, of self-love has led many people, at times, to focus inward, to experiment with encounter groups, drugs, therapy, religion, health fads, casual affairs, communal living, or whatever promises to make them feel better about themselves. The desire to feel good about oneself is an innate part of the human spirit. When this is missing, one can turn to all sorts of outside sources looking for what comes inherently from within.

When you are alerted to the SignPosts and systems for building a balanced self-love, you will be in awe at the different choices you make. Here is one SignPost that is a guide:

*You Can't Really Love Anyone Else Until
You Learn How To Love Yourself*

One point of confusion for many people is their inability to make the distinction between self-love and self-centeredness.

Self-Love Is Not A Dirty Word

For the most part, most of us have been taught misleading SignPosts concerning the way we should feel about ourselves. Philosophy, psychology, and particularly religion, have given us false definitions and teachings about how we are to view ourselves as persons.

Many religions and religious leaders teach that we are "sinners, worms, dust, reprobates" and "are going to hell if we don't straighten up and fly right." We are often led to believe that we are robots with a "holy" umbilical cord connected to God, who controls our every move. We are coerced into thinking we are puppets and do not have value as individuals. Human dignity plays a very small part in many of the religious doctrines throughout the world. It is no wonder that we have a society filled with individuals determined to self-destruct.

Self-Destruction Is Suicide
On An Installment Plan

Most self-destruction occurs when people do not have a healthy balanced self-love. Rather than being a dirty word, self-love is an honorable word, essential for living life in balance and enjoying the life-journey.

Basis For Self-Love

I am often asked: "On what do you base your belief for self-love?" With all the negatives that have been presented throughout civilization, this question is a good starting place for learning about self-love and how to build it. Once you accept that self-love has an intellectual and an emotional foundation, you can begin to incorporate it into your life on a daily basis.

I firmly believe that positive self-love is based on more than just philosophy or psychology. While positive self-love can be viewed through the eyes of thought and mind, I am convinced it also encompasses a "spiritual" dimension.

I purposely use the word "spiritual" as opposed to religion or denominationalism. For me, the concept of "spiritual" is bigger than a religion or denomination. It is empowering to have faith in a source other than myself. Faith in the Creator of the universe and faith in a positive Spirit that surrounds me with power gives me a sense of authority, a feeling of competency, and a presence of who I am. As I have travelled the roads of my life-journey, I have studied various religions and doctrines. While I have learned something from each study, I have come to the conclusion that my spiritual needs are most adequately met from the study and teachings of Jesus.

Many great teachers and philosophers have duplicated His teachings. The teachings of Jesus always acknowledged the value of the individual and encouraged the individual to strive for betterment. He was highly concerned with the plight of people's lives. He was deeply interested in the relationship of people to God and in the relationship of people to people. One of His most prevalent concerns was how people related to themselves. He clearly taught this principle that all religions teach and most people believe to sound good, but few apply:

"Love Thy Neighbor As Thyself"

Regardless of your religious beliefs or particular denomination, you could agree this is a reasonable approach to relating to another person. When this principle is taught, usually the emphasis is put on the "Love Thy Neighbor." However, the significance of this teaching, is **not** in "Love Thy Neighbor." The paramount emphasis should be on "As Thyself." The word "as" means "equal to."

Love Your Neighbor Equal To Yourself

Growing up in a small community, in a very strict religious environment, I was taught every week in Sunday School this rule for living: "Love Thy Neighbor As Thyself." One Sunday I raised my hand and asked: "If that is such a good idea then why don't more people do it?" Around me, I saw gossip, prejudices, back-stabbing, unkindness, intolerance, racism, sexism and a host of other negative behaviors. I was being taught positive principles, and yet witnessed opposite principles being lived out in the lives of the very people who taught me the positive principles. I was confused. My Sunday School teacher had been taught by someone else how to think and teach this principle and so all of the emphasis was on "Love Thy Neighbor."

It was only after becoming an adult in search of alerting, leading and guiding SignPosts that I learned one important fact. I cannot love you, or my children, or my spouse, my parents, my friends or my peers, until I first learn how to love myself in a balanced and positive way.

How can I hope to have a respect for you if I have no respect for myself? How can I value you and your contributions to life if I do not value myself and my contributions to life? I can't and neither can you. It is essential to address this issue of self and self-love in order to establish you, your importance and your value.

Self is an interesting concept. I am partial to Webster's definition that defines self as "the union of elements (body, emotions, thoughts, and actions) that constitute the individuality and identity of a person." You are an individual. You are different in your "body, emotions, thoughts, and actions." Aren't you glad you are different? Just imagine a world where every "self" was just alike. You wouldn't know who was who! You wouldn't know if you were coming or going! I am grateful for the individual self.

Another concept that often gets connected to self is that of the "ego." This is generally thought of as a negative part of the personality, although I do not believe it necessary to categorize it as such. Different schools of thought have different teachings regarding "ego." I suggest, instead, a simple approach to understanding it.

Balanced living simply defines "ego" as "self." Each one of us is a "self" and each one of us has an "ego." It is what makes us unique and different. It is not to be confused with egotism which is defined as "an exaggerated sense of self-importance." Ego is often discussed in the same conversation as conceit. Ego or self can be positive or negative; constructive or destructive. I believe there is a distinct difference between a balanced positive ego or self-love and an egotistical conceited destructive arrogance. We must understand that it is this difference that separates and helps us define constructive and destructive self or ego.

Constructive Ego Or Self-Love

If you will accept that ego means self, then you can accept that there is a difference between constructive ego or self-love and destructive ego or self-hate.

Constructive ego indicates your inherent right to be different and unique as an individual. It further denotes that as an individual you have assets and liabilities. From your assets, you take positive pride in your successes. From your liabilities, you learn discipline and personal development. You learn to value the contributions you make to your home, your family, your relationships, your career, your church, your government and your world. It is important that you understand the value of a balanced constructive self. Once you have this concept as a part of your mind set, you will know that if you do not love yourself in a balanced way, you will make many unhealthy, self-destructive choices.

You will also learn, as you travel the balanced self-love road, you cannot genuinely think of or be concerned for someone else if you are not genuinely interested in yourself. When you have little or no interest in yourself, you may be subjected to serious mood swings resulting in depression, non-productivity or even suicide. Without a balanced self-love feeling inside, you will not be able to weather inevitable events from the outside, i.e.: accidents, illness, financial setbacks, stress, death. If you are void of the power of self-love inside, you will be unable to enjoy fully your successes and your victories. You will be unforgiving and cruel to yourself when you do experience mistakes or defeat. You will be afraid to risk, afraid to do your best for fear of failure.

Destructive Ego or Negative Self-Love

A destructive ego drives one to experience self-defeating thoughts and actions. Many actions, reactions, and responses are the result of self-hate. The braggart, the loud-mouth and the constant attention-getter are examples of a person who has too little self-love. We mistakenly think they suffer from too much self-love. Dislike of one's self, one's image and one's value is a common disease permeating our society.

Look around. What do we see? We see people who are physically ill, mentally and emotionally shattered, spiritually drained, socially outcast, financially impoverished, and family deprived. How does a unique and special creation of God get on these roads? Does an egotistical or destructive self play a part in the choices people make, that drive them to arrive at these conditions? In my opinion, most definitely.

Many people dislike themselves and their entire life-journey is built around self-sabotage. What are the reasons for disliking yourself? Once the reasons have been identified, you can take your own personal self-inventory and choose to change any thoughts or actions that are sabotaging your life-journey.

5 REASONS FOR DISLIKING YOURSELF

1. Childhood Experiences

Certainly, we all know that any kind of positive or negative experience as a child will affect us as an adult. However, we cannot go through life blaming our past, whether good or bad, for the way we choose to act, react and respond today. Self-love or self-hate is not a born trait; it is developed. You can choose to develop self-love even if you have not practiced it up to this juncture of your life-journey. Regardless of what your past has been, you can begin today to learn the principles that can lead you to more balanced self-love. Letting go of the past is a requirement for getting on with today.

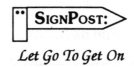

Let Go To Get On

Commit yourself to live in the now and address each experience as it comes with no blame on your yesterdays.

2. Religion

Organized religion has long been a teacher of self-defeating attitudes. Not a single religion is free of responsibility in this area. From Hinduism with its caste system to Buddhism with its self-denial to Christianity with its out-of-balance doctrine of **humility**, many religious teachings in the area of self-love have deprived people of this positive power in their lives.

The organized teachings of many of the Christian principles are misleading SignPosts. I know this first hand, because I was a victim of many of these teachings. Yet, I am completely convinced this was not the goal or plan of Jesus when He left His teachings for us to study and apply on our life-journey.

You might ask: "How did Christianity get so warped?" Actually it began with Aristotle, three hundred years before Christ lived. The Greek philosopher recognized man's almost instinctive inclination toward self-recrimination. Holding a twig in his hand and bending it backward, Aristotle illustrated how people tend to bend backwards and in so doing, condemn, belittle, criticize and run themselves down. Aristotle's solution to this human condition was to advise the human spirit to push forward.

He taught that you have to puff yourself up, strut and boast: "Look at me. Am I Great or what?" Out of this Greek philosophical posture, there evolved a person who was haughty, pushy, puffed-up, boastful. The result? A dangerous and distorted arrogance that found great delight in looking down condescendingly on others.

Against this background, Christianity appeared with its doctrine of humility.

A great problem arose when an attempt was made to translate the Christian concept of self-love into Latin, which is the first language in which the philosophy of Christianity was put into concrete form. A Latin scholar is quoted: "There is no word in Latin which adequately expresses the sense of self-love which Christianity teaches."

The Latin translators, reacting against Aristotle's concept of puffed-up pride, took the teachings of St. Paul and used the Latin word "Humilitas" to describe how you should think of yourself. Unfortunately, the word "Humilitas" better describes the concept of downgrading yourself or running yourself into the ground. Along with the translation came certain connotations. If you think of yourself as a unique, special, important person, you are committing a sin and are a sinner.

In contrast, Christ always gave people's self-image a boost. When He met immoral people, He never called them sinners. Instead, He encouraged them with His teaching of "Follow me and I will help you to become the unique, special and important people you were created to be."

One of the most despised members of His society was the Jew, who was a tax-collecting tool of the occupying Roman army. Such a man was Zaccheus. When Jesus met him, He might have judged him harshly. Instead, He sought to build this man's sense of self-value by offering to spend the night at the house of a man society saw as a two-faced tax collector.

It is interesting that the only persons ever accused of being sinners by Jesus were the very self-centered, narrow-minded, legalistic, self-righteous religious people. "A generation of vipers," He called them. What did they do to deserve this branding? Under the guise of authoritarian religion, they destroyed people's sense of self-love and self-worth. Perhaps nothing destroys one's sense of self-respect more than the finger-pointing, wrist-slapping, fist-shaking religious authorities who claim to speak in the name of God. Mis-taught religion, more than any other social, economic, psychological or political focus, is the primary reason self-hate is a dominating factor in our world. From the mis-teachings of "Humilitas", we were given misleading SignPosts to follow. We must replace these mis-leading SignPosts with those that will alert, guide, instruct, and encourage us on our life-journey. Humility is not putting yourself down, belittling yourself, or shrinking into an unimportant pound of clay. Humility is knowing who you are and who God is and what the two can do together through cooperation.

My personal exploration of "spiritual" has led me to several conclusions about the importance of cooperation between God and me. God won't do anything for me, but God will do everything with me. I need God and God needs me and the two of us working together can make life meaningful and enjoyable.

I strongly suggest that if your life has been negatively affected by negative religious teachings, make a choice to replace the misleading SignPosts. Don't hold on to negative teachings that are keeping you from being the best you.

3. Breakdowns In Family Relationships

Family-relationship breakdowns are caused by several variables and will effect your balanced self-love.

1. Death
2. Divorce
3. Lack of communication

Any one of these will serve to debilitate the positive feelings you have for yourself. (I will address solutions, answers and alternatives for breakdowns in relationships in the chapter on "Family Balance.")

4. Fear And Disappointment

Fear is the most prevalent factor that leads to self-hate or a destructive self. In every way, fear affects the process of developing and maintaining a balanced view of oneself. There are many types of fears and unquestionably, they will keep you on the yo-yo. Here are the fears you face.

F - Fear Of Failure
E - Fear Of Emotional Involvement
A - Fear Of Adventure
R - Fear Of Rejection
S - Fear Of Success

It is critical that fear and disappointment be replaced with faith and confidence. Fear on any level is overcome with thought and action. Whatever fear you may feel in any one of the six areas of life must be dealt with from the "thought-action" process.

Think And Act Now

5. Money

There are two aspects of the money issue and both of them can affect your balanced self love.

1. Affluence
2. Poverty

Poverty, as you can easily understand, can reduce one to little value, not only to the outside, but also to the individuals inside. When one is unable to be productive in a job-related situation, one tends to feel useless and worthless. The human mind connects its value to what it is able to do or accomplish in a work related setting. So when people are not in a work related setting that allows them to be productive, they develop a destructive self.

On the other hand, affluence or having money can also pose a problem for balanced self-love. The abundance of money can reduce a person to a **money-making-failure.** It becomes easy to lose sight of the fact that the real value is not in the money, but in the person who earns the money. I personally know many people who have all the money they can spend, and they too, are on a yo-yo. Money does not insure balance on your life-journey.

A definite balance is needed in the money aspect, in order to develop and maintain a healthy self-love. This can be achieved by:

a. Understanding that money is an exchange for services and goods. It is pieces of paper with old dead people's picture on it. It does not have the ability to be good or bad.

b. Accepting the fact that money does not measure self-value or self-worth. Money is a reward for doing a certain job or accomplishing a certain goal. It is not a measure of you and your value. Just because you are created in the image of God, you have value and worth.

c. Devoting yourself to a career you feel is worthwhile and fulfilling.

d. Using your money wisely and productively.

Now you have a better understanding of some of the reasons behind your feelings of destructive self or ego. To review, they are:

1. Childhood Experiences
2. Religion
3. Breakdowns in Family Relationships
4. Fear and Disappointment
5. Money

As we continue on this journey of learning about self, I want to identify certain aspects of the negative self and then examine certain aspects of the positive self. Knowing these aspects of self will only further give you the information and knowledge you need to develop your balanced self-love.

Aspects Of Negative Self

There are certain aspects and conditions of the negative self that will work against you as you develop a self-love that is balanced and constructive. I have identified 10. When you know what they are and how they affect you toward a destructive self, you can make certain choices that can prevent negative results.

#1 Self-Centeredness

Narcissus was clearly the victim of self-centeredness, not self-love. He was so obsessed with his image that he could not become involved with anyone else. People who are self-centered have difficulty in caring about or relating to others. Also, Narcissus could never satisfy his need for more and still more admiration of himself. This is also a characteristic of self-centeredness. People who are self-centered can never get enough adulation, and perhaps they too, tend to wither away and die, in an emotional sense. Since they cannot accept loving attention from others, their emotional life becomes impoverished.

#2 Self-Defeating

Has anyone ever said to you: "You are your own worst enemy." There is much meaning in this old, but true statement. When you have an out-of-balance destructive self, you tend to act, react and respond in ways that bring about the opposite of your desired results. Have you ever seen a person who desperately wanted to give love and receive love, but through unreasonable behavior and negative attitudes, drove love further away? Self-defeating attitudes creep into every area of your life if you are not fully dedicated to building a constructive self. Even your words can sometimes be self-defeating: "I can't;" "I'm sorry;" "How dumb of me," "I don't really deserve it." From those statements come many of your actions.

What You Think About, You Speak About;
What You Speak About, You Bring About

#3 Self-Will

Self-will is not the same thing as self-determination. Self-will is a negative trait that does deep damage to people on a personal relationship level. The coined phrase to describe it is: "I want what I want when I want it!" It is defined as a "stubborn attachment to one's own desires and ideas, with no concern for others." This is a destructive way of thinking and is responsible for the ruin of countless relationships. Self-will is negative and brings about negative consequences and results. This must be controlled if you are to enjoy a balanced self-love.

#4 Self-Effacing

This is defined as "keeping oneself in the background." Many schools of thought will teach that this is true humility, which I believe is a misleading SignPost. Keeping in the background when you have something to contribute in the foreground is not humility, it is stupidity.

I recall paying a compliment to a young woman who had delivered a beautiful solo rendition of my favorite hymn. She responded, "Oh, you should thank the Lord. It was the Lord singing through me." I replied to her, "No, you should hear the Lord when He sings through me." She, like many, had been taught to stay humbly in the background, to not take credit for that in which she excelled. It certainly does not take away from the supremacy of God when we as His creations excel in using our talents.

#5 Self-Flagellation

This is a condition defined as "extreme criticism of oneself." There are times when self-criticism is not only necessary, it is healthy for you. It is when you go to the extreme that it becomes self-destructive. Have you ever had a friend or loved one say to you: "Don't be so hard on yourself." You usually are harder on yourself than anyone else. Be cautious. Avoid self-sabotage at all costs. Balanced self-criticism is healthy. Extreme self-criticism leads to self-hate and distrust of yourself and your abilities. Replace this extreme execution of judgment with fairness, justice and love.

Other self-negatives that deter you as you move toward balanced self-love are:

#6 Self-Hatred

#7 Self-Pity

#8 Self-Conceit

#9 Self-Glorification

#10 Self-Righteousness

Each of these ten aspects will have a dramatic negative effect upon your balanced self-love. When you replace these negative aspects with the positive aspects, you will then feel the personal power and freedom that a balanced self-love brings into your life. A balanced self-love is a great ally to help you get off your yo-yo.

Aspects Of Positive Self

Now that you know what the aspects of the negative self are and how they lead you to a destructive self or ego, let's focus on the aspects of the positive self and learn how they can build a constructive ego or self-love. For your review, I have also identified ten positive aspects.

#1 Self-Image

This aspect can be either positive or negative. Your self-image is literally the way you see yourself. How you see yourself will determine the way you see and interpret things and people around you. How do you see yourself? What is the picture you have of yourself? Whatever it is, it is like a record going round and round in your head. It is in control of your life. The way you see yourself directs your actions, reactions and responses.

Your answers to the following ten questions will help you identify how you see yourself. They should reveal something to you about the way you picture yourself and the image you have of yourself. Be brutally honest. From your honest self-inventory, you will gain insights to the choices you are making and the changes you will choose to make in order to get off your yo-yo.

Self-Image Self-Inventory

1. YES   NO   Are you satisfied with what you are doing for a living?
2. YES   NO   Do you take pride in your appearance?
3. YES   NO   When you look in the mirror, are you reasonably satisfied with what you see?
4. YES   NO   Do you look forward to meeting people?
5. YES   NO   Do you believe that most people like you?
6. YES   NO   Can you admit a mistake without losing confidence in yourself?
7. YES   NO   Do you regard yourself as a useful, interesting person?
8. YES   NO   Do you consider yourself a person who is worth knowing?
9. YES   NO   Do you know what you want to do with your life?
10. YES   NO   Do you feel fully capable of addressing your problems?

If you have more than four "No's," your self-image needs help. You may want to apply the systems of balanced living and to follow the SignPosts to inform and encourage you as you make changes in the way you see yourself. You want the benefits of a balanced self-love and you can start right now, by building the kind of self-love that will bring you the rewards and benefits you desire, as you travel the roads of your life-journey.

#2 Self-Esteem, Self-Value, Self-Worth

I group these together for I believe they are interchangeable terms and conditions. Esteem, value and worth denote a deep sense of importance. When you accept your importance in the big picture of life, you begin to develop a sense of how valuable you are. You know that you make a difference in life and therefore you make choices that reflect this knowledge and attitude. I have said for many years that when people make destructive choices in their lives, they are demonstrating that they do not understand this aspect of balanced self-love.

Choices Reflect The Degree Of Self-Value

Then, you may ask: "What about the times when I make wrong choices and I make mistakes?" Be of good cheer. Even with a balanced self-love, you will make wrong choices and mistakes, but regardless of what circumstances you may find yourself in, do not forfeit your self-value. You may experience out-of-balance conditions in any of the six areas of life, but you must not allow outside circumstances and conditions to cloud your worthiness as a human being with great potential for life and a beautiful lifestyle. By just being, you are valuable and you are of great worth.

*Just Because You "Made" A Mistake
Does Not "Make" You A Mistake*

#3 Self-Realization and Self-Actualization

To engage in self-actualization is to strive to realize your full potential. To self-realize is to fulfill the possibilities that make-up your individual personality. As you take your self-inventory, think of untapped potential or possibility that could be within your frame of reference to develop. There are unused and unlimited resources within you. However, would it surprise you to know that only about 20% of the people will choose to develop their potential? Most will settle for "just getting by." What a strong indictment on us, as potential giants, to remain dwarfs because we won't choose to take the steps to realize more of our God-given potential. What an insult to our Creator to settle for what we are and not go for what we can become. To not realize more of our potential is to exist and settle for less. To realize more of our potential every day is to live and experience more.

#4 Self-Confidence

We are a society of individuals that need more self-confidence in our homes, our schools, our churches, our government, and our work places. Self-confidence pervades every area of our life. People who have a balanced self-love have a strong positive feel of self-confidence. Confidence is built on small steps of success. When you engage in any activity (love, work, friendship) and succeed, you receive the feeling of a sense of accomplishment. This feeling serves to promote a positive feeling about yourself and your self-value. This, in turn, builds confidence in yourself and your abilities. By the same token, when you do not succeed, you get that feeling of disappointment or failure. This negative feeling of low self-confidence is for a purpose. It drives you to learn about the experience, to correct what can be corrected and to move on to the next experience with a healthy, balanced self-confidence intact Failure does not have to destroy self-confidence. In contrast, failure can help build it. Theodore Roosevelt said this about failure:

"Far better it is to dare mighty things, to win glorious triumphs, even though checkered by failure, than to rank with those poor spirits who neither enjoy much nor suffer much, because they live in the gray twilight that knows neither victory nor defeat."

#5 Self-Respect

Respect is a difficult word to define. We have a sense of what it means, but I want to be specific. Respect is the quality of being decent in character and behavior. When you feel that you have made choices that are decent and when you have set your character values to reflect your decency, you are set in motion to experience self-respect. This is paramount to balanced self-love.

The other five aspects of a balanced self-love will ultimately affect your constructive and balanced self.

#6 Self-Discipline

#7 Self-Dignity

#8 Self-Control

#9 Self-Development

#10 Self-Giving

Each of the ten positive aspects of balanced self-love combine and work together to create the constructive ego or self that becomes the productive, fully alive, fully functioning and balanced you. When you employ the power that these can provide, you can get off your yo-yo.

RECAP FOR "BALANCED SELF-LOVE"

Self: The union of elements (body, emotions, thoughts and actions) that constitute the individuality and identity of a person.
Maximize the positive self.
Minimize the negative self.

Basis for Self-Love:
"Love Thy Neighbor As Thyself."

Constructive ego indicates our inherent right to be different and unique as individuals.

Destructive ego drives one to experience self-defeating thoughts and actions.

5 Reasons For Disliking Yourself:

1. Childhood Experiences
2. Religion
3. Breakdowns in Family Relationships
4. Fear and Disappointment
5. Money

Aspects of Negative Self:

Self-Centeredness
Self-Defeating
Self-Will
Self-Effacing
Self-Flagellation
Self-Hatred
Self-Pity
Self-Conceit
Self-Glorification
Self-Righteousness

Aspects Of Positive Self:

Self-Image
Self Esteem, Self-Value, Self-Worth
Self-Realization and Self-Actualization
Self-Confidence
Self-Respect
Self-Discipline
Self-Dignity
Self-Control
Self Development
Self-Giving

SignPosts For Your Life-Journey:

1. You Can't Really Love Anyone Else Until
   You Learn How To Love Yourself

2. Love Your Neighbor Equal To Yourself

3. Let Go To Get On

4. Think And Act Now

5. What You Think About, You Speak About;
   What You Speak About, You Bring About

6. Choices Reflect The Degree Of Self-Value

7. Just Because You "Made" A Mistake,
   Does Not "Make" You A Mistake

PERSONAL SELF-INVENTORY

1. How do I define self? _____

_____

2. Do I believe that a balanced self-love is essential for productive living? _____

3. Define the following:

   Destructive Ego: _____

   _____

   Constructive Ego: _____

   _____

4. What experiences have I had (past or present) that have influenced me toward a negative self? _____

   _____

5. What experiences have I had (past or present) that have influenced me toward a positive self? _____

   _____

   _____

6. What have I done or what can I do to replace any of my negative attitudes that may be keeping me from enjoying a more balanced life? _____

   _____

   _____

7. Which of the five fears do I experience?

_____

_____

_____

_____

_____

8. What action can I take to overcome my fear(s)? _____

_____

_____

_____

_____

9. How can I continue to develop a constructive balanced ego?

_____

_____

_____

_____

DR. ZONNYA'S FIRST AID

1. In your daily self-inventory, note <u>one</u> asset that you have developed and one liability that you can turn into an asset. This will help you maintain a realistic perception of yourself.

2. You build yourself by building others. Always include a helpful word or deed willingly given to someone else in your daily activities.

3. Release any past experiences (childhood, religion, relationships) that may serve to inhibit your present growth. Do not talk about them. Replace them with a present thought of your improved self and improved conditions.

4. Refuse to allow fear to grow. Whatever your fear, take positive assertive measures through action to find it, face it and fight it.

5. You will experience the feeling of success by building small steps of achievements. Evaluate each day your small steps of success. Then celebrate each one.

AFFIRMATIONS

An affirmation is a positive assertion that expresses a specific belief concerning you and the state of the affairs of your life. It begins with "I" or "My" and always will serve to reinforce all that is unique, special and distinctive about you. Use it often throughout the day. It will inspire, encourage and motivate you as you dedicate yourself to balanced living for a more beautiful lifestyle.

I, _____, accept my

right to have a constructive balanced self-love.

I, _____, know that

with a balanced self-love, I can experience more good in each of the

six areas of my life.

I, _____, maximize my

positive self and minimize my negative self.

"If an individual is able to love
productively, he loves himself too;
if he can love only others, he
cannot love at all."
—Erich Fromm

Chapter 5

BUILD YOUR BALANCED SELF-LOVE

*"This above all: To thine own self
be true, and it must follow, as the
night the day, thou canst not
then be false to any man."*
—William Shakespeare

To build your balanced self-love, you need a system. I strongly believe if you know what the system is, you can then make a choice to work the system. An interesting event happened between me and my husband. I was expressing my displeasure for some minor little thing he had done. My conversation went like this: "Why don't you just get with the program?" He caught me by surprise when he responded: "I would, but I don't know what the program is." I was reminded how important it is to know the system or the program before a proper choice can be made.

I am going to give you a system for building your balanced self-love, but you will have to work the system. You will choose to work the system when, and only when, you are convinced of your benefits. You will benefit in every area of your life when you have working for you a constructive balanced self-love.

This system is primarily built around replacing the aspects of your negative self with aspects of your positive self. Remember, it is not easy to replace; it requires a daily commitment and a daily discipline. But the rewards are valuable and fulfilling.

The first point of this system is to recognize that you, generally speaking, are not taught how to develop a balanced self-love. Tradition teaches a false humility, where self-defeating thoughts lead to self-defeating actions. You must go beyond tradition if you are to acquire the knowledge and skill to build this powerful presence.

I purposely use the term "build" because I think it accurately describes the process that the system needs in order for it to work in your life. In comparison, when you build a house, you start with your elementary plans, then a blueprint is developed and then the structure itself starts to take form. Even after the house is built, you never reach a final point of completion. There is always something that you are repairing, replacing, fixing-up or changing. To "build" is an ongoing process.

The analogy can be made to building balanced self-love. You start with you, as you are now, in the elementary stage of this building process. Then a system is developed that you can implement to help your balanced self-love take form. Even after you have built your self-love, it will always need repairing, replacing, fixing-up and changing. Building your self-love is a road that you will travel throughout your entire life-journey.

A part of every system I develop is built around keeping the system simple. I find great comfort in simplicity. I think my need to keep things simple is directly connected to growing up on a farm. It was a hard life, but it was not a complicated life. You sowed corn, you reaped corn. You sowed cotton, you reaped cotton. You did all that you could do to prepare for a fruitful harvest, and then you knew the rest was in the hands of Mother Nature. If it rained when we needed rain or if the sun shined when we needed heat, our work would be rewarded. On the farm, we were only in charge of doing our part. Mother Nature was in charge of her part.

In today's extremely fast-paced, hi-tech, computerized age, it is difficult to find the "simple" life. Yet, I firmly believe we have made a choice to complicate our own lives. On the flip side of that coin is the opposite choice: to simplify our lives. What the system for balanced living does is simplify, in order to create an environment for application.

Keep It Short And Simple

The system to "Build Your Balanced Self-Love" is developed from the "ABC's Of Self-Love." It is composed of six simple steps that you can take on a daily basis. The steps will guide you as you begin this part of your journey. To get off your yo-yo, you can employ these practical, adaptable, usable and workable steps.

This system is designed for you to apply to your self-growth process. I am confident that, as you utilize these steps on a daily basis, you will be directed toward a new discovery: The discovery of a "new" and more "balanced" you.

SYSTEM TO BUILD YOUR BALANCED SELF-LOVE

Step 1. Accept Yourself

Once you take this first step, you are on the road to building your balanced self-love. To fully accept yourself, you must accept those things about yourself that you cannot change, and must refuse to accept those things that you can change. You must learn to accept your assets and liabilities.

Accept yourself as a vital person who has assets to be developed and used to the fullest. Also, accept yourself as the person who has liabilities that need to be improved and changed. Never reach a point in your life when you think you have nothing to improve or change. When you reach the point of thinking you have arrived, look around and you will probably see that you haven't even left.

One positive aspect of having liabilities is that you do not have to play the game of "perfection." There is something about accepting yourself with your liabilities that takes a lot of pressure off having to be perfect! Once you accept yourself as a human being who does not always act, react or respond in the perfect way, you allow yourself to make mistakes.

From your mistakes, you learn more about yourself and the challenges you experience. Learn to allow yourself to err. Mistakes and errors do not make you less of an effective person.

Remember the SignPost:

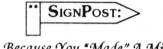

Just Because You "Made" A Mistake
Does Not "Make" You A Mistake

They may very well may make you an even more effective person as you learn and benefit from them. Always look at every experience as a learning experience.

The Only Time You Really Fail Is
When You Fail To Learn

Begin, today, accepting yourself as a vital and vibrant part to the whole. Life is the "whole" and without you, life would be fragmented. Begin to affirm on a daily basis:

I, _____, accept myself as a

unique and special individual.

You are so unique that there is no one who can even compare with you. Nature never duplicates itself; you are the only you. Isn't it exciting to know that when you were created, your Creator did not duplicate you, imitate you or reproduce you in any way? You are one in a lifetime.

I was speaking to a group in Denver and the person introducing me concluded the introduction by saying: "And now I present to you, the one and only, Dr. Zonnya." As I walked to the podium, I marveled at the thought. Truer words have never been spoken. I am the one and only me. You are the one and only you. Wow! That makes me feel pretty special. How about you?

The "accept yourself" process has two points for your consideration.

1. Accept what you cannot change.

2. Refuse to accept what you can change, then change it.

First, how do you accept what you cannot change? Identify the parts of your life that you cannot change. These are people, things and situations over which you simply have no control.

The color of your skin, the way you were raised, the kind of atmosphere you grew-up in, on which "side of the tracks" you were born, what was imposed upon you as a child, the family that you were born into, etc. are all examples of people, things, and situations that were not and are not in your control.

Whatever there is in your life that you cannot change, face it and know if you could change it, you surely would. But since you cannot, you will allow it to be part of your life as you continue to build a balanced self-love. You must choose intellectually, emotionally and psychologically to allow this unchangeable situation to become accepted and approved by you. Many times, you will then find ways to use it to your benefit and advantage.

I share with you two personal experiences of learning to accept myself. The first is a situation that I could not change. The second is a situation that I could change.

I was born a small baby. I grew into a short little girl. I continued to grow, but I did not continue to grow tall. I remained short. And of course, I wanted to be tall. I remember in junior high school, I wanted to be a model. All my friends told me I was too short. Models were tall, willowy, shapely women. There was little doubt that I would ever develop those necessary qualifications.

I remember going home one day crushed. My dream of being a model had been shattered by a guidance counselor. (He had told me to forget being a model. Even well educated educators do not always make right choices. He should have encouraged me to become whatever I wanted to become, but instead, he cruelly shattered my dream). My mother put her arm around me and said, "Honey, you might not be able to be a model, but that's not what is important. What is important is what you can be!" There was nothing I could do about being short, but there was a lot I could do with a person who accepted herself and focused on what she had, not on what she wished she had.

Accept things about yourself that you cannot change by:

1. Fully understanding the situation.

2. Seeking any possibilities that might be available.

3. Thinking well of yourself just the way you are.

4. Acting in such a way as to reinforce the good about yourself.

5. Talking to yourself with a positive affirmation:

I, _____, fully accept myself

and all of me that I cannot change.

My second experience has to do with something I did not have to accept, because I had the ability to change it. I was born with very ugly dark brownish-red hair. For over twenty years, I looked into the mirror to see someone who I did not think looked "pretty." I didn't like myself very much because I had an image of myself that was unattractive. My religion had taught me that if God had wanted my hair to be another color, He would have made it that way. Just think, for over twenty years, I blamed my ugly hair on God.

Then one day I realized that God did not make me have ugly hair. Genetics was the culprit. Once I realized this very important fact, I decided to finally change something about myself that I did not have to accept. To the beauty salon I marched and announced that I wanted "triple-tone" hair: honey blond in the front, bright red in the middle and eggplant in the back.

The hairdresser laughed, but said he would do all he knew to help me reach my goal of change. Several hours later, I was the very proud owner of the most beautiful triple-tone hair ever created. My whole countenance changed. My smile bubbled. My eyes sparkled. My face glowed. I refused to accept something that I could change, so I took action and changed it.

I was speaking in Kansas City and Mr. Negative came up to me during the break. He wanted to tell me he didn't like my triple-tone hair. I don't know why he cared, since he was bald-headed.

It is possible that there are people who don't like my triple-tone hair. That's their choice and they are entitled to it. I know within myself that the color of my hair does not affect the quality of their lives, so I have to confront myself with what my choices will be regarding the quality of my life. I love my hair! I like the way I look and this plays a part in my balanced self-love. It's been many years since that experience and I still love my triple-tone hair. I like me much more because I refused to accept something that I was capable of changing.

You may think "how silly" the hair story is. Silly? Not at all. Nothing, no matter how small it is, is silly if it keeps you from accepting and loving yourself. If you don't have something about yourself that you would like to change and are capable of changing, then it is almost certain that you do not know yourself very well or you are not being honest with yourself.

Take an inventory of you, your assets, your liabilities, your good and bad points in every area of your life. Once you get to know yourself on a more intimate level, you can begin to evaluate yourself more honestly. From your evaluation, you will find many things that need changing and many things that need accepting.

I have a special affinity to the prayer taught by St. Francis of Assisi:

> *"God grant me the serenity to accept*
> *the things I cannot change, the courage*
> *to change the things I can, and the*
> *wisdom to know the difference."*

Step 2: Believe In Yourself

I, _____, believe in me!

You might think the affirmation "I believe in me!" sounds cocky or conceited. While it is possible that it could be said by a self-centered person, its positive application would then be nullified. The "high-hat" who unceasingly tells of self-belief is in fact expressing self-doubt. The "glory seeker" is abusing all that constructive self-value stands for. It is easy to spot the conceited know-it-all. Their self-love, self-respect, self-value, self-belief is always needing to be fed by an outside source. These kinds of people are unsatisfied with their own evaluation of their actions, reactions and responses. They desperately depend on the approval of others.

However, the people who have developed a balanced self-love and self-belief can see themselves as an ever-growing and ever- learning entity. They are satisfied knowing that their actions, reactions and responses are solidly based and may not always win the approval of others. They look for self-approval.

When you demonstrate a belief in yourself, you emanate self-confidence. Self-confidence, or believing in yourself, is a by-product of faith. While faith is a most difficult word and concept to define and understand, I feel that it is a major piece of the self-confidence puzzle. The Bible defines faith as: "The substance of things hoped for, the evidence of things not seen." Webster defines faith as: "A firm belief and trust in someone or something." Please, take just a brief inventory:

Do you believe in yourself?
Do you have faith in yourself?
Do you trust yourself?
Do you have confidence in yourself?

If you answered "yes" to these four questions, you are traveling the road of self-confidence. If you could not answer "yes," you have just taken the first step to getting on the road. The first step is becoming aware of your confidence level. With this awareness operating in your life, you can now begin applying the balanced living systems and you will begin to build your self-confidence.

If you don't believe in yourself, how can you ask or expect anyone else to believe in you? If you don't have faith or trust in yourself, can you ask someone else to have faith or trust in you? Equally important, how can you believe in someone else or have faith and trust in others, if you do not first have it in yourself? Your relationship with other people depends on your self-confidence. Also, it is crucial for you in getting off your yo-yo to develop a belief in yourself. Remember: No one else is just like you and no one can do what you can do.

I am reminded of a little boy who so beautifully demonstrated what believing in yourself means. He told me his story and I learned quite a lesson from this "child" about believing in yourself.

One day this little twelve-year-old boy went into a drugstore to use the telephone. He was a bit too short to reach the phone on the wall, so he went to the Coke machine and borrowed a Coke case. He dragged it over to the telephone, hopped upon it, got his money out of his pocket, dropped it in the slot and dialed a number.

A lady must have answered on the other end of the line because the little boy said: "Ma'am, I'd like to come over and cut your grass." The lady must have said she had someone. The little boy responded: "But Ma'am, he's not as good as me." The lady must have said she was satisfied, but the little boy didn't stop. He said, "But, I'll come over on Saturday and get it all trimmed up nice for Sunday." The lady must have said something else negative because the little boy said: "I'll do it for half-price." Well, the lady must have just got fed up with this little "cocky" kid. She hung up on him.

The little boy smiled and hopped down off the Coke case. As he was returning the case to its place, the druggist yelled at him. "Hey kid. I just heard you on the phone. I like your spunk. You want me to give you a job?" The little boy looked up, smiled, and said: "No sir! I don't need a job. I was just checking up on the job I already have!"

That little boy knew nobody could do what he could do. Nobody could serve his client as he could. No one could contribute to that lady and her yard as he did. He had a genuine case of self-confidence.

Develop faith, trust and belief in yourself and your abilities. Remind yourself of the faith your Creator had in you when only one of you was created. With your faith comes self-confidence and self-belief and with these two, come balanced self-love.

Affirm daily:

I, _____, believe in me.

Step 3: Compliment Yourself

This is the one step of the system that not only builds balanced self-love, but is lots of fun! There is little doubt that you like to do things that are fun. You like to laugh, you like to enjoy yourself and you like pleasurable experiences. I don't want you to be like most people who are so burdened down with their problems that they have very little time for fun.

How does the "Compliment Yourself" step help you build a balanced self-love? A compliment is one way to acknowledge that something has been done efficiently and effectively. A compliment denotes that you have succeeded at a particular attempt. A compliment is an expression of recognition, appreciation and praise. (R-A-P)

I conducted a survey to find out what things people wanted most in life. I was somewhat surprised at the results and you may be, too. Before sex or money, my survey showed that people want and need R-A-P.

Recognition! Appreciation! Praise!

This may be a new concept for you to consider, but before you dismiss it as a possibility of the most important of human needs, let me ask you a few questions.

Do you like to be recognized for what you do?
Do you like to be appreciated for what you do?
Do you like to be praised for your successes and achievements?

Of course you do and please believe me, there is nothing wrong with wanting recognition, appreciation and praise. The main thing is to earn it!

Generally, you think the compliments that you receive should be given to you by outside sources (husband, wife, boss, teacher, children, friends). But compliments should not always have to come from others. Often, you need to compliment yourself.

You are much more inclined to criticize yourself than you are to compliment yourself. Both are necessary for a balanced self-love. Criticism serves as a reminder of your need to change and improve. It is healthy as long as it is balanced with compliments. Too often, self-criticism can get out-of-balance! When that happens, you find yourself being unreasonably severe in your thoughts and actions toward yourself.

When you make mistakes, balanced self-criticism is acceptable. But it is vitally important to remember that because you make mistakes, it does not mean that you are worthless, useless or a big nothing. You are a vital human being who can learn and benefit from each experience.

While I encourage self-criticism, I do not suggest that you take it to the point of self-defeat. Never let an experience go by without dissecting it, microscopically examining it, and taking from it new knowledge about yourself. Criticizing yourself should not be for the sake of punishment; it should be for the sake of learning and improving yourself. It is necessary that you dedicate yourself to keeping a balanced perspective between self-criticism and self-compliment!

Balance Self-Criticism With Self-Compliments

With achievements, successes and progress come compliments. Sometimes they come from others, but always from yourself. Nobody really knows how hard you worked putting that business deal together. No one really understands the time and effort you put into that well-balanced beautifully and tastefully prepared meal. Not everyone notices you as the well-groomed, well coordinated dresser that you are. People are busy and have so much on their minds. You cannot realistically expect them to be ready and waiting to pay you a compliment when you need it. But, you can be ready, willing and able to compliment yourself when you deserve it.

Don't wait on others to compliment you. Compliment Yourself!

Compliments serve to make you feel good about who you are and what you are doing. They are essential to a healthy self-image and self-love. You probably receive at least one compliment every day, but you need more. You need to be reminded of your value and your worth as a unique and special individual. I enjoy giving a compliment to other people and I enjoy receiving a compliment from other people. But I am also dedicated to complimenting myself. I make it a daily practice.

I share with you a truly exaggerated, but humorous event in which my husband, Bob, complimented himself.

The event occurred during the Winter Olympics a few years ago. Everyone was getting gold medals because they could skate and ski, but he was not. However, he knew he was just as good in his field as they were in their field.

First, he went down to the jeweler and had him make a beautiful gold medallion. Next, Bob prepared for the awards ceremony. He had the carpenter make a three tier platform for the awards presentation. Caterers were called in for the celebration dinner. Just the two of us, Bob and Zonnya, were attending this memorable event. After the dinner, he walked to the top level of the platform to receive his gold medal. He nearly wept as he read his accomplishments for the year. As he placed the gold medal around his neck, the only thing that kept him from having a complete emotional breakdown was when I stood and sang the "Star Spangled Banner!"

I agree this sounds silly, even ridiculous, but it worked to reinforce his balanced self-love. You don't have to take a vote from those around you in order to recognize, appreciate and praise yourself. When you have done something big or small, significant or even seemingly insignificant that is worthy of recognition, appreciation and praise, accept it from others with gratitude. Accept it from yourself with sincerity and love.

It is beneficial to do something, in each of the six areas on a daily basis, that deserves a compliment from yourself.
Compliment yourself:

> Physically
> Mentally
> Spiritually
> Socially
> Financially
> Family

When you succeed and compliment yourself, you are propelled by an inner energy to achieve even more success. It is a natural part of the human spirit to want to feel good about yourself. When you do well and feel good, you tend to choose to do things that can keep you feeling good about yourself. It is when you don't feel good about who you are and what you are doing, that you may engage in all types of destructive behavior. When you like yourself you don't want to destroy yourself; you want to build yourself.

Compliment yourself and feel the surge of magnetic power flow through your every cell. You will be inspired and motivated to further achievements. Once you can compliment yourself without any defeating reservations, you will be one step closer to a constructive balanced self-love.

I, _____ , compliment myself.

Step 4: Discover Yourself

What do I mean when I say: "Discover Yourself"?

To begin, what is a workable definition of discover? Webster has a definition that is most appropriate for this discussion:

1. "To make known or visible, expose, display"

2. "To obtain sight, or knowledge of, for the first time"

You have many aspects of yourself that are undiscovered or not known. You have so much potential that is untapped. There are numerous interests that you have not explored. There are unlimited areas awaiting your awareness and attention. Opportunities, challenges, new experiences lie within you and without you. To see them, you will need your own unique system of "obtaining sight and knowledge of them for the first time."

Much has been said, written, and explored in the areas of outer space. At the same time that you may be interested in outer space, remember the importance of exploration into your inner space.

Within your "inner space" lie unexplored interests and hobbies, untapped potential, unused emotions, neglected pursuits, unprepared business endeavors and unnoted possibilities for growth. Now is the time to become aware of and responsible for discovering your own uniqueness. You get so busy with the day-to-day hustle and bustle, the routine of "making a living", that too frequently you seldom choose time to explore yourself. One primary reason for using the technique of "self-inventory" is that it gives you a tool to discover yourself.

There are many reasons for the lack of self-discovery. Fear, lack of self-confidence, inability to change, ego hurts, etc., are all possible reasons. Certainly the reasons need to be confronted and resolved. But one thing you must understand is whatever the reasons are for not discovering yourself, they are not as important as the need for finding the ways to discover yourself.

How do you go about the process of discovering yourself?

First, you take a most valuable self-inventory. List the assets and liabilities about yourself. Be honest! Do not be unduly hard on yourself. Be realistic! Assess yourself in all six areas of life:

Physical
Mental
Spiritual
Social
Financial
Family

Second, make a commitment to develop "funnel vision."

Replace Tunnel Vision With Funnel Vision

It is important you be open to all new ideas, thoughts, philosophies and experiences. Be adventuresome. Get out of the rut. You know what a rut is?

A Rut Is Nothing But A Grave With Both Ends Knocked Out

Do something productive and fun, something you've never done before. Eat a new food that in the past you snarled at. Experiment with a sport or hobby, i.e., art, music, literature, painting, etc. Your funnel vision outlook will begin to open new sights, sounds, tastes, attitudes and desires you were not even aware of in the past.

Third, discipline yourself to experience at least one new thing every day. A new word, a new route to work, or maybe even a new person. Meet someone new on the elevator, in the mall or at the market. Experience a new book, a new magazine article, even a new thought. The more you choose to experience, the more available you will make yourself to the process of discovering yourself.

A good friend of mine in Panama City, Florida had studied my principles and systems for years. While I was there conducting a seminar, he relayed a personal experience of his self-discovery.

He had devoted his entire life to his business and the matter of making money. He had given his undivided attention to just one area of his life, "financial", at the expense of the other five areas.

One day, he discovered a health problem in its beginning stages. Before he knew it, the problem escalated into a serious health crisis. He chose a treatment program and subsequently began his recovery. During this time, he started his personal self-inventory. From it, he discovered many new and different things about himself. He learned he really enjoyed listening to classical music. He uncovered a hidden desire to express himself through the beautiful art of water-color painting.

When he learned that I was to be in the city conducting my seminar, he devoted himself to one of his "creations" just for me. He presented to me a masterpiece with a note that said: "Thank you for encouraging me to discover myself. My discovery has enriched me with a more beautiful lifestyle."

You are never too young and you never get too old to benefit from this step in the system. Now is the time to "Discover Yourself."

I, _____, discover myself.

Step 5: Encourage Yourself

I don't know one single person on the face of the earth that at sometime does not need encouragement. You can look for it outside of you and often times have the right people in place to offer it when you need it. Then, there will be times when the right people won't be there at the time and place you need them. At times like these, "Encourage Yourself."

One system I teach to encourage yourself is: Positive self-talk. I use the power of positive self-talk to give me that special boost when I need it. I particularly like the power phrase: "Yes, I Can."

Everyday, you are faced with obstacles and opportunities.

Beware That You Look For The Obstacles
In Your Opportunities, And Forget To Look
For The Opportunities In Your Obstacles

"Yes, I Can" is just the right stimuli to support you as you confront both your obstacles and your opportunities realistically. As you travel the roads of balanced living, you will set new goals, desire various experiences and make different choices. These distinct events will inherently call upon you to encourage yourself as you get off your yo-yo.

When a problem arises, confront it with: "Yes, I Can Solve This Problem."

When certain issues propose difficult questions, address it with: "Yes, I Can Answer This Question."

When challenges present themselves to you, offer them: "Yes, I Can Introduce Alternatives."

When you employ the power phrase, you activate your personal power. You are stating that you are in charge of you. Your balanced self-love increases when you have an attitude of positive encouragement.

Can you begin to feel the power in this affirmation? Are you aware of the impact this attitude will have on you and the choices you make? Do you feel your shoulders, chest and chin lift just a bit when you affirm: "Yes, I Can?" Can you sense a light of inspiration come alive in your eyes? Are you beginning to glow with a warm flush as this power outlines the strength and determination on your face?

If you choose to allow this power to be a part of your life-journey, the physical effects you will feel will be dramatic. Add to the physical feelings of well-being the positive effects of mental stimulation and emotional uplifting. You are now in a mind-set to further build your structure of balanced self-love.

A word of caution: The "Yes, I Can" system only works when you are honest, realistic and give 100% to the situation. Don't deceive yourself by affirming "Yes, I Can" on something you don't really want to do or believe you can do. Don't cheat yourself by avoiding the facts of a particular situation. Be careful you don't develop unrealistic expectations, only to find that no matter how often you affirm "Yes, I Can," they are unreachable.

"Yes, I Can" works for you when you need just a little extra encouragement in order to reach a realistic desirable result. It is most effective when there is no one around to share that needed encouragement. Remember, it is not other people's responsibility to always be around offering you encouragement. Encourage Yourself.

I share with you a personal experience when I had to call upon the positive power phrase. I had been in the hospital for six days. Several minor surgeries were performed and a barge of laboratory tests were performed. The tests were laborious, discomforting and painful.

I had entered the hospital on a Sunday and was to be released by Wednesday because I had a seminar to conduct in Dallas on Saturday. However, because of complications, I remained in the hospital until Friday evening. I returned home with the feeling that there was no way I could fly to Dallas and present a three hour seminar.

I arose Saturday morning feeling very weak, sore and drained. However, because I practiced balanced self-love and particularly because I knew the power phrase, this condition was only temporary. I had a plane to catch and a seminar to conduct.

I arrived in Dallas with the "Yes, I Can" attitude. On that day, I may very well have given one of the most effective seminars I have ever presented. How? I dared to call upon my own encouragement. I had a goal to achieve, an audience to inspire, and a client who had employed me to give my best 100%. I didn't need pity, sympathy, or "do the best you can" from an outside source. I had deposited within me the encouragement I needed to meet the challenge before me. I relied on my ability to encourage myself.

There are many examples in your own life when you have been called upon to use this power. The secret to this power is that you must develop it and have it as a working part of your being before you can apply it when you need it. Encourage yourself on a daily basis. Then, when the time comes where you need to draw on it, you will have the source of your power charged and ready to perform for you. There is power for your life when you encourage yourself.

I, _____, encourage myself.

Step 6: Forgive Yourself

If you implement the first five steps, but leave out Step 6, you will be unable to achieve the balanced self-love that leads to a more beautiful lifestyle. This step is essential.

Remember Step 3: Compliment Yourself and how you discovered the power of the feeling of accomplishment and achievement.

Also, you discovered that along with self-compliments goes self-criticisms. Both are necessary to maintain a realistic balanced view of your assets and liabilities. Of course, you enjoy the compliments more than the criticism, but now you know that both serve a useful purpose on your life-journey.

While I encourage self-criticism for the purpose of learning, growing and changing, I also strongly encourage that you implement Step 6 in order to free you from any emotional and psychological hang-ups that may accompany self-criticism.

Once you have made a mistake, failed to reach your goal, faltered in expressing your emotions effectively or whatever the situation, "Forgive Yourself" allows you to obtain relief from any guilt and fear that may linger. You will never enjoy your life-journey if you operate in the guilt and fear mind-set.

One of the most difficult tasks you will have as you travel your many roads is to learn to forgive yourself. It is interesting that the principle of forgiveness is taught by every religion. You most probably are familiar with the teachings of the forgiveness of God. You know that when you have wronged someone, the principle of forgiveness is applicable. Do you also know that self-forgiveness is equally important? The forgiveness principle is not totally effective until the "forgiveness trinity" has been addressed. It looks like this:

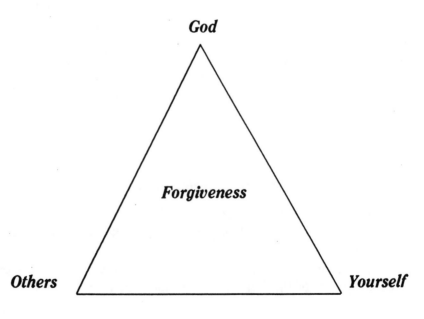

The triangle demonstrates the three entities of forgiveness: God, others and yourself. Without self-forgiveness, you never feel free of the encumbrances that certain choices and actions create. Without self-forgiveness, you continually feel a sense of self-defeat and failure. When you are able to forgive yourself, you automatically feel a burden or weight lifted from your shoulders. You once again feel fully alive and are able to function at a higher level of performance. To get off your yo-yo, implement this step in the balanced living system.

In my years of working with people, I have seen countless lives in ruin because they did not know or practice the "Forgive Yourself" system. When I look around and see people who look like they are bearing the cares and hurts of the world on their shoulders, I know immediately they don't know about self-forgiveness. You will make mistakes in life. At sometime in life, you will fall flat on your face. You will experience failure in the six areas of life. But falling on your face is not nearly as important, as picking yourself up, forgiving yourself, learning from the experience and beginning again.

I practice the fine art of self-forgiveness on a daily basis. Since I know that I am not, nor will I ever be perfect, I accept that I will make mistakes and fail. This is part of the life-journey. I have experienced the guilt and fear of this human condition and I know how debilitating the diseases (dis-ease) of guilt and fear can be. Guilt does more to destroy personalities, marriages, professions, health and friendships, than any other self-imposed limitation. It promotes self-defeating thoughts and actions. You can never experience balanced self-love with a heart, mind, soul, and image full of guilt and fear.

There is a distinct difference in "being guilty" and "feeling guilty." When I learned this distinction, it changed my life-journey. Because I grew-up in a strict, legalistic religion, I thought you were supposed to feel guilty and with this feeling came all those other terrible feelings, such as: self-doubt, anger, frustration, hate, etc. I had to learn the difference in "being guilty" and "feeling guilty."

Example: If I lash-out at a co-worker for no reason and cause hurt to this person, I am guilty of hurting this person and restitution is appropriate. For me to hang on to feelings of guilt serves little purpose. I forgive myself and allow the healing nature of forgiveness to return me to the natural state of balanced self-love.

If I run a red-light and hit a car and injure the driver, I am guilty of a traffic violation, of causing injury and I must answer for my actions. However, through forgiving myself, I need not choose to allow the feelings of guilt to inhibit me from living a fully functioning life. I face the penalty and I forgive myself.

When I implement the forgiveness triangle, I ask the forgiveness of God and others, then I ask for self-forgiveness. Every night before I go to bed, I apply this step. I look into my mirror and I say: "Zonnya, forgive me. For any and all that I said or did this day that was unproductive or injurious to others or myself, forgive me." What this does is set in motion powerful dynamics of fairness, faith and freedom.

How do you rid yourself of the disease of guilt and fear? Certainly not by drugs, alcohol, self-pity or other destructive behavior. You gain your freedom when you practice self-forgiveness. I encourage you to choose time to engage in self-forgiveness. You will discover a brand new you each day of your life when you are not carrying the baggage that guilt and fear imposes upon you.

I, _____, forgive me.

To "Build Your Balanced Self-Love, learn from these six steps. Now that you have the knowledge, you can make the choice to implement it into your life on a daily basis. It will not suffice to do these steps just one time. Balanced self-love requires you to develop it daily. You will experience your life-journey with so many more positive and powerful forces in your life and you will get off your yo-yo the minute you make your choice and begin your action.

RECAP FOR "BUILD YOUR BALANCED SELF-LOVE"

System: ABC's For Building Balanced Self-Love:

Step 1: Accept Yourself
Accept what you cannot change.
Refuse to accept what you can change, then change it.

Step 2: Believe In Yourself
Know that you are a unique and special individual.
Develop trust, faith and confidence in you and your abilities.

Step 3: Compliment Yourself
Three things you want before sex or money:
Recognition - Appreciation - Praise.

Step 4: Discover Yourself
Take a valuable self-inventory.
Develop "funnel vision," instead of "tunnel vision."
Enjoy one new experience daily.

Step 5: Encourage Yourself
Use positive self-talk and the power phrase: "Yes, I Can."

Step 6: Forgive Yourself
Employ the forgiveness triangle to free you of guilt and fear.

SignPosts For Your Life-Journey

1. Keep It Short and Simple

2. Just Because You "Made" A Mistake
Does Not "Make" You A Mistake

3. The Only Time You Really Fail Is When You Fail To Learn

4. Balance Self-Criticisms With Self-Compliments

5. Replace Tunnel Vision With Funnel Vision

6. A Rut Is A Grave With Both Ends Knocked Out

7. Beware That You Look For The Obstacles In Your Opportunities, And Forget To Look For The Opportunities In Your Obstacles

8. Separate What Is Important In Your Life From What Is Not

PERSONAL SELF-INVENTORY

1. Do I accept myself as a valuable and unique human being? _____

2. Can I accept my assets and liabilities? _____

3. Do I change the things about myself that I can? _____

4. What are some changes that I have made or can make? _____

    _____

    _____

5. Do I have a genuine or false self-confidence? _____

6. What can I do to build my belief in myself? _____

    _____

7. Do I compliment myself when I deserve it? _____

8. Do I criticize myself realistically or too harshly? _____

9. What three things do I want most in life?

    1. _____

    2. _____

    3. _____

10. Do I attempt to discover something new about myself every
    day? _____

11. List some new discoveries about myself and my lifestyle: _____

    _____

    _____

12. Do I practice the "Yes, I Can" principle? _____

    If so, how and when? _____

_____

_____

13. What does forgiving myself mean to me? _____

_____

_____

_____

14. What action am I taking to build my balanced self-love? _____

_____

_____

_____

DR. ZONNYA'S FIRST AID

1. Get yourself a notebook or diary and write down the six steps for building your balanced self-love. On a weekly basis, enter your own personal thoughts and actions toward each one.

2. Do something on a daily basis for someone else you consider to be worthwhile.

3. You have taken the first step toward building your balanced self-love by learning this system. Now, take action by using each of the six steps.

4. Schedule a specific time (morning, during the day or evening) for your own personal time. Make an appointment with yourself and keep it. You deserve it and this time will help you focus, think and make choices about the roads of your journey.

5.
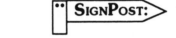

Separate What Is Important In Your Life From What Is Not

6. Each night before you turn out the light and go to sleep, look into your mirror and say: "I forgive me."

AFFIRMATIONS

An affirmation is a positive statement that expresses a specific belief concerning you and the state of the affairs of your life. It begins with "I" or "My" and always will serve to reinforce all that is unique, special and distinctive about you. Use it often throughout the day. It will inspire, encourage and motivate you as you commit yourself to balanced living for a more beautiful lifestyle.

I, _____, accept myself

as a valuable and unique human being who contributes much good

to life.

I, _____, like me.

I, _____, understand that

both compliments and criticisms are necessary for a balanced self-

love. I realistically evaluate each experience and compliment or criti-

cize myself in order to enhance my growth.

I, _____, forgive myself daily.

This insures fairness, faith and freedom in my life.

*"The greater our scientific and technological
advances become, the more emphasis
we must put on the importance
of the individual."*
—Chief Justice Earl Warren

PART II

SYSTEMS FOR BALANCED LIVING

The goal as you study the systems for balanced living is to identify where you are out-of-balance and then implement the systems to put you back in balance and off your yo-yo. A chapter will be devoted to each of the six areas of balanced living. Along with the questions, problems and challenges of each area, I will offer simple, practical, adaptable, usable and workable answers, solutions and alternatives. Please adapt each idea, each system, each SignPost to yourself and your individual lifestyle.

As you read and internalize this material, you may think that it is common knowledge. As a matter of fact, a person attending one of my seminars made that very statement to me. He said: "Dr. Zonnya, all of the stuff you teach is common sense. It's just common knowledge." Interestingly enough, I agreed adding just one slight insight. I replied: "Yes, sir, it is, but it's not common practice."

Knowing the "stuff" is only step one; practicing the "stuff" is what will bring you results. You can't practice it until you know it and then once you know it, you make the choice to practice it. In each chapter of Part II, I will remind you of things you may already know, but need a refresher course on. Also, I will offer you new ways of looking at things, with new ideas for practicing what you know.

Yes, you can get off your yo-yo and enjoy a balanced living lifestyle.

Chapter 6

PHYSICAL BALANCE
Life Looks Better When You Do

*"If anything is sacred,
the human body is sacred."*
—Walt Whitman

Physical "out-of-balance" is no fun!

Yet, you most probably have experienced or are experiencing some out-of-balance problems related to your body. Some of these can be prevented; others will have to be treated. Please note: when a problem exists that cannot seemingly be solved through your own reasonable means, do consult a specialist in the field of the problem area.

Feeling well and looking well is the normal, natural way to be. In spite of the way you feel or look right now, the basic fact remains that it is the nature of things that the life you live should be healthy and every function and action of your body should be perfect. However, because of the misuse and abuse you give your body, you more often than not, live in a body that does not feel or look as nature intended. The time is now to restructure your thinking and your actions toward your physical being and its balance.

Remember, balanced living is built on three basic pillars and these apply to physical balance:

1. Individual awareness daily to your physical area
2. Individual importance daily of your physical area
3. Individual responsibility daily for your physical area

From these three, you can begin your personal self-inventory. Listed below are ten statements. Use them as a guide. Add your own statements and answers to insure that you are seeing your physical area as it really is.

1. My diet is typically: Balanced or Out-of-balance

2. My weight is: Balanced or Out-of-balance

3. My exercise program is: Balanced or Out-of-balance

4. My health habits are: Balanced or Out-of-balance

5. My work time is: Balanced or Out-of-balance

6. My rest and relaxation is: Balanced or Out-of-balance

7. My physical awareness and care of my body is: Balanced or Out-of balance

8. I allow my stress to be: Balanced or Out-of-balance.

9. My time of sick days each year is: Balanced or Out-of-balance

10. My knowledge of my body is: Balanced or Out-of-balance

What you have done with just these few statements is to verbalize the pluses and minuses regarding your physical life. This knowledge allows you to be aware, assign value to and accept responsibility in a way that promotes change in your physical area.   If there would be one word that I would choose to describe "physical balance", I would choose "HEALTH." I want to use "HEALTH" as an acronym to brighten your vision of the "HEALTH" concept. Health is not about being skinny, eating fad foods, or looking like a magazine model. Health is so much more than those things. When you add this information to your mental computer, you will be able to make many different choices as you travel the roads of your life-journey.

Physical balance, not physical yo-yo, should be your way of life and a part of your daily living. Let's look at "HEALTH" and see the powerful benefits that it has to affect your life. There are six characteristics that compose "HEALTH."

H - Humor
E
A
L
T
H

Humor

Laughter Is What We're After

Everybody likes a good laugh and we need more laughter in our lives. I contribute much of my physical balance to learning how to develop a sense of humor. We are not born with more humor or fun or laughing ability than someone else. We learn and develop our ability to smile, to laugh, to look for the **fun** in life. Since I came from a family who was serious about life, about religion, about every aspect of life, I did not grow-up with much laughter and fun. When I was growing up, I did not watch cartoons or read the funny papers or even know what comedy was. I had to develop my sense of humor and learn how to laugh. What a difference this made in my physical balance.

Endless research has been done on the relationship between humor and health. It is encouraging to know that with a fun-loving belly-laughing approach to life, you can live life more in balance and can live a longer and more fulfilled life.

Saturday Review editor Norman Cousins, suffering from a physician-diagnosed incurable disease, reviewed Candid Camera episodes and Marx Brothers films and, in part, belly-laughed himself into health.

He felt so strongly about this part of his health that he devoted his last years to speaking and writing about the effects of laughter on the life process.

Humor has a "profound connection with physiological states of the body," writes Raymond A. Moody, Jr., M.D., in *LAUGH AFTER LAUGH*. He goes on to say that "over the years I have encountered a surprising number of instances in which, to all appearances, patients have laughed themselves back to health, or at least have used their sense of humor as a very positive and adaptive response to their illnesses."

There is a link between sense of humor and longevity. Research shows those who laugh the loudest live the longest.

Grow Old Better, Not Bitter

There are two ways to grow old: better or bitter. A sense of humor will play a major role in the attitudes you choose toward things and people.

Some researchers have suggested that by laughing you provide a healthful massage for your internal organs. Other studies point to the possibility that by defusing anger, laughter can prevent some heart attacks. Still other studies state that by alleviating depression, laughter may very well play a role in reducing the risk of developing cancer. In addition, laughing is good exercise. Norman Cousins called it "internal jogging" and he was right on target.

It is suggested that the average person needs 15 or more laughs a day. On some crazy level this might be a good yardstick for you to use to evaluate what kind of day you are having. I often challenge myself to see what kind of day or week or month I'm having by the volume of laughter I experience.

Fifteen Laughs A Day Keeps Sickness Away

If you find yourself not enjoying laughter each day, you can assess that you are out-of-balance. There is a balance needed between seriousness and lightness. The ratio needs to be balanced on a daily basis.

Besides making you feel better, the use of humor can be a major tool for insight. It can point out your own idiosyncrasies and eccentricities and can help you learn to laugh at yourself. Laughing at or with others at their strange ways can be fun, but often, it's different when it comes back to you. Learn to laugh at yourself. Humor is a healthy technique for putting events, people and yourself in the proper perspective.

"There are three things which are real," wrote John F. Kennedy. "God, human folly, and laughter. The first two are beyond our comprehension. So we must do what we can with the third."

"Laughter is like a medicine," notes the Bible. It is good for whatever ails you. Develop your humor, your laughter and your love of living, to enjoy your journey to it's fullest.

Health Can Be A Laughing Matter

H - Humor
E - Exercise
A
L
T
H

Exercise

The phenomenon of physical fitness is an international past-time. It has captured our attention. Hundreds of books, television programs, spas, diet and exercise centers are just a few of the by-products of our interest in physical balance. Everybody talks about exercise, many actually do it, but few seem really to enjoy it. I think it should be fun.

From our early experience in school with gym classes, most of us were left with the impression that being fit has to involve sacrifice and even pain. I offer a different interpretation of the fitness concept.

For those of us who do <u>not</u> want to be Olympic champions, but <u>do</u> want to look and feel like champions, there is another alternative. I understand the concept "with gain comes pain," however, pain runs against human nature. To minimize it is the best alternative. It has been said that all living organisms move away from pain. I am convinced more people would develop a life-time exercise program if it was more fun and had less pain connected to it. We are looking for what makes us feel well, look well, be well.

Why do so many exercise programs fail? Because they do not offer enough pleasure. Any fitness program that does not afford at least as much pleasure as pain will fail. You are designed to feel good, not bad. Exercise does not have to be painful, boring, or limiting. There are many ways you can get the exercise you need and make it a fun experience.

Here are some ways to get yourself up and going.

1. Determine specifically why you want to exercise. Is it to lose weight? Just thinking about the calories you're burning can sometimes keep you going. You burn 300 calories an hour when you walk, for example. That may sound like a mere droplet of fat, but it all adds up over weeks if you combine regular exercise with a reduction of calories. And the good news, experts say, is regular exercise actually diminishes your appetite, particularly your appetite for junk-food. Also, regular exercise changes your metabolism. You burn more fat all day and all night, not just while you are exercising.

    Perhaps weight-loss is not your primary motive. Perhaps you simply want to be fit. Fitness is an admirable motive for getting off your exercise yo-yo. Consider these statistics: the average person has a fifty-fifty chance of experiencing a stroke or developing heart disease. Without exercise, your muscles, including your heart muscle, lose strength and begin to waste away. Blood vessels actually disappear. But regular exercise helps prevent heart disease, keeps bones strong, controls blood circulation, gives you energy and rejuvenates you.

2. Determine specifically what keeps you from exercising. Is it time that you use as an excuse? Remember: time is about choosing, not about having. Consider getting up half an hour earlier. The

extra energy you get from exercising will more than compensate you for the loss of sleep.

3. Set aside a specific exercise time in advance. Even if your timetable must change day-to-day or week-to-week, pre-plan your exercise time.

4. Follow a regular routine for just twenty-one days. It's easy enough to keep going if you know it's for a limited time only. (This applies to a diet, too). Behaviorists say new habits become ingrained in just three weeks. Also, after three weeks, you will feel such a noticeable improvement that you would not want to relax your efforts.

5. Reward yourself for sticking to your schedule. Be imaginative. Don't use food as a reward. Be creative.

6. Increase your everyday activity. Park at the far end of the shopping center instead of right by the door. Get off the bus a stop or two before your destination. Get out of the elevator on the floor below or above the floor you're going to. Pace the subway platform. Walk down the hall to see your office colleague, rather than using the phone. Think of the jugs of water you lift as weights. When you bring in the groceries, think of your time as getting physical exercise. Lift and lower them several times before you stock them away in the cupboard. Think of household tasks as calisthenics.

  There are many ways to "get up and going". Use each experience throughout the day as an advantage. Open up to the many possibilities you encounter on a daily basis. Once you are convinced of the benefits of exercise, you will find ways to keep it fun and exciting.

Tips For Keeping Exercise Fun

1. First, if you are hard-driving and success-oriented, don't let today's accomplishment become tomorrow's obligation. Take each day as it is. Remember yesterday is gone and tomorrow is not here. Do what you do today. Live up to what you do today, not what you did yesterday. Each day is a new day.

2. Remember that variety is the spice of fitness, as well as the spice of life. If you find your exercise routine is getting boring, then change it. Change your surroundings. Change your activity. In terms of actual weight loss, there is an advantage to changing your activity. Studies have shown that you burn fewer calories at any given activity as you begin to get better at it. Clumsiness, in a word, burns more calories than expertise.

3. Choose something that doesn't feel like exercise.

4. Go easy on yourself. You are a pleasure-seeker at heart, not a "pain-o-maniac".

5. Exercise at different times of the day. Routines can create boredom. If you get bored by a routine, change it around.

6. Don't be afraid to miss a day. Laboratory tests show it takes about five days of doing virtually nothing to bring about any loss of heart or lung capacity. Muscle tone holds up even longer. Stop the panic at the mention of business trips, family affairs or weather conditions that might prevent you from making your appointed rounds with the exercise doctor. Fitness is more durable than you may think.

7. Feel free to suit your exercise to your moods. Today, you might feel like a real intense game of tennis; tomorrow, a slow easy walk on the beach.

8. Learn to listen to your body. For all its apparent shortcomings, it has an undeniable sense of justice. Treat the body too hard by exercising too much, eating too little or working too hard and it will express its disapproval by hurting or by being grouchy. Treat it too softly and it will announce its concern by feeling heavy and lazy. Somewhere in between there is a balance. It will be your individual choice to find and develop your own physical healthy balance.

    While I enjoy a variety of exercises, my favorite is walking. It is the exercise of choice that I recommend.

A report made public by the National Institutes of Health, reveals that walking regularly has been found to diminish demineralization of bones, reduce aging of the lungs and cardiovascular systems, help control obesity, improve circulation, reduce arthritic problems, greatly reverse late onset of diabetes in overweight people, lower high blood pressure and improve mental attitudes.

Most of us don't realize that even a short walk causes the heart to beat rapidly and work harder, raising the pulse rate. If that happens for a short time every day, the heart's stamina is increased. A moderate walk is comfortable and safe for most people.

One misconception about walking is that it stimulates the appetite and will cause you to eat more. On the contrary, a half hour walk will make you feel more keenly alive and you will be less bored, hence want to eat less.

Walking puts every part of your body to work, particularly the muscles of the feet, calves, thighs, buttocks and abdomen. As these muscles expand and contract, they will help your heart pump its 24 hour quota of about 72,000 quarts of blood through some 100,000 miles of capillaries, veins and arteries that make up your body's circulatory system.

Exercise is essential to your physical balance and it is fun!

H - Humor
E - Exercise
A - Appearance
L
T
H

Appearance

Life Looks Better When You Do

How you look, from head to toe, to yourself and to others makes a significant statement about your interest in your balance. It has been said that you don't have a second chance to make a first impression.

Although it is not my intention here to go into details of proper dress, color coordination, etc., how you look cannot be overlooked as an important factor in physical balance.

It is important that I add to this discussion about appearance, a note regarding weight. The world of advertising has been highly successful in programming us that to "look good" we must be thin. Many people have suffered physical, mental and emotional hurt because of this misleading SignPost. I strongly emphasize that how much you weigh is a part of "health" and it is an individual issue based on body size, bone structure, genetics and personal preference. I know first hand how the weight issue can get you on an endless yo-yo. Consult with a professional, review the facts concerning you and your body, make a determination of how much you can weigh to enjoy optimal health and then make your choices to move toward that result. Do not weigh yourself everyday; do not discuss your weight; do not allow yourself to get into a mind-set that will drive you crazy. Stop the craziness!

Appearance begins with awareness. Awareness leads to action when you accept your own individual responsibility for the way you look. Certainly, some of the old sayings are true: "You can't judge a book by its cover" or "Beauty is only skin deep" or "Beauty is in the eyes of the beholder." It is, also, certainly true you should want to look as good as you can look, given what you have to work with or change. Sometimes, it is appropriate to make changes in your appearance in order to achieve your best look and feel. New knowledge must be gained and new habits must be developed.

I remember many of the stages and changes I have encountered to enhance my health and physical appearance. I've heard it said that we've become a society concerned only with looking young. Maybe yes — maybe no! What is more important than looking young is to dedicate yourself to putting your best foot forward; not for the benefit of others, but for the benefit of yourself. I take good care of me for me! Take good care of you for you!

From head to toe, I have chosen to do things that are to my advantage. With appearance, goes hygiene. My dentist was always on my case because I did not use dental floss! One day, he really got my attention when he showed me a picture of a mouth that was diseased and out-of-balance. He made the point by illustrating to me what my mouth would be like unless I got my teeth, gums, and tissue healthy. From that point on, I began to develop my dental hygiene. Also, I had to have crowns put on five of my teeth, due to an automobile accident. It was scary, painful, and uncomfortable, but I knew that for me to enjoy good dental health and good physical appearance, this was the course of action I needed to choose. Now, I work daily on an important part of my appearance, my smile! It's bright; it's confident; it's healthy. No, it is not easy and yes, it is worth it!

I also remember changing my hair color and how it affected my entire appearance. With today's world of miracles, you can almost do the impossible. Your appearance deserves your awareness and responsibility. There is always a way available to help you reach your goal for a healthy and balanced physical appearance if you are dedicated to finding it!

Not only are women concerned about their appearance, but men have also learned how important their appearance is to their balance. I have observed my husband as he made choices about his appearance. As he got older, he discovered that to read he either needed longer arms or larger print. As a minister/speaker, he did not want the bothersome task of always having to push his glasses back upon his nose as he was delivering his most energetic and expressive talk. He wanted his audience to remember what he said and not how many times he took his glasses on and off. So, he set out to find an alternative to this challenge. Strange as it may sound, he found an answer: wear one contact in one eye and nothing in the other eye. One eye would see the distance; the other eye would see the close-up. Although it sounds crazy, it works for him.

The point to be made here is you have a choice and it is your responsibility to do what needs to be done to promote your good health and pleasing appearance. As you take your personal inventory, give special attention to your appearance aspect. Start at the top of your head and examine each part of you all the way down to your toes. Identify those things about your appearance that give you a feeling of well-being. Give equal attention to those things that you want to change or need to be changed in order to bring a sense of health and balance to you as you travel your life-journey.

Once you have made your identification, it is your choice to take action.

Add Years To Your Life While Adding Life To Your Years

1. Exercise regularly.

2. Don't smoke.

3. Keep your weight at a moderate level.

4. Drink only in moderation.

5. Minimize stress.

6. Use prescription drugs cautiously.

7. Always look your best.

> H - Humor
> E - Exercise
> A - Appearance
> L - Leisure
> T
> H

Leisure

Leisure is what you do just for you and in today's hurry-and-worry world, you most probably do not do just for you very often. You may be so caught up in your work, in your duties, in your responsibilities or in your routines that you have allowed yourself to get out-of-balance where leisure is concerned.

One fundamental SignPost for your life-journey:

Choose Time For You

I don't mean in a selfish self-centered way. I mean in a balanced and healthy way, allowing you to replenish and revitalize your own physical balance.

Leisure activities are expressed in many ways. From pitching horseshoes to cross-country skiing, people experience leisure differently. There is no one way that is right or wrong. Whatever you do that gives your body a change of pace and is fun and exhilarating to you, choose to go for it. You always have a choice of the kind of leisure in which you engage. Make the right choice that is suitable for you. Leisure should serve as a diversion. It should redirect and refocus your body and mind. It helps to alter your perspective. Leisure should be just plain ole **fun!**

Leisure Alternatives

1. If you feel regimented or feel you have little control over your life, maybe you could try photography, or collecting, playing a musical instrument. For something more active, try hiking, roller skating, or swimming.

2. If your personal life is full of tension and frustration, I suggest that you get into tennis, touch-football, throwing darts, working out at the gym or sky-diving. Do an activity that releases your aggressive feelings in a productive way.

3. If your work offers you little opportunity to be creative, look into painting, sketching, sculpting, photography, home decorating, landscaping or flower arranging. These will give you the opportunity to be expressive as only you can be.

4. If you work under a deadline pressure, you may need to give yourself an open-ended amount of time in your leisure activities. How about target-shooting, roller skating, hiking, or walking on the beach or biking?

5. If you work with machines, you will need to get out into nature and find the soothing comfort that nature will bring to you. Cross-country skiing, camping, fishing or any type of water sport will offer you a new viewpoint of the world.

If these have not quite "caught your fancy," pursue some other form of leisure that is more suitable to your personality and needs. There are too many activities available for you to deny participation in the one just right for you.

If you do not allow yourself time for yourself, you will soon run dry. My dad used to tell me when I was growing up on the farm that if you continued to take water out of the well and water did not get put back into the well, it would soon run dry. Just like the well, if you give out of yourself and don't put back into yourself, you too will run dry. You will lose the lust for living that brings about a more beautiful lifestyle.

H - Humor
E - Exercise
A - Appearance
L - Leisure
T - Tranquility
H

Tranquility

Tranquility is defined as "free from disturbances or turmoil." Very few people I know live life with tranquility. To be quite honest, I don't think it is possible to travel the roads of your life-journey completely free from disturbances or turmoil. However, I do think you can position yourself for certain blocks of time in which you do not experience disturbances or turmoil. The statistics on crime, drug and alcohol abuse, stress, divorce, and finances are just some of the out-of-balance situations that rob us of our tranquility. How can we be free from turmoil when we live in a world so full of turmoil?

Tranquility is a major part of the physical balance. Certainly, throughout any given day you experience turmoil and disturbances of one kind or another. There are no easy answers, but there are some alternatives that you can choose to use in your daily living.

Two mechanisms that can help you effectively cope with disturbances and turmoil are:

Rest
Relaxation

Without the proper rest and relaxation, you cannot function effectively. They are essential to a healthy and balanced body.

There are literally hundreds of techniques for learning to relax. Books specifically designed to teach you how to relax are available. Transcendental meditation, yoga, relaxation response, prayer or religious rituals are just a few of the techniques available for your use. You will want to experiment with different techniques until you find the ones that can key you into a relaxed mind and body.

Personally, I use several techniques. Because I am the very energetic type, I often have to concentrate to wind myself down. My exercise and leisure time are vitally important as I focus on relaxation. I employ meditation, affirmation, prayer and controlled positive thinking as other methods for relaxing. And there is nothing quite like watching a beautiful sunset and marvelling at nature and her wonders for quieting my mind and body.

Experiment with many different techniques until you discover what works for you. You will experience, however briefly, a time free of disturbances and turmoil and this will greatly contribute to your physical balance.

How important is it that you get the adequate rest you require? Many health problems begin to develop when you do not receive proper and adequate rest and sleep. Every person is different when it comes to the number of hours of sleep needed per night. Through your personal inventory, you will discover the right amount of sleep you require to function at your optimum level.

Several factors can contribute to a good night's sleep. Let's review just a few of them.

1. Light
   Light is a stimulant to wakefulness.
   Darkness provides the quiet and calm for sleep.

2. Temperature
   Ideally, the room should be around 70°F. Proper temperature is essential for going to and remaining asleep.

3. Noise
   Quiet is basic to sound sleep. The rule is that any level of extraneous sound, especially if it is non-rhythmical and atonic, is anti-

sleep. There are exceptions, such as the person who leaves the radio or TV on all night, or has a fan humming in the background, etc. While this is not the typical case, it is not considered to promote good sleep.

4. Air circulation
   Still air is stale air and stale air is not conducive to sound sleep. Open the door or window. Get the air moving.

5. Humidity
   Ideal room humidity is ordinarily in the range of 30% - 35% and it furthers the continued sleep process.

6. Bed
   The mattress should be of a firm nature to give better body support.

These are just a few of the factors that can contribute to or detract from the quality of your sleep. Adequate amounts of sleep, along with the proper kind of sleep, will insure you the rest you need to cope effectively with turmoil.

Another form of rest is napping. Many cultures employ the technique of napping as a way of increasing productivity. The regularity of afternoon naps (between 1:00 p.m. and 3:00 p.m., averaging 20 minutes each) has been said to be a major factor in easing fatigue, reducing tension and preparing you for better sleep at night.

There is no question that sleep deprivation affects people in a variety of ways, mainly by changing their moods. A sleep deprived person becomes irritable, short tempered and even depressed. Unquestionably, decision-making is also affected. Even though our society does not recognize the napping technique as an official one, many people use it to increase physical balance.

Develop your own unique and individual style for getting the rest and relaxation that you need to cope effectively with disturbances and turmoil. There is no way to rid yourself totally of the turmoil and disturbances in your world, but you can be prepared to meet them head on with the highest effectiveness and efficiency possible, by practicing the systems of rest and relaxation.

H - Humor
E - Exercise
A - Appearance
L - Leisure
T - Tranquility
H - Habits

Habits

Your habits play a determining role in the kind of health you will enjoy. Your habits will guide you to balanced living or out-of-balance living. It's time to take a physical self-inventory and identify your physical habits.

If You Don't Take Care Of Your Body,
You Won't Have A Place To Live

You only have one body and one life to live with it! Your habits can be your friends or your enemies; they can help you or hurt you. They are first cobwebs, then cables. They are bobs or sinkers; cork or lead; holding you up or pulling you down!

There are productive habits and non-productive habits. The key is to increase the productive habits and replace the non-productive ones. Here are a few prominent non-productive habits:

1. Smoking
   Cigarettes are the chief cause of preventable death in the world. Yet, millions persist in the habit. Thousands will die this year of smoking related cancer. Remember the SignPost: Everything is a matter of choice; choice equals results.

2. Excessive drinking
   The numbers continue to rise and the problems created by this choice continue to affect thousands. Not only is the drinker adversely affected, but so is anyone who is a part of the life of the drinker, many times including innocent victims.

3. Consumption of salt, sugar and flour
    These contribute to the aging process and to the free flowing of
    the circulatory system. I was told by a deep-caring friend how
    pretty I was. Then he grabbed my cheek, shook it a little and said:
    "Honey, your looks won't make it to 35 if you continue eating
    and drinking all that sugar." I was a "Coke-aholic" and he ap-
    pealed to my sense of vanity. I reviewed the facts and have since
    replaced my sugar habit with natural foods and drinks.

4. Dieting
    You knew I would get to this sooner or later. Well, here it is!
    There is no one diet for everybody. There are many good aspects
    of the many hundreds of diets available. They key is balance. Fad
    diets usually are out-of-balance. Your body is not a fad, so why
    treat it with a fad? Good eating habits are essential to a balanced
    body. You are familiar with the basic food groups. You know to
    reduce the amount of fat in your diet. You know to push back
    from the table. If you're like me, you don't have a thyroid gland
    problem. You have an elbow gland problem! Research the diet
    that best suits you and your lifestyle. Start and don't stop. This is
    the challenge.

*Dieting Is One Of The Few Games Where
Losers Win And Gainers Lose*

Here are some suggestions:

1. Never use food as a pick-me-up.

2. Remember food is not your best friend.

3. Got the blahs? Don't eat. Get active. Stay busy.

4. Avoid eating when you are angry. Take a walk to "cool-off".

5. Learn to celebrate without food. It is not a reward.

There are many habits that you choose. One sure way to find out their plus or minus value in your life is to ask: "Does it add to my balance or contribute to my out-of-balance?"

To enjoy a physical balance and health, add two more ingredients:

Commitment
Dedication

You can choose to become committed and dedicated to your body. You can choose to activate willpower and self-discipline to reach and maintain the kind of physical balance and health that will end your yo-yo living and bring you a more beautiful lifestyle.

RECAP FOR "PHYSICAL BALANCE"

Physical Balance Requires: Individual Awareness Daily
Individual Importance Daily
Individual Responsibility Daily

Physical Balance As Defined By: "HEALTH"

H - Humor
E - Exercise
A - Appearance
L - Leisure
T - Tranquility
H - Habits

Two Additional Ingredients For Health: Commitment
Dedication

SignPosts For Your Life-Journey

1. Laughter Is What We're After

2. Grow Old Better, Not Bitter

3. Fifteen Laughs A Day Keeps Sickness Away

4. Health Can Be A Laughing Matter

5. Life Looks Better When You Do

6. Add Years To Your Life While Adding Life To Your Years

7. Choose Time For You

8. If You Don't Take Care Of Your Body,
    You Won't Have A Place To Live

9. Dieting Is One Of The Few Games Where
    Losers Win And Gainers Lose

PERSONAL SELF-INVENTORY

1. List five of my own physical out-of-balance conditions:
   1. _____
   2. _____
   3. _____
   4. _____
   5. _____

2. Do I enjoy at least 15 good laughs a day? _____

3. What are some of the things about myself I find to be humorous?

   _____

   _____

   _____

   _____

4. Describe my exercise program: _____

   _____

   _____

   Do I need to develop an exercise program? _____

   Do I accept my responsibility to my body? _____

5. Are there things about my appearance I would like to change?

   _____

List three:

1. _____

2. _____

3. _____

6. What one thing do I do that is purely for the sake of fun? _____
_____

7. Do I have a tranquil presence about me? _____

Do I get my needed rest? _____

How many hours of sleep are required for me to function at my highest level of performance? _____

8. List three "good" habits I practice daily:

1. _____

2. _____

3. _____

9. List three "bad" habits I need to replace:

1. _____

2. _____

3. _____

10. Am I fully committed to my body? _____

11. Am I fully dedicated to my body? _____

12. Do I accept my full responsibility for my physical balance? _____

DR. ZONNYA'S FIRST AID

1. Read something every day that will increase your knowledge about your body. There are many articles and books available on diet, exercise, dress, color, etc. Knowledge is imperative for you to have in order to apply it accordingly.

2. Experience one good laugh during the day that you can share with someone else. If nothing happens in your day's activities, read something that is humorous. It is essential that you get that "internal massage" on a daily basis. It's so much more fun when you share laughter with others.

3. Allow at least fifteen minutes each day for some sort of planned exercise. You can choose to spare 15 minutes. It will make a significant difference in your physical balance.

4. Plan one activity each week that will enhance your appearance. Try a manicure, a facial, a new haircut, a new shade of lipstick or nail color, a different shirt or pair of pants, etc. There are endless things you can do to contribute to a more pleasing appearance that will not break the bank. You deserve one treat a week.

5. If you smoke: STOP!

6. Include in your daily routine a time for something that helps you relax. Something that is FUN! However short the time maybe, it is necessary for you to use a diversion for good physical health.

7. Ease up on the salt, sugar and flour intake. It is amazing how good food tastes without them. It will take a little getting used to, but you can do it and be so much better for the effort.

8. Celebrate each day. Life, in and of itself, is a celebration, but you need a little extra "rah-rah" on a daily basis.

9. Never let a day go by without doing at least one thing to improve your physical balance.

AFFIRMATIONS

An affirmation is a positive statement that expresses a specific belief concerning you and the state of affairs of your life. It begins with "I" or "My" and will always serve to reinforce all that is unique, special and distinctive about you. Use it often throughout the day. It will inspire, encourage and motivate you as you commit yourself to balanced living for a more beautiful lifestyle.

I, _____, accept that good

health is my natural state.

I, _____, choose to do those

things that will help me enjoy my good health.

I, _____, accept my

responsibility for my humor, my exercise, my appearance, my leisure, my tranquility and my habits.

"Health is a precious thing, and the only one,
in truth, which deserves that we employ in its pursuit
not only time, sweat, trouble and worldly good,
but even life: inasmuch as without it, life comes to
be painful and oppressive to us."
—Michael Montaigne

Chapter 7

MENTAL BALANCE
If You Don't Use It, You Lose It

"All men desire by nature to know."
—Aristotle

The mind and the body have many common characteristics. If you do not exercise the parts of your body, you can experience what is called "atrophy," which is the degeneration of the parts you don't use. Like the body, the mind will also degenerate if it is not stimulated and stretched. I know many people who have hung a door-sign on the door knob of their mind that says: "Do not disturb."

Get A Check-Up From The Neck-Up

While I encourage you to get an annual physical check-up for your body, I more strongly encourage you to take a monthly, weekly, even daily check-up of your mind.

While each of the six areas of balanced living is equally important, I do feel that special attention must be given to the mental area. The mind is the home of your attitudes and thoughts, and from your attitudes and thoughts all your actions, reactions, and responses will unfold. The mind consciously, unconsciously and subconsciously directs all processes for the six areas of your life.

Hundreds of years of study still have not revealed all the possibilities and potentials that the human mind contains. Even with all the research, experiments, publications, etc., all professionals recognize that we have just begun to discover the capabilities that the mind possesses. The mind is the center of existence and the more you know about it, the more you can use it to your best advantage. Your mind can be your best friend or your worst enemy.

Respond to the following ten statements and you will get a glimpse of just how formidable the challenge of your mind really is.

1. My learning is: Balanced or Out-of-balance

2. My knowledge about my work is: Balanced or Out-of-balance

3. I tend to look on the brighter side of life: Balanced or Out-of-balance

4. My temper is: Balanced or Out-of-balance

5. My skills regarding my job are: Balanced or Out-of-balance

6. My attitudes tend to be: Balanced or Out-of-balance

7. My emotions and feelings are: Balanced or Out-of-balance

8. My worry is: Balanced or Out-of-balance

9. The stimulation of my mind with subjects other than my work is: Balanced or Out-of-balance

10. My actions to change the things in my life that I can change are: Balanced or Out-of-balance

These statements are designed to open to you new awareness concerning the many different aspects of mental balance. If you answered out-of-balance to any of these statements, do not feel alarmed. Awareness is the first step toward more balance and to getting off your yo-yo.

Think of the mind as the center of your existence. Every thought, every word, every action, every reaction and every response you experience begins in your mental center. When you improve your mental center, you will improve your lifestyle. The nature of your life is determined by the nature of your mind. What goes on inside your mind affects every part of your life. If you want to change the external aspects of your life, you must begin with internal changes. Where do you begin? I choose the acronym "LEARN" to guide us as we delve into the mystery of this great concept: the mind.

As the mind is the center of existence, it has five components that merge together to give you what I call "mind power." When I use the term "mind power," I am referring to your power over your mind, not the power someone else can have over your mind. Your greatest asset is your mind power and you begin to develop that power through your learning. Each of the five components are centers that enhance your mind power.

L - Learning Center
E
A
R
N

Learning Center

It is within the capability of the mind to store hundreds upon hundreds of megabytes of information. Your mind is the greatest computer that has ever been computed. IBM and NCR cannot begin to compete with the unlimited power and possibilities that you have right between your ears. Research indicates that people only use 10% to 12% of their potential. Can you just imagine what kind of lifestyle you would have if you just used 5 more percent? You increase your potential by your learning.

Our country promotes the need for learning, yet we see our school systems not meeting the needs of our youth. (I could write another book on that subject.) After our formal education is completed, most of us become satisfied with adding little, if any, knowledge to our learning center. What we do learn is usually demanded if we are to continue in our careers.

Learning is a road you choose and as you grow older it should be a continual part of your life-journey. Learning is the master key to growth, better living and balanced living.

When You Stop Learning, You Start Dying

How many people do you know who are content with where they are in life? One main reason for this passive, mediocre existence is the absence of learning. Learning keeps you alive, interested and interesting.

To Be Interesting, You Must Be Interested

One of the greatest challenges you will face in your life is to keep on living until you die. One way to keep living is to keep learning. Learning guarantees you will keep growing.

An older gentleman was asked by the president of my Rotary Club to give a presentation on how to grow old gracefully. The man responded: "What are you talking about? I'm not growing old, I'm still growing up." He knew the one sure way to stay young, interesting and alive was to keep growing and keep learning.

Cardinal John Henry Newman, 19th Century English theologian and author, wrote: "Growing is the only evidence we have of life."

Learning is a personal commitment you make for your life-journey. You must become a **self-motivated** student of life if you want to enjoy the rewards of a beautiful lifestyle.

There are three ways you learn: by reading, listening and observing. Here are a few suggestions as to how you can enhance your learning center.

1. Read
   Reading is a main contributor to successful, happy, productive living. It is also the major difference in people who have developed a sense of adventure and those who have not. Challenge yourself to read something you may think you don't like; you may surprise yourself and develop a new interest.

2. Listen

   Listen to people, television, radio, audio, music, etc.
   Listen with your ears open. Tune out the negative; tune in the positive.

3. Observe

   Look with your eyes open. Clean your mental windshields so you can see things differently.

You Can't Do Things Differently Until
You First See Things Differently

These are just a few ideas that will add to your learning and growing. Choose to invest in your learning center.

L - Learning Center
E - Emotion and Feeling Center
A
R
N

Emotion And Feeling Center

The mind is not only the learning center of your life, it also is the center of your emotions and feelings. Much research has been done in the fields of emotions and feelings. While I respect the ideas and opinions of others, I have arrived at my own personal assessment of these two. There are two emotions: love and fear. From these two emotions, all feelings evolve. There are numerous feelings that you experience, both positive and negative. Positive feelings emerge from the emotion of love; negative feelings, from fear. Love and fear, more than logic or reason, determine how you act, react and respond on your life-journey.

To travel your many roads productively, you will want to develop a balance between emotions and feelings, logic and reason. You cannot simply be an emotional person, nor on the other hand, simply a logical person. You will want to combine and balance these two for gaining the most productive results.

The mind is the center for your emotions and feelings. Exactly how powerful are the emotions of love and fear? They can create your health or sickness, happiness or sadness, friends or enemies. Review the following chart for an inside look at what the negative emotion of fear creates. Then check the positive emotion of love and the results it brings into your life.

CHARACTER TRAITS THAT CREATE ILLNESS OR HEALTH
—NEUROTIC ANONYMOUS—

Fear = Illness	Love = Health
Self-pity	Empathy
Resentment	Understanding
Anger	Acceptance of Reality
Defiance	Tolerance
Intolerance	Humility
False Pride	Service
Selfishness	Generosity
Greed	Honesty
Blaming Others	Compassion
Indifference	Satisfaction
Dissatisfaction	Patience
Impatience	Faith
Dread	Not Being Judgmental
Self-hate	Concern for Others
Envy	Gratitude
Disdain	Happiness
Depression	Richness
Anxiety	Joy in Living
Guilt	Energy
Remorse	Laughter
Psychosomatic Illness	Responsiveness
Insomnia	Warmth
Irritability	Motivation
Tension	Peace of Mind
Suicidal Thoughts	Optimism
Homicidal Tendencies	Usefulness
Abuse of Loved Ones	Adjustment
Loneliness	Purpose
Withdrawal	Long-Suffering

©Neurotic Anonymous International Liaison, Inc.

Of course, you prefer the results listed under "Love = Health," yet you experience many of the results listed under "Fear = Illness." While it would be unrealistic for you to never expect to experience fear and its many results, I suggest there are things you can do to minimize the fear in your life that creates such devastating results. Here is a straight-forward plan for minimizing negative results.

1. Face the feeling clearly and candidly

If you feel anger, hate or jealously, face the fact that you are choosing to feel it. Acknowledge to yourself that these feelings are within you. You own your feelings. You are entitled to your feelings and no one can argue that what you feel is what you feel. This will create for you an increased level of awareness and a sense of control. Once you are aware of the feelings you are choosing, you have the power to make other choices.

2. Take action on the feeling

Begin by understanding how you arrived at a particular feeling. Ask yourself if the feeling is justified and reasonable. Write down on paper how you are feeling. This helps add a dimension of logic to the emotion.

3. Replace the destructive feeling with a constructive feeling

You must be fully convinced that no matter how much you have the right to feel as you do, the one person that your negative feelings most affect is "you"! Usually replacing a negative feeling begins with an act called "forgiveness". You may need to forgive someone for a certain reason, but most of all, you will need to forgive yourself for developing the negative feeling. Once you do this, replacement is a cinch. Replace hate with feelings of good will. Replace envy with feelings of gratitude and acceptance.

The reality of your life today depends upon the balance of the centers of your mind. Your mental power directs your life. Your emotion-and-feeling-center can build you up or keep you down. It can create for you a heaven or a hell. Your emotion-and-feeling- balance is necessary if you want to enjoy a more beautiful lifestyle.

L - Learning Center
E - Emotion and Feeling Center
A - Attitude and Thinking Center
R
N

Attitude And Thinking Center

Some people are easily upset; others aren't. Some people always seem to find what's wrong; others seem to always find what's right. Some look for the bad; others look for the good. What makes the difference? Attitude and thinking make the difference.

What Happens To You Is Not Nearly As Important As Your Attitude Toward It

You are in total charge of your attitude and your thinking. No one can make you think what you do not choose to think. You may blame someone else for your attitude and thinking, but to do so is to follow a misleading SignPost.

No Blame Is Allowed

Assume your personal power over what you choose to think. There are three mental attitudes or ways of thinking that will increase your balanced living and help you get off your yo-yo. If these attitudes are used negatively, they can ruin your life-journey:

1. Your Attitude Toward Yourself
2. Your Attitude Toward People
3. Your Attitude Toward Problems

Your attitudes toward these three are determined by the way you think and you are in charge of the way you think. Unfortunately, thinking has a poor reputation in many people. It has almost become an extinct species.

Thinking Is Not Hazardous To Your Health

It has been said: "Five percent of the people think. Ten percent think they think and the rest would rather die than think."

Henry David Thoreau wrote: "The millions are awake enough for physical labor, but only one in a million is awake enough for effective intellectual exertion; only one in a million to a poetic or divine life. To be awake is to be alive."

And even before Thoreau, an anonymous writer expressed his sentiments sarcastically when he said: "Learn to think. It will profit you well, for there is so little competition."

These descriptions may have exaggerated the challenge of thinking, but they do point out a most important fact: thinking is essential for productive living. Reserve the right to do your own thinking. Do not give someone else the right and privilege to think for you. It is an individual process. Make good use of yours. Remember: thoughts are things.

What You Think About, You Speak About; What You Speak About, You Bring About

Everything in your world begins as a thought. To control your thinking is the greatest achievement you can pursue. It is in fact, the only thing over which you have complete control.

What is your attitude about life? What do you think is the purpose of your life? What are your attitudes about yourself, people and problems? The answers to these questions will give you an insight into your mental balance. Let's examine each of the three basic attitudes individually and learn more about how they affect mental balance.

1. Your Attitude Toward Yourself

What is your attitude toward yourself?
How do you think and feel about yourself?

The attitudes you hold about yourself will color every aspect of your life. It is essential that you develop positive, constructive, realistic attitudes about yourself.

Accept yourself as an important part of life. Develop a good opinion of who you are, what you are doing and where you are going. Recognize that you have assets and liabilities. Don't judge yourself too harshly. Like yourself, in spite of your imperfections.

Not only do you need a liking-you attitude, you need to set a goal to improve yourself every day. Self-improvement creates a good feeling toward yourself.

Go Into Competition With Yourself

Because of our highly competitive society and work-place, we are taught from a very young age that we must compete with others. This teaching has created some extreme out-of-balance feelings for many people. One reason why so many people get depressed, discouraged and feel down on themselves is because they are always comparing themselves with others. This is a big mistake and a misleading SignPost.

The most important person and the only person you can ever really compete with is yourself. There is no one else like you, so how can you realistically compete with someone who is so different than you? Can you compare apples and oranges? Not really, because they are two different foods. If you understand the competition principle, it will relieve you of many tensions, pressures and stresses that are needless for you to experience.

Wherever you are in life and whatever successes or achievements you have enjoyed, work at improving you. Don't get caught in playing the game of "keeping up with the Joneses" or "being better than the Smiths." Be better than you!

Don't compare yourself with anyone else. Forget all about the position or success of others. Measure yourself on your own standards and by your own merits. Your standards should be:

1. What you have done
2. What you are doing
3. What you can and will do

You are in a race with yourself and you can always be the winner. Your attitude toward yourself will determine whether you win or lose. Where and when you start and where and when you stop is all up to you! You are in charge of your attitude and thinking about yourself.

On a daily basis employ the power of these three attitudes toward yourself:

1. "Self-Love" Attitude — I like me.
2. "Self-Confidence" Attitude — Yes, I can.
3. "Self-Improvement" Attitude — I improve me.

Your mental balance depends on your attitude toward yourself.

2. Your Attitude Toward People

How do you generally feel about people?

Do you have a positive feeling of expectation or a negative feeling of doubt?

Your continued mental balance is served better when your attitude toward people is constructive. This is difficult to maintain sometimes, especially when you have been disappointed or hurt by someone that you believed in and trusted. But your happiness and success are enriched when you maintain a general attitude of: I like people and accept people in spite of their faults.

"People who need people are the luckiest people in the world" are words from a song and every time I hear Barbra Streisand sing them, I am reminded that life is made for interaction with one another.

As John Donne said, "No man is an island." I need people and people need me. You need people and people need you. We need each other.

Trust, faith and confidence are things you must believe in and look for in others. Never will you feel so good as when you feel good about those around you. When people disappoint you, don't let it taint your picture of humanity. Remember: no person is perfect, including you. Accept people, knowing they have the ability to improve.

Accept People As They Are,
Not As You Wish They Were

Three attitudes to develop toward people are:

1. Attitude of Acceptance
    Accept people as they are, knowing what they can become.

2. Attitude of Trust
    Trust people to always act, react and respond in a positive, constructive manner. They may not always respond as you want them to, but always trust that the best of them will shine.

3. Attitude of Forgiveness
    Forgiveness is a major link to happiness and a well balanced mind. Never harbor ill feelings toward others. Even if you have reason to feel negative toward a person, don't. Grudges create out-of-balance; forgiveness creates balance.

Feel good about people. Send out the emotion of love and the feelings of trust and faith to others. You will be surprised how much you will get in return.

3. Your Attitude Toward Problems

Life presents many experiences we call problems or challenges. For some people, their attitude will be: "Too much to handle;" "Poor me;" "I can't cope;" "Why me"? For others, problems are looked at as opportunities. Just imagine a given day with no problems, no opportunities, no challenges. How boring, dull and uninteresting it would be. Of course, most of us would like to have a few less problems each day. But since that may or may not be possible, what we must do is develop a balanced attitude toward them.

Look For The Opportunities In Your Obstacles And
Not Just The Obstacles In Your Opportunities

Welcome obstacles because you know they can present you with opportunities. When you are faced with a problem, immediately feel a surge of energy in you that says: "Be creative. Use your imagination. Look for the alternatives." Don't ignore a problem in hopes that it will go away; don't pretend that it does not exist; don't blame someone else. Instead, acknowledge it and put to work your problem solving abilities.

You do have those abilities. Develop your problem-solving attitude. Think alternatives, not excuses. When you are faced with a problem that needs alternative solutions, remember the three-question system:

1. What is the problem?
2. How did the problem evolve?
3. What can I do to solve the problem?

Once you have satisfied yourself with realistic and reasonable answers to these questions, you will be open to problem solving systems.

If you assume a confident "problem-solving" attitude toward the problems you face in each of the six areas of life, you are certain to gain self-respect and a sense of your own balance.

Three attitudes to develop toward problems are:

1. Attitude of Welcome
   Be grateful that you have problems to solve. Cemeteries are filled with people who would change places with you no matter how difficult your problems seem to be.

2. Attitude of Alternatives
   No problem has just one solution. Generally there are several possibilities that can be examined. Never jump to the first or easiest answer. Give yourself the opportunity to be creative.

3. Attitude of Solution
   There is no problem that cannot be solved. You may not always like the solution, but there is always a solution to every situation. Don't leave problems hanging. Assume the position that you have the ability and capability to create the right solution.

When you think about problems, people and yourself, use the "Think Power Daily Dozen." These are twelve attitudes that you can reinforce every day into your mental computer as you stay in charge of your thinking on a daily basis.

"Think Power Daily Dozen"

1. Think Of Yourself As Successful
2. Think Of Yourself As Loving
3. Think Of Yourself As Attractive
4. Think Of Yourself As Friendly
5. Think Of Yourself As Helpful
6. Think Of Yourself As Generous
7. Think Of Yourself As In Charge Of You
8. Think Of Yourself As Strong
9. Think Of Yourself As Courageous
10. Think Of Yourself As Optimistic
11. Think Of Yourself As Affluent
12. Think Of Yourself As Having Peace Of Mind

Balanced Living Does Not Come "The Way" You Think;
It Comes "From The Way" You Think

If You Think You Can - If You Think You Can't;
Either Way, You're Right

You have now added attitude and thinking to the power of your mental center.

L - Learning Center
E - Emotion and Feeling Center
A - Attitude and Thinking Center
R - Reason Center
N

Reason Center

Reason and logic unite with all of the other centers to build a strong, sound, productive and balanced mind. As I noted earlier in the discussion of the emotion and feeling center, emotion and feeling must be balanced with reason and logic. They demand to be balanced for the highest performance of productivity.

To use reason and logic in your day-to-day living, incorporate the following three steps into your mental center for approaching any situation. Remember: reason and logic is a process.

1. Separate Facts From Opinion, Then Analyze Them
   It is easy to play into the game of taking things at face value without looking at what lies beneath the face. Emotion and feeling sometime override fact. To use reason and logic, you must be able to distinguish fact from emotion and feeling. Once you have the facts separated from opinions, you can begin to examine each for clearer understanding. Define the situation as it is, not as it appears to be.

2. Research Possible Solutions, Backed-Up With Evidence
   The solution must be acceptable in terms of the facts that will back it up. Be sure not to jump to conclusions. The facts must support your choice. Look for the assurance that the solution can be implemented.

3. Take Appropriate Action
   Action is the only thing that brings results. You may not always be right in your action, but it will never be said that you do nothing and take no action. There are some people who never make mistakes; they are the ones who do nothing. Refuse to be a do-nothing person.

Always remember: you live in an imperfect world. The people you live, work and associate with are all imperfect. Even when you use reason and logic, along with emotion and feeling, solutions may also be imperfect. One obvious sign of your balanced living will be when you develop the capacity to live with an imperfect solution to a human situation.

L - Learning Center
E - Emotion and Feeling Center
A - Attitude and Thinking Center
R - Reason Center
N - Now Center

Now Center

To fully enjoy mental balance, you will want to live in the NOW! Your mind has the ability to look back or to look ahead; to live in the past or to live in the present; to forget or to remember.

Remember What You Should Remember;
Forget What You Should Forget

Most people remember what they should forget and forget what they should remember. The only time that you can choose to forget or remember is now.

Your yesterday is gone. Nothing that you do can change your yesterday. You can feel good or bad about it. You can see it as a success or failure, but you cannot change it! You may ask: "What do I do with my yesterday?" Learn from it, enjoy it, forget it! Sure you will reflect on it from time to time. Reflection should serve only to help you as you are changing and growing. Never should you look back with regret nor bitterness nor disappointment. To live a healthy balanced life you must free yourself of looking back.

You Will Never Move Forward Looking Back

I tell my audiences that I am trying to get the mechanic to take the reverse out of my car, because it is usually when you are backing up that you hit something. Just put it in high gear and keep on going.

When you choose to live life in the rear-view mirror, you never enjoy the scenery ahead. You don't know where you're going; you only know where you've been. You'll miss the turns on the roads of your journey because you won't see them until you're past them. You can't avoid the bumps and potholes because you won't see them up ahead. Choose to live life with a full front view of your roads. Choose to travel your roads with a clean and clear mental windshield. **You can enjoy your journey.**

Just as you can do nothing about your yesterday, you also can do nothing about your tomorrow, because when it gets here, it is today. Certainly, I believe in planning and I teach goal-setting. But the purpose of planning and goal-setting is to prepare you for a day called "today"; a time called "now."

The time is now!

Now is when you are in charge of you.

Now is the time for you to use your mind and your mental balance to get off your yo-yo and enjoy all the rewards and enrichments you choose for your life-journey.

RECAP FOR "MENTAL BALANCE"

Five Centers For Mental Balance:

    L - Learning Center
    E - Emotion and Feeling Center
    A - Attitude and Thinking Center
    R - Reason Center
    N - Now Center

To Enhance Your Learning Center:

    1. Read
    2. Listen
    3. Observe

Two Emotions That Feed All Feelings: Love
                                                Fear

To Turn Negative Feelings Into Positive Feelings:

    1. Face The Feeling Clearly And Candidly
    2. Take Action On The Feeling
    3. Replace The Destructive Feeling With A Constructive Feeling

Three Mental Attitudes To Develop:

    1. Your Attitude Toward Yourself
    2. Your Attitude Toward People
    3. Your Attitude Toward Problems

To Use The Reason Center Effectively:

    1. Separate Facts From Opinion, Then Analyze
    2. Research Possible Solutions, Backed-Up With Evidence
    3. Take Appropriate Action

SignPosts For Your Life-Journey

1. Get A Check-Up From The Neck-Up

2. When You Stop Learning, You Start Dying

3. To Be Interesting, Be Interested

4. You Can't Do Things Differently Until
   Your First See Things Differently

5. What Happens To You Is Not Nearly
   As Important As Your Attitude Toward It

6. No Blame Is Allowed

7. Thinking Is Not Hazardous To Your Health

8. What You Think About, You Speak About;
   What You Speak About, You Bring About

9. Accept People As They Are,
   Not As You Wish They Were

10. Look For The Opportunities In Your Obstacles, And
    Not Just For The Obstacles in Your Opportunities

11. Balanced Living Does Not Come "The Way" You Think;
    It Comes "From The Way" You Think

12. If You Think You Can - If You Think You Can't;
    Either Way, You're Right

13. Remember What You Should Remember;
    Forget What You Should Forget

14. You Will Never Move Forward Looking Back

PERSONAL SELF-INVENTORY

1. Am I fully aware of the possibilities that lie within my mind to be explored? _____

2. Do I believe that a continuing education is necessary for me to grow? _____

3. What one new thing have I learned today? _____

    _____

4. List the title and author of the last book I read: _____

    _____

5. Do I resist learning new things? _____

    Am I in a rut? _____

6. List my general attitude toward myself: _____

    _____

7. List my general attitude toward people: _____

    _____

8. List my general attitude toward problems: _____

    _____

9. Am I generally a happy, fun loving person? _____

10. How can I increase my happiness? _____

_____

11. List one feeling that seems to dominate my life: _____

12. Am I changing things about myself to create a more balanced life?

_____

13. List five such changes:
    1. _____
    2. _____
    3. _____
    4. _____
    5. _____

14. List three problems that I have faced and solved in the past week:
    1. _____
    2. _____
    3. _____

15. List five things that I think of myself as:
    1. _____
    2. _____
    3. _____
    4. _____
    5. _____

16. Do I use more logic or feeling in handling my day-to-day activities? _____

17. Do I tend to live in the past, always reflecting back on how bad or good it was? _____

DR. ZONNYA'S FIRST AID

1. Dedicate yourself to your self-improvement. Nothing is more important than you becoming a better you.

2. Make a list of four books that you want to read this month. Set a goal to read one book each week.

3. Meet one new person every day. You be the one to start the conversation. Look a person straight in the eyes when you are talking.

4. When a negative feeling enters your mind, immediately get up and do something. Fight it with action.

5. Make at least one change in yourself every week. It can be in any of the six areas of life, but don't let a week go by that you don't make a change.

6. Begin each day by encouraging yourself that you can handle, effectively and efficiently, any situation that arises.

7. In your next argument, employ the techniques of reason instead of feeling. You may be surprised who comes out ahead.

8. Forget those things which are behind and live in the now.

AFFIRMATIONS

An affirmation is a positive statement that expresses a specific belief concerning you and the state of the affairs of your life. It begins with "I" or "My" and always will serve to reinforce all that is unique, special and distinctive about you. Use it often throughout the day. It will inspire, encourage and motivate you as you commit yourself to balanced living for a more beautiful lifestyle.

I, _____, am optimistic about

life. I look forward to, and enjoy, challenges.

I, _____, know that people

feel better when they do things well, so therefore, I trust people to do

their best.

I, _____, enjoy improving

my knowledge about myself and my attitudes and thoughts toward

others.

"To learn how to think is
to learn how to live."
—Ernest Holmes

Chapter 8

SPIRITUAL BALANCE
Love Cultivates, Never Dominates

*"Be useful. That is the first and final commandment
for those who would be useful and happy in
their usefulness. If you think of yourself only, you
cannot develop because you are choking the Source of
development, which is spiritual expansion
through thought of others."*
—Charles W. Eloit

The word "spiritual" denotes different definitions and images to every different person. As each individual is different, so is the interpretation of a spiritual adaptation to the life-journey. Some people will define spiritual as religion; others, as doctrine or denomination; still others, as a church, creed or dogma. Spiritual is bigger than Christian, Jew, Muslim, Hindu, Islam or any other organized or recognized group. While spiritual may encompass many or all of these, I strongly feel that spiritual is much more. As I share "spiritual balance," I offer for your consideration a more expanded definition. In order to experience and enjoy balanced living as you travel the roads of your life-journey, it is critical for you to come to terms with what spiritual is for you and to understand how very important it is that you live and express a spiritual balance in your life.

The primary definition of spirit is: a vital principle held to give life to physical organisms. While this does apply to the human species, it also applies to all living organisms. Yet, by most standards, living organisms, other than the human species, are not capable of experiencing a spiritual aspect of life. Spirit is more than a vital principle.

Spirit is also that immaterial essence or activating cause of individual life. It expands to include emotions, feelings, energy, animation, hope and courage. Further, it embraces individual choices regarding ethics, morals, values and integrity. How you live your life and what you take from and give to life is an integral part of your spirit. At the end of the life-journey, one of the most vital aspects of spirit is its eternal quality.

If you can focus an encompassing meaning for spirit, I feel that you will be better prepared to increase your awareness, importance and responsibility for your spiritual balance. This area or road of balanced living is surrounded by controversy. No one will present an argument that the physical, mental, social, financial and family areas of life are roads on your life-journey, but there is much discussion regarding the spiritual road.

There are some people who believe that the spiritual part of life is the most important. Then, there are others who place little value on it in their lives. I firmly believe spiritual balance is just as essential to getting off your yo-yo as any of the other five areas. Just as you will define your balance in each of the other five areas different from other people, so too will you define your spiritual balance from your individual point of view.

You begin travelling your spiritual balance road by formulating a personal belief, philosophy and code of living. This is necessary in order for you to know what it is that guides you as you travel your life-journey. You may make changes in your personal belief, philosophy and code of living, as you travel your many different roads and this will come as a direct result of your personal growth.

Your personal belief, philosophy and code of living will include the earlier mentioned aspects of spiritual: emotions, feelings, energy, animation, hope, courage, choices, ethics, morals, values, integrity, how you live your life, what you take from and give to life, and finally, how you prepare for the end of your life-journey.

To travel the spiritual road of life is an adventure well worth taking. Give 100% of your mind, heart and soul to it, for you will travel this road of your journey every day of your life. Keep an open mind to the many possibilities within your spiritual nature.

Live Life With Funnel Vision,
Instead Of Tunnel Vision

I personally know the limitations tunnel vision imposes. The early years of my spiritual life was experienced through tunnel vision. Once I learned this SignPost, I assumed my responsibility to free myself from the prison of tunnel vision.

While I know that your background, environment and circumstances will be completely different from mine, let me share with you my personal journey to spiritual balance. From my experiences, you may be inspired, encouraged and motivated to pursue your own individual spiritual balance.

I grew up in a very strict, conservative, authoritarian, fundamental religious home and church. I was taught misleading SignPosts from day one. I was taught there was only one belief that was right and it was ours. Everybody else was wrong and going to hell. I was taught that God was up in heaven with a stick, and if I did not cross every "t" and dot every "i," I was "gonna get it and going to hell if I didn't straighten-up and fly right." We were against everything, i.e., dancing, going to movies, sports, females wearing pants or shorts, make-up, watching television, listening to "worldly" music, and on and on. Our religion consisted of a bunch of rules made-up by some person or persons, based on **their** interpretation of the Bible.

Our religion gave us the authority to judge wrongly everyone and everything different from us. We were the only ones right and we were proud of it. We could criticize and condemn because we represented God. Preachers would yell, rant and rave, about sin and judgement and hell. One of the most misleading SignPost was the one that kept people "in line" by the use of guilt and fear.

Was what I experienced in my childhood and teenage years spiritual? Absolutely not. It took much de-programming and re-programming for me to arrive at a spirituality that works for me. But I did! If you have had or are having problems in this area of your life, please know you can work through the difficulties and the misleading SignPosts. You can enjoy a spiritual balance in your life.

What I was taught in my early experience was taught from people who were out-of-balance. It is sad, but there are still people just as out-of-balance living in your community today. If you are one of them, wake-up. If you are associating with them, move.

I know people who have "their halo on so tight that their horns are sticking up." They are out-of-balance.

There are people who "Praise the Lord" for everything: "Mamma just got shot, well, Praise the Lord." Out-of-balance. There are those who think if you don't believe just as they believe, you're wrong and going to hell. Out-of-balance.

One major cause of mental and emotional breakdown is religion. Religion can bug you; spiritual balance can bless you. Religion comes out of the head; spiritual balance comes out of the heart. Religion, you endure; spiritual balance, you enjoy.

As I researched this material, I looked for ways to present a system for spiritual balance that is adaptable, liveable and usable. As I have done in previous chapters, I have chosen an acronym to personalize spiritual balance. I have chosen the word: "PRACTICAL." The ideas, concepts, principles and systems presented here provide me with deep inspiration, motivation and encouragement, and I know your life will be touched as you experience them.

Before we begin to discover the "PRACTICAL" of spiritual balance, please take a self-inventory by responding to the following questions, as being either Balanced or Out-Of-Balance.

1. I am basically a truthful person.
    Balanced or Out-Of-Balance

2. I consider ethical and moral values important in my life.
    Balanced or Out-Of-Balance

3. It is important to me to help others.
    Balanced or Out-Of-Balance

4. I am continuing to develop a stronger character.
    Balanced or Out-Of-Balance

5. I participate in the institutions that reflect my religious beliefs.
    Balanced or Out-Of-Balance

6. I have strong personal beliefs.
    Balanced or Out-Of-Balance

7. I follow the Golden Rule in the affairs of my daily life:
   "Do unto others as you would have them do unto you."
   Balanced or Out-Of-Balance

8. I give of my time and financial support to organizations that
   serve others.
   Balanced or Out-Of-Balance

9. I am too critical or judgmental of others.
   Balanced or Out-Of-Balance

10. I have the ability to forgive others rather than hold grudges.
    Balanced or Out-Of-Balance

This short self-inventory will help you develop further insights into
your beliefs about the importance of spiritual balance.

While it is not my intention to write a thesis on spiritual balance,
it is my intent to inspire you with a more encompassing definition of
it. There are nine powerful systems that I offer you to incorporate
into your spiritual life. I address each of these, direct and to the point.
I am confident each will alert and guide you on your life-journey.
Whatever your present religious beliefs are, I am confident the following systems will complement them. Should you be at a juncture on
your spiritual road where you are looking for leading SignPosts, you
will find them here. If you are just beginning the formulation of your
personal belief, philosophy and code of living, this is your starting
point. Now let's examine the systems in the word "PRACTICAL" and
learn the power they can give you as you move away from spiritual
out-of-balance toward spiritual balance.

P - Pardon
R -
A -
C -
T -
I -
C -
A -
L -

Pardon

Pardon, or forgiveness, is one principle that is a foundation-builder, if you are to experience and enjoy spiritual balance. Every religion, philosophy and doctrine throughout the ages have taught the value of forgiveness. Once you learn how to forgive, you begin to learn how to live. Forgiveness is a thought turned into an action. It allows you freedom from the troublesome encumbrances, such as: guilt, fear, anger, hate, and bitterness. These will prohibit your personal growth and will keep you on that endless yo-yo.

As I have previously stated, my spiritual journey has led me to an adaptation of Christian principles in my life. From this point of view, I believe in the forgiveness of God through Christ. From the Scriptures, I have learned that God is a God of love and grace, and that God understands our human frailties. It is the love of God that creates the dynamics of forgiveness. Divine forgiveness is achieved by simply acknowledging wrong-doing and asking for a pardon. Human forgiveness is achieved in a similar manner, only sometimes with resistance. Often, it is easier to ask and receive forgiveness from God than it is to ask and receive forgiveness from people. However, there is a great liberating power that you feel once forgiveness has been requested and/or given.

Because you are human, you err. To have the courage to admit your errors and your mistakes and ask for forgiveness builds your spiritual character. To offer forgiveness to someone who has wronged you, is to be understanding, compassionate and tolerant.

You can shout from the rafters about your religion and its teachings, but if you are unable to give or receive forgiveness, you are spiritually out-of-balance.

The Scriptures teach, yet, another principle that accompanies forgiving and that is the principle of forgetting. Christ, in the New Testament, tells us that He forgives and forgets. While it may be difficult to explain how this happens, by my faith I accept that God forgives and forgets. There is no doubt that faith plays a great role in the development of your spiritual self.

Without faith, you will have to have a human explanation for things to which there is no human rhyme or reason. When God forgives and forgets something, it is as if it never happened. There is no record of it; there is no memory of it. It just never happened.

To Forgive And Forget Is
As If It Never Happened

However, dealing with the human mind is somewhat different than dealing with the God-mind. No, it is not easy for us as human beings to find it within our hearts and minds to forgive someone and never remember it again. Yet, the great example has been set: forgive and forget.

I was teaching a single's seminar and was sharing SignPosts on forgiving and forgetting. One hand went up, and a middle aged lady spoke rather sharply as she said: "Forgive, maybe; forget, never; not after what he did to me." I heard the hurt in her voice and saw the pain on her face. She needed a SignPost. I began to share with her that I believe even on a human level, we can forgive and forget. While the human mind is not structured to just forget the event, the human mind can replace the negative feelings that accompanied the event. In so doing, you can forget the hurt, the pain, the anger, the betrayal and all of the negative feelings connected to the event, while at the same time, remembering the event.

To Forget, Replace Negative Feelings
Connected To A Hurt

I have shared this SignPost with many through the years, and whether you are a victim of rape, incest, relationship betrayal, financial embezzlement, fraud, child abuse, etc., you can indeed invoke the system of forgive and forget. Spiritual balance requires you to offer and receive pardon.

Steps To Forgiving And Forgetting

1. Acknowledge the situation of hurt or pain.

2. Identify the person, place or thing that created the hurt.

3. Remind yourself of your humanness and the humanness from whom your hurt was created.

4. Speak aloud: "I Forgive."
Say it as often as you need to until you feel that you have released all negative feelings.

5. Replace any negative thought with a thought of peace and goodwill for any person, place or thing.

6. Do not think or speak negatively of the situation or person.

7. Bless the person or situation.

P - Pardon
R - Reasonable
A -
C -
T -
I -
C -
A -
L -

Reasonable

Spiritual balance asks you to be reasonable. It is most difficult to approach any subject without recognizing that it is composed of reason and emotion. So it is with your spiritual balance.

You are a combination of thoughts, emotions, feelings, actions, reactions and responses. These work together to bring balance to your spiritual life. Without emotion, you would be a robot with a hair-do. Without reason, you would be reduced to a mere form of guttural expressions. The key to getting off your yo-yo is to bring balance between your reason and logic and your emotions and feelings.

When you focus on such intangibles as God, faith, and trust, it can be most difficult to apply reason and logic to every issue. For people who demand a human explanation for every situation, there can be no reasonable explanation for many of the issues and situations you will experience on your life-journey. I am not here to argue the point of applying reason to what some would call unreasonable. However, in the Scriptures, Christ recommends to the people: "Come and let us reason together." I interpret this as a clue that using reason and being reasonable is a part of spiritual balance.

As I have travelled my spiritual roads, I have studied many religions, doctrines, denominations and spiritual teachings. I continue to learn from my studies. I also encourage you to study and learn more. Never take the word of a rabbi, priest, minister, teacher, writer, or anyone else on the grounds that they are the powers that be who "know" the right and only way to spiritual balance. It is within you to search and research the teachings and principles that you embrace. Outside sources can offer you assistance and direction, but ultimately, you are in charge of how you will travel your spiritual road. Never give-up your God-given heritage to "choose this day whom you will serve."

Most spiritual laws and spiritual principles that apply to earthly living seem to have reason. Review just three such laws and principles and ask yourself if reason applies.

1. The Ten Commandments? Every one of them is for your improvement and benefit. Reasonable? Yes, I believe so!

2. The law of sowing and reaping? "You reap what you sow." If you sow happiness, you reap happiness. If you sow bitterness, you reap bitterness. If you sow to good health, you reap good health. If you sow to sickness, you reap sickness. Reasonable? Yes, I believe so!

3. Love thy neighbor as thyself? Does it seem reasonable that you cannot love someone else without first having learned to love yourself. Reason is a primary element in learning how to love yourself and certainly in learning how to love others. It is vital that you be reasonable in dealing with others. Many relationships do not last over the long haul, because one or both people are unreasonable. Expectations are often unreasonable. Demands or needs are often unreasonable. In order to enjoy balance, you must use good judgment, common sense and intelligence in dealing with others. Reasonable? I believe so!

Spiritual balance requires that you be reasonable. Your ability to learn and apply reason to your life will move you forward on the road toward spiritual balance.

Tips On Learning To Be Reasonable

1. Read many different kinds of materials on faith, religion and spiritual aspects.

2. Question yourself and others as to how certain beliefs are accepted.

3. Give your beliefs the test of: Does this make sense?

4. Test your beliefs as to their practical application to living in the now.

5. Always keep your mind open to new ideas, new beliefs and the possibility of change.

Use the powerful dynamics of "practical" as you travel your life-journey.

P - Pardon
R - Reasonable
A - Alive
C -
T -
I -
C -
A -
L -

Alive

Alive means living and experiencing the most; existing means settling for less. Spiritual balance should create a keen awareness into your personal aliveness. If you accept that you are created in the image of God, you must then accept that the image of God is alive. It is this alive quality that makes you unique, special and vital. Look all around you and you will see people walking around who are not alive. Except for the breathing process, they are dead. They have no excitement, enthusiasm or purpose for living. They are dead, they just haven't had the final service. How sad!

Living life "alive" is an alternative to this sadness; living life "alive" is a choice. Spiritual balance gives you a foundation upon which your aliveness can grow. What are some things that can suck the life out of your "alive" being? Two things will be the kiss of death to your aliveness:

1. Being critical, judgmental and condemning of others

2. Engaging in self-defeating thoughts and actions

These will rob you of your joy, your creativity and your ability to be a fully functional alive being. Spiritual laws and principles build your awareness for living life alive. Certainly I am concerned about life after death and I am equally concerned about life after birth. I am interested in the here-after and I am equally interested in what we're after here.

Living life alive begins in your thinking; it develops into a state of mind. Once you are convinced that living life alive will add more fulfillment to each area, you can then choose to employ systems to move you toward more aliveness.

Tips To Increase Your Aliveness

1. Acknowledge the image of your Creator in the qualities of: happiness, imagination, potential, creativity, problem-solving, abundance, and prosperity and then accept this as you.

2. Look for the good and praise it!

3. Devote a portion of each day to some type of self-improvement.

4. Affirm on a daily basis: "I live life alive."

As you use the different systems embodied in "practical," you will feel more and more in charge of your life and will gain a stronger sense of balance in each of the six areas of life. "Practical" has so much to teach us. Let's review the "C".

P - Pardon
R - Reasonable
A - Alive
C - Communication
T -
I -
C -
A -
L -

Communication

When you think of spiritual communication, you may, as do most of us, think of prayer. There are many great prayers that we have been taught. I am reminded of two: The Lord's Prayer and the Serenity Prayer of St. Francis of Assisi.

The Lord's Prayer
"Our Father which art in heaven, hallowed be Thy name. Thy kingdom come, Thy will be done, on earth as it is in heaven. Give us this day our daily bread and forgive us our trespasses, as we forgive those who trespass against us. And lead us not into temptation, but deliver us from evil. For Thine is the Kingdom, and the power, and the glory forever. Amen."

The Serenity Prayer
"God grant me the serenity to accept the things I cannot change, the courage to change the things I can, and the wisdom to know the difference."

However meaningful these two are to you, the most meaningful spiritual communication to you will be that of your own. In addition to prayer, you can engage in spiritual communication by mediation, music, affirmation, creating, giving, etc. Spiritual communication is an individual choice. There is no one right or wrong way. The method of your spiritual communication is not nearly as important as you using it on a daily basis to guide you, as you develop your balance.

Thoreau and Emerson experienced a heightened sense of communication through their experiences with nature. Nature teaches so much that you can learn and use.

Rather than tell you how to communicate, which would be totally against my philosophy of sharing, let me share with you a few thoughts for enhancing your spiritual communication.

Tips On Spiritual Communication

1. Set aside a special time that you can have just for you. Start with just a few minutes. As your communication becomes more enriched, you may want to allot more time for it.

2. Read something of a spiritual nature (Bible, philosophy, inspirational thoughts, Upper Room, etc.).

3. Focus on creative power: The God force, nature's creative force, your own ability to create.

4. Audibly speak and express the feelings and emotions that are within you. The main part of this exercise is to verbalize your thoughts, emotions, feelings and ideas.

Spiritual communication is refreshing. It has qualities of cleansing and healing. And since there is no one right or wrong way, there is also, no right or wrong time. Your spiritual communication can be any time, for any reason, for any result. It is a power for unlocking hidden potential and releasing you to unlimited possibilities.

> P - Pardon
> R - Reasonable
> A - Alive
> C - Communication
> T - Thankful
> I -
> C -
> A -
> L -

Thankful

Spiritual balance is impossible without being "thankful."

In All Things, Give Thanks

This is a most difficult system to practice, because there is no room for exception. "In **all** things give thanks."

Are you thankful? Can you be thankful for the things that happen to you that you don't understand? It's easy to be thankful when everything is going well; but what about when things aren't going so well?

Learning to be thankful in all things brings peace and harmony within the body, mind and spirit. Without thankfulness, you tend to take people and things for granted. You tend to expect more and more from others. You tend to be demanding of life and people. You will grow old bitter, instead of better.

Thankfulness, on the other hand, helps you develop long suffering, mercy, kindness, understanding, compassion, and a grateful heart. It helps you to keep your perspectives in balance.

Tips For Being Thankful

1. Develop a habit of saying "Thank You" for everything good and bad that happens to you.

2. Remind yourself that the opposite of "thankfulness" is "thanklessness."

3. Watch the expression on the face of the person that you show thanks toward. What a great sight to see.

P - Pardon
R - Reasonable
A - Alive
C - Communication
T - Thankful
I - Individuality
C -
A -
L -

Individuality

Your spiritual balance inherently carries with it your own individuality. As an individual, you were created. You are not a duplicate of any other creation. Therefore, it will be you who will study, learn, pick and choose each aspect that will compose your spiritual balance.

Just as you have the inherent right and privilege of creating your individual spiritual balance, you must allow other individuals the same right and privilege. This is a vital point for me having grown-up in my particular environment where there was only one way to address spirituality. Be aware that you do not get so caught up in the fervor of your personal belief system, philosophy, and code of living, that you arrive at the juncture where you expect or insist others think, act, react and respond just like you. This attitude will greatly distress your spiritual balance.

You are entitled to your beliefs and your opinions. Because you allow that same position to others, disagreements will many times arise out of discussion and communication. Disagreements about faith, religion, beliefs, ethics, morals and the whole gamut can become part of the discussion. What SignPost can you follow when you encounter others who hold different ideas to yours?

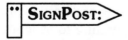

Disagree Without Becoming Disagreeable

Every individual will express individuality in faith, in beliefs, in convictions, viewpoints, ideas, thoughts and interpretations. It is certainly possible for you to entertain the individuality of others without losing your own. Individually develop your own spiritual balance. It should not be left up to chance, or to someone else to develop for you. The spiritual part of your life gives meaning and purpose to your life and should not be over-looked. It must be protected at all costs.

Tips To Maintain Individuality

1. Recognize yourself as a unique and special person created in the image of God.

2. Study spiritual teachings of all different beliefs. This should add to your knowledge and understanding of others, but more importantly, it will add to your knowledge and understanding of you.

3. Respect the rights of others to disagree with you.

> P - Pardon
> R - Reasonable
> A - Alive
> C - Communication
> T - Thankful
> I - Individuality
> C - Creative
> A -
> L -

Creative

Spiritual balance includes your creative power. Because you were created in the image of your Creator, you also have the potential and ability to be creative. This quality is what makes you most like your Creator.

Create means to cause, to originate, to imagine, to produce. These qualities are within you, waiting to be ignited to their full potential. Your spiritual nature allows you to search and research all of the avenues of expression. You are the only creation that has the ability to express yourself creatively and not just instinctively. This indicates just how very much you are like your Creator.

I get very excited and enthusiastic when I stop and take an inventory of how important I am to God and to life. I can't think of anything that turns on my life-juices more, than to think I am created with the fullest ability and capability to create. It is a power that can revolutionize your life when you get plugged into it.

Would it amaze you to know how many people do not use their creative power? It is surprising to learn that most people are so caught up in the ruts of day-to-day survival, that they never take time to explore this most special part of their lives.

Take a self-inventory to discover your own power to create. Remember, everything you touch, enjoy and benefit from today is a product of someone's creativity. Every problem solved is the result of creative thinking.

You have heard of the I.Q.: Intelligence Quotient. Let me introduce you to C.Q.: Creative Quotient. You are in total charge of how you develop it and how you use it. What is your C.Q.? Are you developing your creative power?

Tips For Developing Your Creativity

1. Spend time each day meditating on the creative power within you.

2. When solving a problem, always have more than one alternative.

3. Develop a hobby in which you are able to use your imagination.

> P - Pardon
> R - Reasonable
> A - Alive
> C - Communication
> T - Thankful
> I - Individuality
> C - Creative
> A - Active
> L -

Active

Spiritual balance requests you to be active. Activity in its many different forms of expression is what outwardly demonstrates your thought for others.

Love In Word And In Deed

Activity means involvement. Spiritual activity has many forms of expression. There is no pre-described right way for you to demonstrate your involvement. It may include: praying, Bible reading, church attendance, tithing, witnessing, service to hospitals or rest homes or volunteering. There are endless number of people who need you to be active.

Being active and involved serves many purposes. First, it is a great diversion for you to be able to involve yourself in an activity that gives of yourself. It enriches your life when you do something for others.

Second, the persons or institutions that you involve yourself with receive long-lasting benefits from your involvement.

Third, I believe when you are active and give of yourself, time, talent, energy or money, you get so much more than you give.

It Is More Blessed To Give Than To Receive

People need you and your contribution to life, but more importantly, you need people and what they can contribute to your life. Get involved. Stay active.

Tips For Being Active

1. Set aside time to engage in activities that enhance your spiritual balance.

2. Devote time to service in your community.

3. Write or call a person that you think could use some encouragement.

P - Pardon
R - Reasonable
A - Alive
C - Communication
T - Thankful
I - Individuality
C - Creative
A - Active
L - Love

Love

While this system falls last in the acronym, it certainly is not least. If I had to choose one system that spiritual balance is predicated upon, it would be the system of love. Millions of words have been written about love and its power to change the life-journey, and yet, many people travel their roads never fully experiencing this ultimate force of good.

Spiritual balance can never be experienced without employing the system of love in your life. When you realize that love has its roots in creation, it gives a deeper meaning to your life. God loved and needed to express love. You are created from love and have an intrinsic need to love and be loved. To give and receive love is a mandate for spiritual balance. There are many SignPosts to direct you as you empower your life with the system of love.

Love Thy Neighbor As Thyself

*Do Unto Others As You
Would Have Them Do Unto You*

Greater Love Hath No Man Than
He Lay Down His Life For A Friend

Love Cultivates, Never Dominates

There is one aspect of love that I believe is fundamental to understand, and incorporate into your life, and that is learning to love unconditionally. Unconditional love is not the same as conditional love. To love in spite of; to love even though; this is the true meaning of love. Love is not love when it must meet certain conditions.

I frequently hear people exchanging communication about their feelings and I hear the conditions built into their love. "I'll love you if you...." This is love on condition and it will deeply limit your love experience and your spiritual balance. No one will always be able to meet all of your requirements or conditions. Love is what you give even when others don't meet all the requirements. Love is accepting even when understanding is lacking. Love is the ultimate answer to many of your out-of-balance situations.

Tips On Love

1. Learn to love yourself.

2. Accept others who are different from you even when you disagree.

3. Practice thinking only good of others.

4. Allow others the same rights and privileges you cherish.

Spiritual Balance is: "PRACTICAL"

Apply these nine systems of "practical" and you will begin to feel the development of your spiritual balance. Whatever your doctrinal beliefs are, however you choose to express your faith and whenever or wherever you practice your religion, these nine systems will serve to complement your spiritual growth and your spiritual balance.

RECAP FOR "SPIRITUAL BALANCE"

Spiritual Balance Means: "PRACTICAL"

P - Pardon

R - Reasonable

A - Alive

C - Communication

T - Thankful

I - Individuality

C - Creative

A - Active

L - Love

SignPosts For Your Life-Journey

1. Live Life With Funnel Vision,
   Instead of Tunnel Vision

2. To Forgive And Forget Is
   As If It Never Happened

3. To Forget, Replace Negative Feelings
   Connected To A Hurt

4. In All Things, Give Thanks

5. Disagree Without Becoming Disagreeable

6. Love In Word And In Deed

7. It Is More Blessed To Give
   Than To Receive

8. Love Thy Neighbor As Thyself

9. Do Unto Others As You
   Would Have Them Do Unto You

10. Greater Love Hath No Man Than
    To Lay Down His Life For A Friend

11. Love Cultivates, Never Dominates

PERSONAL SELF-INVENTORY

1. Do I have a spiritual value system that directs my life? _____

2. Do I practice a recognized faith? _____

3. Am I aware of the need for spiritual balance in my life? _____

4. Is forgiving others a part of the way I relate to others? _____

5. List three of my spiritual values:

_____

_____

_____

6. Do I apply reason and emotion to my beliefs? _____

7. List three vital things for which I am thankful:

_____

_____

_____

8. List two ways that exemplify my being spiritually out-of-balance:

_____

_____

9. Do I comply with the spiritual laws and principles that can make my life more fulfilling? _____

10. Is my love generally conditional or unconditional? _____

DR. ZONNYA'S FIRST AID

1. Through your self-inventory, come to terms with your spiritual self. Identify the aspects of your spiritual life.

2. Recognize that you are a unique and different creation, created in the image of your Creator. List all the qualities that you feel describes your Creator. Use it as a guide in directing your life. Remember: Your God wants only the best for you.

3. Give some type of daily attention to developing your spiritual self. Read, listen, participate, etc. Get involved to learn more about what you can incorporate into your life to enhance your spiritual balance.

4. Develop and record your personal belief.

5. Create your personal philosophy.

6. Define your code of living.

AFFIRMATIONS

An affirmation is a positive statement that expresses a specific belief concerning you and the state of the affairs of your life. It begins with "I" or "My" and always will serve to reinforce all that is unique, special and distinctive about you. Use it often throughout the day. It will inspire, encourage and motivate you as you commit yourself to balanced living for a more beautiful lifestyle.

I, _____, believe in the

existence of God, a Higher Power, a Force of Love, that is external and

puts meaning into our lives.

I, _____, accept that my

life- force is an extension of the God force working within and through

me.

I, _____, have no doubt

that the God power within me can help me to enjoy a more beautiful

lifestyle.

"Beloved, I wish above all things that thou
mayest prosper and be in health as thy soul prospers."
—3 John: 2, New Testament

Chapter 9

SOCIAL BALANCE
To Be Interesting, Be Interested

*"A man wrapped up in himself
makes a very small package."*
—Anonymous

The social area of life is equal in importance to the other five areas of your life. Your social balance involves your ability to encounter and effectively address people and situations on a daily basis. You may consider yourself to be a people person or you may think of yourself as a loner. In fact, you probably are both. At times, you prefer being with people; at times, you prefer your solitude. However, regardless of how people-oriented you are or are not, life requires you to learn the necessary fundamental social skills to operate within the human element.

Achieving social balance in your life will be a challenge. The meaning of the word "social" includes a broad spectrum of relationships, companionships, and associations with others. I know many people who get on a social yo-yo. This can literally make your life-journey difficult to travel. It is easy to get out-of-balance in this area if you are not aware of the systems that you can choose to keep you on the right road.

There are many evidences of social out-of-balance. Unhappiness, loneliness, unfulfillment, alienation, lack of involvement, complacency and disregard for others. Everywhere you look, you can see unhappy eyes and faces. Could there be a connection between happiness and social balance? I am convinced there is a major link to a happy productive life and the way you interact with others on a social level.

It bears repeating: "No man is an island," said John Donne. It is true you need people and people need you. While you are unique to yourself, you have an intrinsic need to interact with others for pleasing and fulfilling results.

On the other hand, you can also experience out-of-balance by over extending your interaction with others. You can become so socially involved with others that you lose sight of your priorities in life.

There are several systems you can employ to assist you in moving toward social balance. It is good to remember that just like in each of the other five areas, your social balance will be different than that of anybody else you know. To identify where you are on your social road, your self-inventory will provide you insights to where you are headed on your journey. It is much easier to strengthen your weaknesses when you know what they are. Please address the following statements designed to help you as you increase your awareness about what social balance is and how it contributes to your more beautiful lifestyle.

1. I feel at ease in a social gathering.
    Balanced or Out-Of-Balance

2. I am courteous and thoughtful of others.
    Balanced or Out-Of-Balance

3. My trust of people is:
    Balanced or Out-Of-Balance

4. Making new friends for me is:
    Balanced or Out-Of-Balance

5. My self-confidence is:
    Balanced or Out-Of-Balance

6. My ego is:
    Balanced or Out-Of-Balance

7. My regard for others and their needs is:
   Balanced or Out-Of-Balance

8. My involvement in social, civic, or community activities is:
   Balanced or Out-Of-Balance

9. I like most people.
   Balanced or Out-Of-Balance

10. I enjoy socializing with myself.
    Balanced or Out-Of-Balance

Your responses may have turned on some mental light-bulbs as to areas that need more light. Social balance is not just about your interaction with others; it also includes your interaction with yourself.

You are by creation a social creature. Seneca, a first-century Roman philosopher, wrote that we are born to live together. "Society," he said, "is an arch of stones, joined together, which would break down if each did not support the other." Though there are times when you need to be alone, there is an innate need to feel connected to others. The human mind, heart and soul hungers for meaningful and purposeful involvement with others and seeks to find in it an escape from loneliness.

There are many mental images that arise when I use the words social balance. As in each of the six areas of balanced living, I have chosen an acronym to describe the systems you can use for achieving more balance. The word I have chosen to describe social balance is "FRIEND." Social balance is "friendship" and so much more. It is looking at all of your relationships, companionships, and associations with others at work, at home, at play, in your community, in your politics, in your religious institutions, etc. and applying the systems for rewarding benefits.

F - Fulfilling
R -
I -
E -
N -
D -

Fulfilling

"Fulfilling" is a way of describing what you feel when you know you have contributed to someone else in a positive and uplifting way. It certainly can be a close friend or it may be with a person that you meet for a brief moment, as you travel the many roads of your life-journey. Fulfilling means that you dare to give and share with others unconditionally.

Your capability to receive and enjoy social balance is limited only by your capacity to give. Giving is a natural part of life.

When You Learn To Give,
You Learn To Live

Giving involves more than money. It involves time, a smile, a note, a phone call, a touch. There is no more fulfilling event in the world than to know inside yourself that you have given something of yourself. You enjoy a fulfilling feeling when you give to or share with someone else. When you manifest your good-will by an air of openness or through a specific gesture, it returns to you in far greater measure.

So, you may ask: "Isn't it selfish to do something for someone so that I can feel fulfilled?" Two thoughts: first, you don't do something for someone in order to be fulfilled; you do so, knowing that you will be. Second, everything you do in life is done from a motive. There is one basic motive for everything you or anyone else does: **benefits**. You do what you do in life for your benefits. As long as all parties involved benefit, you have a win-win lifestyle. When others benefit from your giving and you benefit by giving, here is another win-win. It is wise to keep your motive fair, just, and helpful not only to yourself, but to others. In order to know what is fulfilling to you:

1. Make a list of things that you do for others or of ways you give to others.

2. List their name, the date and what you did.

3. Write how you feel inside when you give of yourself.

When you put in to life, you have the right to take from life. A fulfilling experience motivates you forward toward other fulfilling experiences.

Life Is Like A Bank;
You Can't Take Out What You Haven't Put In

Note: If you get disappointed in others, don't let it affect your future fulfilling experiences with people. People are disappointing at times. While you may get disappointed in people, keep in mind that even sometimes, you get disappointed in yourself. Sometimes, the only thing that helps you as you address the many people who come in and out of your life on a daily basis is a smile. The following poem suggests what even just a smile can add to your fulfilling social balance.

The Value Of A Smile

It costs nothing, but creates much.

It enriches those who receive it, without impoverishing those who give it.

It happens in a flash, but the memory of it sometimes lasts forever.

It creates happiness in the home, fosters goodwill in a business and is the countersign of friends.

It is rest to the weary, daylight to the discouraged, sunshine to the sad and nature's best antidote for trouble.

Yet it cannot be bought, begged, borrowed, or stolen, for it is something that does no earthly good to anyone until it is given away.

And if in the course of the day some of your friends should be too tired to give you one, why don't you give them one of yours?

For nobody needs a smile so much as those who have none left to give!

Social balance in your life will bring you that fulfilling sense
of joy, peace and good-will.

> F - Fulfilling
> R - Resourceful
> I -
> E -
> N -
> D -

Resourceful

For social balance, resourceful means that you develop new and
interesting ways to keep your social interactions alive and growing.
When you are well-read, well-informed, have interesting hobbies and
an interest in life, you are better able to contribute to life in a more
productive way. Friendships, casual or intimate, must have resources
upon which they can draw. It is difficult to enhance your resources if
you are content to stay just as you are right now. To grow, change,
and make meaningful contributions to your relationships, companionships and associations in life, you will be required to keep learning. To stop learning is to start dying.

To Be Interesting,
Be Interested

There are several systems you can employ to enhance your resourceful abilities.

1. Reading
   Read everything available about everything. Don't just read about
   what you are particularly interested in; read about things that
   others might be interested in. Be interested in everything.

2. Listening
   Listen to positive, uplifting and encouraging materials. With tech-
   nology, it is more convenient than ever to increase your knowledge in as many subjects as you care to learn. Your cassette player

should be with you at all times. Any time, any place, you can feed your resources. It is imperative in such a changing, fast-paced world that you keep up with as much new information as possible, on all kinds of subjects. Listening is a powerful resource to keep your social interactions alive and growing.

3. Asking Questions
   You only know what you know. The only way you can know what someone else knows is to ask. To increase your resources, you must be willing to ask questions. Do not be embarrassed or intimidated by anyone or anything. You have the individual right to increase your resourcefulness and you can choose to take the necessary steps to do it. Asking questions will give you added insight into others, their needs and wants. It will also enlighten you as to your needs and wants. There is no substitute for asking questions to increase your resourceful ability.

To add to your resourcefulness: read, listen, ask questions.

F - Fulfilling
R - Resourceful
I - Involved
E -
N -
D -

Involved

Involved indicates you are not willing to sit on the sidelines of life and let the game be played by others. You want to be a part of all the plays. The game of life requires involvement in order for it to be rewarding.

Life Is Not A Spectator Sport

Involvement in every aspect of living is what social balance encourages. Just as with every system, you must balance it as it applies to your life. There are so many aspects of life in which you can involve yourself that you must be aware of getting out-of-balance in your involvement.

Involved means that you participate. Your participation is needed in all areas of life: Politics needs you and your involvement; the church, the school system, the business community, and the civic and social organizations need you and your involvement. Certainly your money, your thoughts and prayers and your caring is needed, but nothing is needed like your active participation.

This does not mean that you have to be a joiner. I do not advocate joining just for the sake of joining. At the same time, if there are certain groups you feel close to or can contribute to, I feel your social life will be more balanced if you choose to give of yourself in a meaningful way, as an active participant. You will want to structure your priorities and your time organization in order to fit your involvement into your already busy schedule. Here are two tips:

1. Set aside a time to explore exactly what you are interested in and with what groups or people you are most comfortable.

2. Make a commitment to yourself and to those who need you and your involved balance.

Never settle for less in any area of life when you can experience more, better and greater. Being involved in worthwhile projects is just one alternative to existing. Start today traveling your social road with balance. **Get Involved!**

> F - Fulfilling
> R - Resourceful
> I - Involved
> E - Emotional
> N -
> D -

Emotional

Using your emotional system to move toward social balance is a powerful dynamic. When you realize just how powerful your emotions can be in affecting your life-journey, you will be driven to learn all you can about them.

There are two emotions: love and fear. All feelings have their beginnings in these two emotions. Relationships, companionships, and associations are developed from love, and destroyed by fear. It is crucial to your balanced living to realize, internalize and actualize the concept of emotion.

The word "emotion" creates many different images. You may think of it as an outward expression. While you express love or fear and all of the feelings these two invoke externally, you must be alert to the knowledge that emotion, love or fear, begins internally. Everything is first thought. When the thought of love or fear is developed internally, you then make a choice as to how you will externally demonstrate your feelings.

The two emotions of love and fear are the seeds for all the positive or negative feelings you experience. Without question, how you use these two powers will sharply affect your ability to balance your life. On each of the roads you travel, you will be called upon to address many challenges. Your initial response to life's challenges will begin from a position of love or fear.

In my many years of working with people, I have not found a system that is more important to understand than this system of "emotion." When I see people in a relationship that thrives, I know they are operating from the position of love. When I see people in a relationship that fails, I know they are operating from the position of fear.

Racial discrimination, prejudice, sexism or abuse of any kind operates from fear. Any time that you are experiencing a negative feeling or situation in your life, ask yourself: "What is the fear that is operating in my life?" Once you identify the fear, you can choose to replace the fear with love. Once you have replaced fear with love, you immediately begin to experience positive feelings. What is it about love that it "makes the world go round?"

Love

One of the maximum rewards of social balance comes when you know you have internally and externally expressed yourself from the position of love. When you close your eyes to go to sleep and know within yourself that you have given and received love and friendship today, you experience a sense of calmness, peace and tranquility that more people need more of. That sense of deep gratification develops when you have given of yourself. While you help others when you give of yourself, that good feeling inevitably rebounds, perhaps helping you most of all.

Giving love is often joy enough in itself. The encouraging thing about giving is that you cannot give without receiving. You should not have the attitude that I will give love because I want to receive love. The attitude should be that I give love knowing that I will receive love.

Those who live selfishly, only within themselves, build a prison around themselves. One test of your social balance is how you treat people who aren't likely to be able to reciprocate with some favor. The act of loving and giving is severely limited if you require a return. To love and be loved is the balance you are moving toward on your life-journey.

There Is Only Misfortune In Not Being Loved; There Is Misery In Not Loving

On the other hand, when you love others, care and befriend others, you gain in every area of your life. You will never grow **old** when you love; you will just grow **older**. You will reach the end of your journey called death, but you will arrive there young in spirit. Loving others unconditionally and without expecting anything in return, keeps you feeling ever alive and ever enjoying life.

Love is the emotion that will help you grow old better, instead of bitter. So many people experience things in life that can cause bitterness. Bitterness is a feeling from the position of fear and it kills! Bitterness kills energy, enthusiasm, and happiness. Eventually it will literally kill your life. Love is a shield against this deadly killer.

When you give and receive love and friendship, you accept that the power of love empowers you to treat others with respect, fairness and equality. In gazing into the eyes of another, you are in a very specific way looking into a mirror and seeing a reflection of yourself. What you give or withhold is reflected back to you.

One strong feeling that love invokes is **kindness**. Johann Wolfgang Von Goethe, the German poet and philosopher of the 18th Century, wrote: "Kindness is the golden chain by which society is bound."

Without sensitivity to the needs of others and the touch of kindness which endeavors you to meet those needs, there can be no true society. There is only a group of individuals, each fending for themselves, without regard for the other. Without kindness there are no growing relationships in which people relate constructively to one another. Remarkably, it requires little effort to decide to behave kindly toward another person. It sometimes requires much more stamina to carry out that decision. Yet, when the relationship is important, kindness may be the very quality which will make the necessary difference in its life or death. A kind word or action will usually bring rewards far greater than the effort exerted.

Kindness is a principle that you can use to help you grow in all of your relationships, both intimate and casual.

Tips On Developing Love And Kindness

1. Look at each individual as a unique expression of life.

2. Refrain from judging.

3. Ask yourself: "Am I talking to others the way I'd like to be talked to by them?"

4. Think before you put your mouth in gear.

5. Always build the other person up.

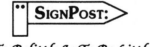

To Belittle Is To Be Little

Love and fear determine the quality of your life-journey. To balance your life and your social area, commit to traveling the many roads of your life-journey from the position of love, replacing the position of fear whenever it rears its ugly head.

Learning about social balance from the acronym "FRIEND" gives you insights into just how many aspects there are in just this one area of your life.

F - Fulfilling
R - Resourceful
I - Involved
E - Emotional
N - Needful
D -

Needful

As a human being, you have certain needs that must be fulfilled, in order for you to enjoy a balanced and more beautiful lifestyle. Interaction with others is one of those basic needs, along with giving and receiving. You have the need to share and to contribute in a constructive way to not only yourself, but to others. You have the need of friends in your life; both casual and intimate. In addition, you have the need to be a friend.

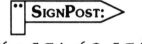

To Have A Friend, Be A Friend

Friends offer these power-positives to your life:

1. Friends can help you when you are in need.

2. Friends can encourage you when you are discouraged.

3. Friends can help you release tension by being a sounding board for you in your decision-making.

4. Friends can comfort you in times of grief, sickness, death, etc.

5. Friends can reinforce your self-worth.

6. Friends are good for your mental health.

Just as a friend can add all of these to your life, so too, can you be a friend, and contribute power-positives to the lives of your friends. This is needful for social balance.

To stay healthy, develop friends. Without the circle of supportive friends, stress can have a serious effect on both mental and physical health. Socially isolated people have a greater risk of dying, independent of traditional risk factors such as smoking, drinking, or obesity. Friends can be good medicine. There are many great benefits to receive from being involved in personal relationships.

While you read a lot about the effects of diet, exercise, smoking and drinking on health, seldom do you hear about the effects of friends for a healthier life. I strongly suggest that the kind of lifestyle you enjoy or endure is a direct result of the kind of health, good or bad, that you experience. If your lifestyle includes meaningful friendships and relationships, I guarantee you are healthier, happier and more alive. It is imperative that you understand the need for friendship and take the necessary steps to build lasting quality relationships. You can fulfill many of the needs in your life through your relationships, companionships and associations with others.

F - Fulfilling
R - Resourceful
I - Involved
E - Emotional
N - Needful
D - Developed

Developed

Anything having is worth working at and developing. The same is true of social involvement and friendship. In a social situation, there will always be one who is the leader. There will always be one who takes the initiative to make things happen. If you are to enjoy social balance and a rewarding life, decide now that you will assume the responsibility for developing the necessary skills to make friendship work for you. You are not born with the necessary information or skills to make and keep friends, but there is no question that you can develop those techniques.

I have developed "Ten Commandments For Building Rewarding Friendships At Home, At Work, At Play." Use these to help you develop your relationships and increase your social balance.

Ten Commandments For Building Rewarding Friendships At Home, At Work, At Play

Thou Shalt:

1. Guard Against Taking Each Other For Granted.

2. Refuse To Allow Fear To Destroy A New Friendship Or Damage An Old One.

3. Share Interesting Activities Together.

4. Establish Realistic Expectations.

5. Do Unto Others As You Would Have Them Do Unto You.

6. Be Generous With Praise; Courteous With Criticism.

7. Choose Quality Time Over Quantity Time.

8. Be A Giver And A Taker; It Keeps The Relationship Balanced.

9. Put In As Much As You Want To Take Out.

10. Forgive And Forget.

Social balance, like balance in the other areas of your life, is not easy to attain. However, when you see the results of unhappiness and loneliness, you will agree that it is necessary to take the time to develop your skills for creating meaningful relationships, companionships, and associations with others.

RECAP FOR "SOCIAL BALANCE"

Social Balance Is: "FRIEND"

F - Fulfilling
R - Resourceful
I - Involved
E - Emotional
N - Needful
D - Developed

SignPosts For Your Life-Journey

1. When You Learn To Give,
   You Learn To Live

2. Life Is Like A Bank;
   You Can't Take Out What
   You Haven't Put In

3. To Be Interesting,
   Be Interested

4. Life Is Not A Spectator Sport

5. There is Only Misfortune In Not Being Loved;
   There Is Misery In Not Loving

6. To Belittle Is To Be Little

7. To Have a Friend, Be A Friend

PERSONAL SELF-INVENTORY

1. Do I like people? _____

2. Are my expectations realistic of others or do I tend to expect too much? _____

3. Is it easy for me to talk to others? _____

4. Do I look forward to new social situations? _____

5. List two assets that I have that make people like me:

    1. _____

    2. _____

6. Do I do at least one good deed every day without expecting it to be returned? _____

7. List three things that I have done this week to help someone:

    1. _____

    2. _____

    3. _____

8. Do I stay up to date on things that are happening in the world, so I can effectively communicate with others? _____

9. List the organizations that I participate in and are a vital part of:

    _____

    _____

    _____

10. How do I show someone I love them? _____

_____

_____

11. Am I quick to judge others? _____

12. Name my two closest friends:

    1. _____

    2. _____

13. List the name of one new person I have met this week that I would like to develop into a closer friend:

_____

14. Do I practice the "Ten Commandments For Building Rewarding Friendships At Home, At Work, At Play?" _____

15. List any of the "Ten Commandments" that I am weak in and need to make stronger: _____

_____

_____

_____

_____

_____

DR. ZONNYA'S FIRST AID

1. Make a habit of doing or saying something that is helpful to someone else on a daily basis. Do it unconditionally.

2. Practice giving and receiving. To be a good giver you must also know how to receive.

3. Read something new each week that you can use in your conversations with others. Don't get in a rut in your conversation.

4. Make a list of questions about things that you would like to learn. Talk about them with others.

5. Every day, tell someone you love them. The words "I Love You" are the three most powerful words for bringing about healing, happiness and health.

6. Practice the "Ten Commandments For Building Rewarding Relationships At Home, At Work, At Play."

AFFIRMATIONS

An affirmation is a positive statement that expresses a specific belief concerning you and the state of the affairs of your life. It begins with "I" or "My" and always will serve to reinforce all that is unique, special and distinctive about you. Use it often throughout the day. It will inspire, encourage and motivate you as you commit yourself to balanced living for a more beautiful lifestyle.

I, _____, learn to grow more

loving and compassionate toward others.

I, _____, experience each

person I meet with reasonable expectations.

I, _____, accept my

responsibility to be involved with people in my life and to make things

happen in my friendships.

*"The only ones among you who will
be really happy are those who will
have sought and found how to serve."*
—Albert Schweitzer

Chapter 10

FINANCIAL BALANCE
Proper Preparation Prevents Poor Performance

*"We have too many people living
without working, and altogether
too many working without living."*
—Charles R. Brown

Financial out-of-balance devastates your life-journey. You can be on the minus side or the plus side in your financial life and still be out-of-balance. Financial balance is certainly connected to the facet of money, but as you will discover, there are many facets on the road to financial balance.

Of the six areas of balanced living, the area of finances and money is probably the area that gets most of your attention. Because it is so important and necessary to you in your daily living, it can become easy to feel that it is the most important area of your life. Money, your job, your career, and your livelihood consumes a major part of your 24 hour day and often you allow it to get out-of-balance.

The issue of money is individual and personal. I know people who believe that money is the answer to every question, problem or challenge. These people are usually people who do not have the money they need to enjoy the lifestyle they have chosen. On the other hand, I know people who have all the money their bank can hold and they live life out-of-balance. I call these people "Money Making Failures."

While they have succeeded in one area, they have failed in one or more of the other five. Even with money, you can be out-of-balance, and of course, if you don't have money, your condition becomes obviously out-of-balance.

If financial balance is not about how much money you have, then what is financial balance about? While I am the first to agree that most people immediately have the image of dollar bills when they hear the word "financial," I also want you to expand your perception of this area. Remember: Money is just paper with old dead people's picture on it.

Financial balance is about money and so much more, including all of the dynamics that combine to get you off your yo-yo. As I have done for each area of balanced living, I have chosen an acronym to use in the discussion of systems for financial balance.

However, before I present the systems, please take a brief self-inventory. Use the questions, statements, and your responses to prepare your mind for new thoughts and alternatives to approaching the financial area. Please keep your mind open and objective. While you already have your own ideas about this controversial subject, please allow yourself to review new ways of looking at a very old subject. Please respond to the following as either: Balanced or Out-Of-Balance:

1. My emphasis on the financial area of my life is:
   Balanced or Out-Of-Balance

2. My plans for my financial future are:
   Balanced or Out-Of-Balanced

3. The importance I place on money is:
   Balanced or Out-Of-Balance

4. My money management is:
   Balanced or Out-Of-Balance

5. The time I devote to my job or career is:
   Balanced or Out-Of-Balance

6. My retirement plans are:
   Balanced or Out-Of-Balance

7. The manner in which I handle the ups and downs of my job is:
   Balanced or Out-Of-Balance

8. The stress I experience is:
   Balanced or Out-Of-Balance

9. I do what I do because I choose to, not because I have to.
   Balanced or Out-Of-Balance

10. I deal fairly and ethically with those who are a part of my financial world.
    Balanced or Out-Of-Balance

Now that you have further insights into just a few areas that will be included in "financial balance," let me offer you the systems in the acronym "POWER" as a guide on this road of your life-journey.

I considered many acronyms before choosing "POWER," such as: LIFEWORK, FLOURISH, PROSPER, ACTION, and WEALTH. However, "POWER" embodies the systems I want to present for your consideration.

The systems in "POWER" follow two most alerting SignPosts.

K-I-S-S:
Keep It Short And Simple

S-I-B-K-I-S
See It Big - Keep It Simple

There is no need to choose to live life with daily complications and confusion. There is too much of that in your life right now. You can simplify your life, therefore increasing your pleasure and profit. Operate every area of your life from the two stated SignPosts and you will feel and see immediate results.

You will further understand "POWER" as I begin to unfold each system and apply it to financial balance. Indeed, you do have the

"POWER" to get off your yo-yo and enjoy a more beautiful lifestyle. When you are in financial balance, there are many constructive side-effects. When you are in financial balance in its full meaning, you are healthier and happier. You feel a deep sense of satisfaction from your work and your relationships grow more meaningful. As you can see, this particular area affects every other area. Since it demands so much of your attention and time, it is important to know and apply the systems that will lead you to financial balance.

There are many systems you can employ and you will want to research many of them. To get you started, consider the five systems of "POWER."   When I use the term "POWER," I certainly do not mean the kind that is misused and abused. Rather, I am referring to the kind that will guide you along the roads of your life and give you control of your life-journey.

Financial Balance Is: "P-O-W-E-R"

P - Plans
O -
W -
E -
R -

Plans

The first system for "POWER" in your financial balance is "plans." Two similar terms for plans, which you are familiar with, are: "goals" and "objectives." What term you use is not as important as implementing this system into your daily life. You can never get anywhere in life without your plans being well defined.

I compare life without plans to playing football without goal posts. Without goal posts, you would never know when you score. A football player could run himself to death if he did not know where his goal was. Without the goal, he would never know he scored. With a goal, he knows exactly when he scores. So it is with the purpose of plans in your life. They guide you toward your goal and then help you know the score.

So much has been written about setting goals and recording them. I must join the ranks and reiterate that it is essential that you record your plans in a manner that you can see them. You can write them on paper and post them. You can enter them into your computer and review them daily. However you record your goals, be sure you have easy access to them. Your plans and goals are the foundations on which you will continually build your life. Of course, you will want to revise them from time to time, but you must first have something to revise. You need to set goals in every area of your life. Often, it is easier to set goals in the other five areas of life and a bit harder to get a clear picture of where you are going financially. Your planning and goal-setting must be clear to you.

Of course, if your planning makes you reach for too many goals, such fragmented targeting can be just as self-defeating as drifting about aimlessly. With her experienced wisdom, Eleanor Roosevelt warned that many individuals proceed "on the sea of life without any chart or compass or any special port in view. They are drifting and they don't know where they are going. They will never enter the harbor of success."

The person who has no definite purpose, who aims at nothing in particular, is almost sure to accomplish nothing. Whatever your purpose is financially, you are not likely to score a bull's-eye if you don't set up a clear, visible target to shoot at. You will stay just like you are if you have no plans or goals.

SignPost:

The First Step To Getting Somewhere Is To Choose That You Are Not Going To Stay Where You Are

When you make the choice that you are not going to stay where you are, it will be your plans that help you get somewhere else.

I have developed a system for planning or goal-setting that will assist you in getting started and maintaining your plans. It is called: "Six Time Zones For Successful Planning." Whatever you want to accomplish in your life will be done by achieving success on a scheduled basis. Set your plans and move toward them with these time zones.

Time Zones For Successful Planning

1. Daily Plans
2. Weekly Plans
3. Monthly Plans
4. Short Term Plans (6 months to 1 year)
5. Intermediate Plans (1 year to 5 years)
6. Long Term Plans (5 years and up)

As you plan your life-journey and your financial involvement and as you record your plans, use each time zone to direct and guide you. For each plan or goal, attach a time zone to it.

The following questions will further prepare you as you analyze your financial plans and balance and assign a time zone to them:

☑ What income level do I want to achieve?
☑ What responsibilities will I assume?
☑ Will I start a new business, expand my present business or continue to work for another?
☑ What net worth do I want to have?
☑ What investments do I want to pursue?
☑ Will I be financially independent?

When you are involved in the planning process, you are constantly in motion. Movement denotes life, and your life will move forward with balance, when you implement the system of plans. Your planning is also connected to your enthusiasm for living. Definite plans give you added enthusiasm for living and an increased energy supply.

Take an inventory of your financial area of life and determine what new plans need to be set and what old plans need to be revitalized. In order for you to not get too discouraged in your planning, be sure to set realistic plans for your financial area. It is important to be positive about your plans, and it is equally important to be realistic. If you set unrealistic plans for yourself, you will set yourself up for self-sabotage.

Remember, without plans you are going nowhere. You can't get where you want to go in your financial balance, if you don't know where it is you want to go.

Financial balance means that you must have plans.

Plans give you "POWER."

P - Plans
O - Order
W -
E -
R -

Order

Financial balance needs you to have your time, your plans, and your surroundings in order. When the system of order is out-of-balance in your life, you will forfeit the opportunity to be the successful person you want to be. The masses of people do not practice order in their lives and therefore self-sabotage their success. Lack of order in your life creates loss of time, money, accomplishment, fulfillment and constructive action. Without having your life in order, you will never know who you are, where you are going, or what you are doing. With no or little order in your life, you will be on the proverbial yo-yo forever. The good news is you can get off!

Order means the accurate arrangement of things. Everything has a place, a home. From the paper clips on your desk to the towels in your closet to the important financial papers in your deposit box, everything about you can be accurately arranged. When you use this system, you will greatly diminish your frustration, your stress, your negative feelings. I personally know the benefits that order will bring into your life.

This is one system that I honor in my own life. As a matter of fact, some of my family and friends feel that I am even a fanatic regarding order in my life. Over the years, I have discovered the powerful results in my life from having my life in order.

Benefits Of Order In Your Life

1. Order sets up productive action dynamics.
2. Order removes procrastination.
3. Order brings you information.
4. Order minimizes frustration.
5. Order causes preparation.

6. Order creates vision.
7. Order takes you to your destination.
8. Order helps you enjoy your relaxation.

Amazing benefits from something so simple, but not so easy to attain.

The financial world is highly competitive and without order in your life you will not be able to effectively and productively address the inevitable pressures that you will experience. Apply the system of order to your goals, your time, your money, your spending, your budget, your investments and your retirement plans.

Having your life in order gives you the feeling of having some control of your life. When you are in control you are better able to determine the outcome of certain situations and therefore, remain in charge. Remember: You are in charge of getting your life in order and maintaining order in your life on a daily basis.

Listed below are some tips to help you get further organized:

1. Keep a written list of the things you want to achieve.

2. Keep a daily plan of action as to how you will go about achieving your goals.

3. Make files for everything. This will save time when you need them at your finger-tips.

4. Set aside a certain time to do certain things.

5. Get your home, your desk, your car, and your records in a systematic order.

Initially, it will take a focused amount of time to get your life in order. Do not become over-whelmed by the task. Just begin. Start with a small area. Get it in order, then step back and feel your sense of accomplishment. Your sense of accomplishment will propel you forward to the next area and then the next. You will receive immediate results in your life once you have activated the system of order. Every area of your life will be positively affected and you will gradually begin to feel the yo-yo balance.

A Life In Order Is A Life In Balance

Financial balance includes the accurate arrangement of things in your home life and work environment that combine to guide you to financial success. Financial balance means that you have your life in order. Order gives you "POWER."

Financial Balance Is Power!

P - Plans
O - Order
W - Work
E -
R -

Work

In order to attain a sense of financial balance, you need to know the system of **work**. Unfortunately, with the increasing ease in the marketplace, you don't hear the word **work** very often. In many homes and businesses, it is an unknown tongue, a foreign language. It's getting to be a dirty four-letter word. Next time you're in a rest room, write **work** on the wall. I guarantee it will clear the stalls. It seems fewer and fewer people know and appreciate the system of **work**.

Nothing Is Ever Accomplished By What You
Are Going To Do; Only By What You Do

To achieve anything in life that is meaningful and worthwhile, it will require you to "do," to "work."

I often wonder where is it that people learn what work is. It's not taught in most homes and certainly not in most schools. When young people go to college or business school, they don't hear about work. Instead, they hear words like career, position, fringe benefits, etc. Very seldom do they hear that to make things happen, you've got to work.

Without work, you become lazy, unproductive and bored. Aren't you happier when you know you are involved in something that you ˌoy doing and are at the same time making money at it? Of course, you are. That is the natural way things are to be. Your work should be something you are challenged by and enjoy doing. If you don't like your work, either change your work or your attitude toward it. Without fulfilling work, you get irritated and angry, not to mention broke. Your work is a means by which you make that all encompassing exchange called "money."

Money in and of itself is neither good nor bad. It is what you do with or without it that makes you good or bad. Money is simply an exchange for services and goods. It has no value until you exchange it. Your money is earned from the work you do.

Money is a vital part of your life-journey. Your financial balance, in part, will depend upon how you define and structure your need and want of money. Being in financial balance is not about the amount of money you have, but rather, it is about having the amount of money that you need for the lifestyle you have chosen. Money allows you to be and do the things you choose. Money gives you the opportunity to enjoy more of the things there are to experience on the roads of your life-journey.

It is important to realize that money does not make one happy or sad. It is the means by which you can enjoy things more. It has been said that money can't buy happiness; but you can rent it so long, you think you own it.

Money is not evil. It is the love of it or lack of it that can make you evil. Everything you do in life, you can do better if you have more money. The key to productive money-use is to keep your money principles in balance so as to help and not hurt you.

To enjoy the results of money, you earn it and you do that through your work. Work gives you "POWER."

Financial Balance Is Power!

P - Power
O - Order
W - Work
E - Enthusiasm
R -

Enthusiasm

Your enthusiasm guarantees you "POWER" for traveling your life-journey. The original Greek definition of enthusiasm is: "God within you." In the creation process, the God-force is instilled within you. Through this force, you emanate life.

Along with the Greek definition, I want to embrace an expanded definition. Enthusiasm expands to include: energy, excitement, zeal, eagerness, spirit, devotion and motivation.

Enthusiasm is the electricity that turns you on to life. It ignites energy inside you to set goals financially and develop game-plans to reach them. It gives you excitement to start a project, and then to stay with it to completion. If you think that enthusiasm is just about feelings, think again. Enthusiasm works even when you don't feel like it. You can never achieve balance in your life if you operate by just your feelings. There are many times in your life when you don't particularly feel like doing what you do, but you do it anyway. That is motivation in its purest form.

SIGNPOST:

*Motivation Is Doing What You Choose
To Do For A Specific Benefit,
Whether You Feel Like It Or Not*

Your enthusiasm for living life to the fullest is a major factor in achieving balance in your life. When you sow enthusiasm into your financial area, you will reap bountiful benefits. Enthusiasm gives you the "POWER."

It is highly important that you like what you do, where you live, the people you work with and the type of extra-curricular activities you are involved in. All of this contributes to the kind of energy level you enjoy. Energy is the surge you feel inside that drives you to set your goals and then to action to meet them.

Along with energy, develop qualities that make for enthusiasm in your life. I intentionally use the term "develop," because you do, in fact, develop enthusiasm, eagerness, zeal, devotion and motivation. These are power-drivers for your balance in every area, and specifically to your financial area. There is no substitute for enthusiasm in your business or in your work or in your life.

There are many systems to use to keep your enthusiasm alive and thriving. One system that I employ is to celebrate whenever I achieve a goal or something I have set out to do. Celebration is a most important part of balance in any area, but particularly in the financial area.

When you get the raise, celebrate. When you start your own business, celebrate. When you close the sale, celebrate. When you figure out the computer problem that no one else could figure out, celebrate. Celebrate every day. Do not let a day go by that you do not allow yourself the pleasure of patting yourself on the back. Treat yourself kindly, for not everyone will.

Your celebration does not always have to be over something big that you have accomplished. It can be over the little things that you choose to do. How much you spend on the celebration is, also, not important to the system of celebration. It is the very act of acknowledging your achievement that will be the generator for your continued enthusiasm.

Enthusiasm gives you "POWER."

Financial Balance Is Power!

P - Plans
O - Order
W - Work
E - Enthusiasm
R - Rewards

Rewards

With proper use of your time, involvement in a job, career and work that you love, productive investments of your time and money, you inevitably reap the rewards of your labor.

Rewards can be spelled:	Money
Rewards can be spelled:	Material Things
Rewards can be spelled:	Personal Gratification and Satisfaction
Rewards can be spelled:	Respect From Others For A Job Well-Done

There are many ways to spell "rewards." When you have your financial life in order, when you have plans and are organized, have meaningful work, are enthused about your life and what you are contributing to life, I am confident that you will experience the kinds of rewards you are looking for.

For many people financial balance denotes money, fame and wealth. There is no question that all of these things can be used to help make life more productive. However, it should be noted that there are other things that make for financial balance. One thing that adds to financial balance is happiness. You can have all the investments, all the money, all the wealth and still not have learned how to be happy. There is something about happiness that balances out a fully-involved financial area.

Money can buy conveniences, luxuries and material things that can help you to enjoy a more beautiful lifestyle. But truly satisfying, enduring happiness flows only from one Source. All the inner qualities you build and develop will ultimately honor you with the rewards of a balanced life. These include self-respect, gratifying daily endeavor, peace of mind, giving and getting, etc. Money can buy none of these things.

It has been humorously noted: "Money can't buy love, health, happiness or what it did last year."

An anonymous soldier was quoted as saying: "I wished for all things that I might enjoy life and was granted life that I might enjoy all things."

When you combine the systems of plans, order, work, enthusiasm and rewards, you have put together a power-team for guiding you to financial balance. Indeed, you have the "POWER."

RECAP FOR "FINANCIAL BALANCE"

Financial Balance Is: "POWER!"

> P - Plans
> O - Order
> W - Work
> E - Enthusiasm
> R - Rewards

SignPosts For Your Life-Journey

1. K-I-S-S: Keep It Short And Simple

2. S-I-B-K-I-S: See It Big - Keep It Simple

3. The First Step To Getting Somewhere
    Is To Choose That You Are Not Going
    To Stay Where You Are

4. A Life In Order Is A Life In Balance

5. Nothing Is Ever Accomplished
    By What You Are Going To Do;
    Only By What You Do

6. Motivation Is Doing What You Choose
    To Do For A Specific Benefit,
    Whether You Feel Like It Or Not

PERSONAL SELF-INVENTORY

1. Am I working at what I really want to do? _____

2. What changes can I make in what I am doing for a living?

   _____

   _____

3. Have I found the right balance-point in over-working and under-working? _____

4. List three things that are most important to me in the areas of finances:

   1. _____

   2. _____

   3. _____

5. Do I feel a sense of accomplishment each day? _____

6. List two investments that I currently have, that are helping to insure my financial balance:

   1. _____

   2. _____

7. Am I a good manager of money? _____

8. List two ways I can improve my money management:

   1. _____

   2. _____

9. Do I use stress to my benefit or to my detriment? _____

10. Do I record my plans? _____

11. Write four plans that I currently have in the works regarding my finances:

    1. _____

    2. _____

    3. _____

    4. _____

12. Do I use the "Time Zones For Successful Planning"? _____

13. Do I consider myself to be organized? _____

14. Can I be more organized? _____

    If so, how? _____

_____

15. What does the word "reward" mean to me? _____

_____

_____

_____

_____

DR. ZONNYA'S FIRST AID

1. Take a self-inventory regarding your financial area. Ask yourself the questions that pertain to you individually. Develop a personal philosophy concerning the direction you will choose to take in your financial area.

2. Define success as it applies to you and your lifestyle.

3. Incorporate "Time Zones For Successful Planning" in your goal-setting. It is imperative to record your plans.

4. Your self-inventory will help you become aware of any area of your life that is not in order. Develop a system for getting every area of your life in order. It won't be easy at first nor will you get it done overnight. Begin today.

5. Learn to like your work or change your work.

6. Celebrate every accomplishment, large or small. This propels you toward future achievements.

AFFIRMATIONS

An affirmation is a positive statement that expresses a specific belief concerning you and the state of the affairs of your life. It begins with "I" or "my" and always will serve to reinforce all that is unique, special and distinctive about you. Use it often throughout the day. It will inspire, encourage and motivate you as you commit yourself to balanced living for a more beautiful lifestyle.

I, _____, know

that my prosperity helps me be of service to myself and others.

I, _____, accept

my right to financial success and prosperity.

I, _____, realize

that there is an ample supply of good for everybody.

"People are always blaming their circumstances for what they are. The people who get on in this world are those who get up and look for the circumstance they want. If they can't find them, they make them."
—George Bernard Shaw

Chapter 11

FAMILY BALANCE
Relationships Are Built, Not Born

"If we want better people to make
a better world, then we will have to begin
where people are made: in the family."
—Anonymous

Since the beginning of the first family, the subject of family has captured the interest of philosophy, religion, politics, psychology and every study regarding human development. Also, from the first family, we learn the balance and out-of-balance that a family, as a **unit** can experience. Equally from the first family, we learn the balance and out-of-balance that an **individual** of the family unit can experience.

I was asked in a media interview: "How can the family unit be improved?" I replied: "The family unit can only be improved when each individual in the unit improves." The family unit is composed of individuals; individuals make the family unit. The family unit has two components: first, the centrifugal family: husband/father, wife/mother, children; second, the extended family: grandparents, uncles, aunts, cousins, nieces, nephews, and it can expand to include anyone whom the family unit invites into this extended relationship.

When an individual of the unit experiences out-of-balance situations, it usually affects the family unit with out-of-balance conditions.

There are many situations that exist indicative of family out-of-balance. They are labeled: divorce, child abuse, spouse abuse, substance abuse, aging bitterly, lack of effective communication, run-aways, child-snatching, suicide, teen pregnancies, sexually transmitted diseases, etc. Indeed, the family institution seems to be on an endless yo-yo and dangerously out-of-balance.

In today's society, in addition to the traditional family unit, there are many unconventional modes of family living. The material presented here is primarily focused toward the traditional family unit as it is defined by the majority. However, I do want to note that whatever family structure exists, it is important to define family-balance for the family unit. I am confident this material can be translated to address the most unique family unit. Again, the conventional traditional family unit is husband/father, wife/mother and children.

When we talk about family-balance, it is necessary to look at some foundations on which balance can be built. Also, we must address to whom the balance concept can be applied. In addition, we must look at the over-all structure of the family unit, what composes it and how it functions within the social structure.

I believe the systems that apply to one individual of the family can apply to every individual of the family; how the principles are implemented will be an individual decision. It is the responsibility of each individual to dedicate himself/herself to his/her own self-improvement. Without this, there will be no family-balance or improvement. Once each member accepts his/her responsibility for individual improvement, then the unit improvement will follow.

In this chapter, I offer simple, practical, adaptable, usable and workable systems to build family-balance. The systems apply to men and women, boys and girls. As previously done in each chapter of the six areas, I have chosen an acronym to identify the systems you can use to get you off your yo-yo and help you enjoy more balance in your family.

The acronym for family-balance is "CARE." However, before we examine the systems of "CARE", please take the following brief inventory. This will assist you as you begin to openly address the many issues that family-balance includes. The statements are designed to assist you in realistically looking at yourself and some of the attitudes, actions, reactions, responses, or habits which may be preventing you from enjoying the beautiful lifestyle you want and deserve in your family. Please respond to the statements with the answer of Balanced or Out-Of-Balance.

1. I maintain open communication with all members of my family.
   Balanced or Out-Of-Balance

2. I show courtesy and consideration for each member of my family.
   Balanced or Out-Of-Balance

3. I am willing to accept my family members even though we disagree.
   Balanced or Out-Of-Balance

4. I never make derogatory comparisons between the behavior of my family members and someone else.
   Balanced or Out-Of-Balance

5. I can forgive and forget after a disagreement.
   Balanced or Out-Of-Balance

6. I plan and act on entertainment and relaxation time that is designed to bring my family members closer together.
   Balanced or Out-Of-Balance

7. I express my love and affection for each member of my family.
   Balanced or Out-Of-Balance

8. I do not feel jealous of the time that members of my family spend with outside friends.
   Balanced or Out-Of-Balance

9. I am willing to compromise when differences exist.
   Balanced or Out-Of-Balance

10. I love unconditionally.
    Balanced or Out-Of-Balance

The preceding statements probe into the way you act, react and respond to those closest to you. It was once said, "If we would treat our friends like family, we'd have none. But if we would treat our family like friends we would have many."

Let's begin the journey of exploring just how you can better interact with your family, to bring about more balance and harmony in your relationships.

Family Balance Means "CARE"

C - Communication
A -
R -
E -

Communication

The term "lack of communication" is used to describe the absence of communication. This can be death to your family-balance.

The term "breakdown in communication" is frequently used to describe what happens when there is a misunderstanding. While this can be detrimental to your family-balance, it is repairable.

There is a term that will guide you to your family-balance: "effective communication." This is what you are striving to achieve in each of your communications within in all of your relationships, and certainly with your family.

It is not difficult to communicate. The challenge comes in effectively communicating the message you want to send to your listener. Let's review what happens in a spoken communication.

1. I choose to say something to you. I know exactly what I am saying.

2. You hear something. I have no idea what you heard.

The Message Is Not The Message Sent;
The Message Is The Message Received

3. You choose to say something back to me based on what you heard, not on what I said.

4. Then, I respond to you based on what I heard and the process continues.

If we were articulate enough and lucky enough, we heard the messages that were sent. If we did, then our communication was effective. If we did not, then we experienced a breakdown in communication. Too frequently, the latter is the norm.

While I am writing a book on effective communication that gives detailed systems for avoiding the pot-holes and blow-outs on the road of communication, I feel compelled to offer you a few systems to assist you on your road toward effective communication. These systems apply to each member of the family. Within the family, there are many pairings and even more situations that call for communication, i.e.: communication between spouses, communication between parent and child, communication between siblings, etc. If you know some of the systems for effective communication, then you can choose to implement them and decrease the breakdowns. To know and use the following systems will help you get off the communication yo-yo.

There are four basic communication techniques. They are:

1. Listening
2. Speaking or Writing
3. Acting
4. Touching

Listening

To increase or improve your listening techniques, consider the following systems.

1. Listen with your ears open and your mouth closed.

2. Sit forward as you listen. This shows you are interested. When you sit back, it indicates you may be bored.

3. In addition to your ears, listen with your eyes, face, hands, and body.

4. Don't interrupt.

5. Ask questions, only after the speaker is through speaking.

6. Look your speaker in the eyes. When you look away or stare into space, even though you may be listening, the speaker will read your body language to mean you are not.

7. Concentrate. It shows in your face.

Your Face Is Your Billboard;
Check Your Billboard

8. Listen between the lines to what the speaker may not be literally saying.

9. Refrain from looking like you are ready to speak while the speaker is speaking. You will get your turn.

These systems apply to whomever you listen to on a daily basis. Often the hardest part of effective communication in the family is listening. It is essential for the person who listens to understand that without listening there is no effective communication. It becomes a one sided conversation and usually accomplishes nothing.

You are familiar with the proverbial statements: "My parents don't listen to me," "My wife never listens," "My husband doesn't hear a thing I say," and "My children never listen to me." Generally, when people think they are not being listened to, it is because they have not been given the feedback that you, the listener, has heard what was said. To acknowledge with a response to someone who has spoken to you is the only way he/she will know they have been heard. This is crucial for effective communication between family members.

For parents, here is a SignPost just for you, regarding your children listening to you:

Don't Worry That Your Children Never Listen To You;
Worry That They Always Watch You

Speaking

To increase or improve your speaking techniques, consider the following systems:

A. Use words that move "forward" such as: You, yourself, yours, we, our, please, thank you, excuse me, forgive me, pardon me.

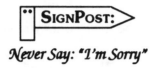

Never Say: "I'm Sorry"

What you did may be sorry, but you are not sorry. You are created in the image of greatness, not sorryness. Replace this with: excuse me, forgive me, pardon me.

B. Drop the hold-back words such as: I, me, my, sorry, later, maybe, try, but.

Never Say: "I'll Try"

You either do something or you don't, but you don't try. Example: Try to stand up. You can't try to stand up; you either do or don't. Try is a cop-out.

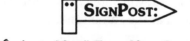

Eliminate "But" From Your Communication

Replace "but" with "and." "But" sets up walls, barriers, defenses and resistance. Example: "Honey, thank you for a nice evening, but you really embarrassed me when you made the remark about the restaurant." By using the word "but," your listener did not hear what came before it, only what came after it. Replace "but" with "and" for more effective communication. Listen to your communications throughout the day for how many times you sabotage it with this simple, but threatening word.

C. Use simple words to express yourself. Don't complicate the conversation.

D. Go easy on slang and eliminate profanity. It helps no one and hurts all involved. Once said, it can never be recovered.

E. Avoid sarcasm.

F. Say what you mean and mean what you say.

*It's Not What You Say That
Hurts Or Heals; It's How You Say It*

Verbally expressing oneself effectively is essential for a healthy and balanced family. While some members may be more expressive than others, it is vitally important for every member of the family unit to express feelings, desires and displeasures, as well as pleasures.

Often times, there are valid reasons why a family member does not feel secure enough to speak. If the family environment is abusive or authoritatively governed, it will be difficult for family members to be open and share their feelings, desires, likes and dislikes. It is extremely important for each member of the family to do his/her part to build a warm, loving and accepting environment that will encourage communication. This does not happen overnight. It takes time to build a strong foundation that will support the family as a unit, while supporting each individual at the same time.

Relationships Are Built, Not Born

Family-balance will require each member to contribute to the building process, through listening, speaking, acting and touching.

Acting

To increase or improve your acting, reacting and responding skills, please consider the following systems:

A. Think before you act, react or respond.

B. Consider the consequences (good or bad) of your actions, reactions and responses.

Choice Equals Results

C. Do not act, react or respond in haste.

D. Your behavior is always considered an example to someone in the family. Remember you may very well be a role-model.

E. Once an action, reaction or response has been decided upon, be firm, yet understanding of others in the family.

Words and actions have power. They can build or destroy a relationship. It is imperative as you move toward more family-balance, to increase your awareness level for improved effective communications.

I fully understand that I have only opened the proverbial "can of worms" for effective communication. I do hope that with this brief review of just a few of the systems, you can clearly focus on how vital they are to your family-balance. Also, I am fully aware that the systems I am sharing will only be used by the family and its members who are dedicated to improving and growing together. These systems are, however, for every family, traditional or non-traditional. The key for family-balance, whatever the make-up of the family, will be to use them on a daily basis.

Touching

To increase or improve your touching techniques, review and consider the following systems:

A. There are two levels of touching: literal and figurative. Literal is physically touching others, skin to skin. Figurative is touching by what you think, say or do towards others.

B. Only touch others with respect and integrity. Never abuse the communication technique of touching.

C. You must first get in touch with yourself before you can be effective in getting in touch with others.

D. Reach out and touch somebody's hand. We all are touch-hungry and touch-starved.

E. Use your time, energy, effort, creativity and money to touch the lives of others.

To Touch Is To Live

A Hug A Day Keeps Emptiness Away

You can never get too many hugs and you can never give too many. You communicate to others through the technique of touching. Touching produces powerful results between people. It can heal hurts that words can only begin to address. I am convinced you cannot achieve effective communication, which leads to family-balance, without the proper use of touching between family members.

Family Balance Means: "CARE"

C - Communication
A - Attitudes
R -
E -

Attitudes

Family balance is predicated on the attitudes of each individual member that translates into a family unit attitude. As an individual, you can only contribute those attitudes which you have first developed toward yourself. This process begins by developing healthy and loving attitudes toward yourself.

Attitude means the way you think about yourself, other people, issues, places and things. There are many attitudes that contribute to the family unit enjoying a more beautiful lifestyle and getting off the yo-yo. The following five attitudes will serve as systems for you to employ, as you move away from out-of-balance, toward more balance, in your family:

1. Attitude Of Unconditional Love
2. Attitude Of Goal Setting
3. Attitude Of Individualism
4. Attitude Of Changing
5. Attitude Of Togetherness

1. Attitude Of Unconditional Love

Love is only a four-letter word that surrounds hundreds of roads you will travel on your life-journey. To be such a small word it surely has significant impact on the quality of your life-journey. You normally think of love as being a natural part of the family structure. You are taught from birth about this feeling you are supposed to feel toward your family.

In reality, family love is often taken for granted. You assume that because you are part of a family love is an automatic emotion. It takes very little time or effort to realize that nowhere is love automatic, even within the family. Love, both giving and receiving it, requires the traits of effort, time, commitment and patience, just to mention a few. Love is more than an emotion or a word you use, it is an action you take.

While there are many aspects of the love process, I want to address the aspect of unconditional love. During the years of my encouraging people, this one aspect seems to present the most difficult challenge for family members. It is a given point that people are imperfect and make imperfect choices. Yet the SignPost still leads the way:

Everything Is A Matter Of Choice;
Choice Equals Results

To offer unconditional love is to offer love in spite of the actions, reactions or responses of a family member. This is much more difficult to do than to say. To verbalize the words "I Love You" is easy. To actualize the words "I Love You" in the face of imperfections is the challenge you will be called upon to meet, if you are to enjoy family balance. "I Love You" are just words if you cannot put them into action.

Love In Word And In Deed

When you are disappointed, or when you experience mistrust, disloyalty, hurt or pain from someone you love, it becomes more difficult to express and give love without strings attached. It is easier to say, "I will love you if...." However, this kind of conditional love will not build stronger and more balanced family relationships.

Unconditional love is what you offer no matter what the actions, reactions or responses are. Unconditional love forgives and forgets.

Forget What You Should Forget;
Remember What You Should Remember

Let me share with you a "Statement Of Unconditional Love" which you can apply to every relationship within the family unit.

Statement Of Unconditional Love:

"I love you and I will always love you. There is nothing that you have ever done, are doing, or can ever do that will cause me not to love you. As a person who is making your own choices, you are receiving the productive or non-productive results of those choices. I, too, receive the results of my choices. You will live with the results of your choices, just as I live with the results of my choices. I love you and I will always love you."

A family that demonstrates unconditional love is a rarity. However, the family that offers unconditional love on a daily basis will enjoy the results of a more beautiful family lifestyle.

2. Attitude Of Goal-Setting

The family that enjoys the results of family balance is the family who understands the process of both goal setting for each family member individually and for the family as a unit. Think of the family as a team. Each member helps to make the team complete. While each member has individual goals, the ultimate goal is a healthy, productive and balanced family unit.

In addition to the family area, you have five other areas in which you set individual goals: physical, mental, spiritual, social, and financial. At the same time you are setting individual goals, you are part of a team that works together to set team goals.

Family goal setting is an opportunity for each team member to contribute to the whole. It is also an exercise in learning to work together for a common purpose. As a team, you work together to set goals and enjoy the benefits in many areas, i.e., defining household duties, planning vacations, setting times for family recreation, developing a financial savings program for individual needs or for needs of the unit, creating a positive environment for each family member to develop and grow, formulating morals, values, and a code of living for traveling the life-journey.

The family is a unit, a team, a whole, and should be treated with the highest respect and dignity. No one person in the family is more important than the other. It takes each member of the family to make the whole unit. If one member does not contribute to the unit, the unit sacrifices. Each member should feel a certain responsibility to the team and should contribute his/her individual part to making the unit whole.

In today's society, the family unit that I have just described seems almost extinct. It is not extinct; it is alive and it needs encouraging. The family unit has taken some justified criticism, along with much that is unjustified. The modern family is different than it has ever been in it's history. The modern family can certainly make improvements, just as modern religion or modern politics can improve.

It is my goal to encourage every individual who is a member of today's family unit. You are valuable as an individual and you are valuable as a member of the family unit. Many of your choices not only will affect you, they will have effects on others, especially the members of your family who love you unconditionally. Make your choices carefully. Set your goals wisely and work within the unit as it moves toward balance.

3. Attitude of Individualism

In the discussion of "attitude of goal setting," the point was made that the family consists of individuals. Each individual is unique, special, different and valuable. Without any one member, the entire family-unit would be different.

To express individualism within the family-unit is essential to individual, as well as unit growth. You must be allowed to be yourself within the parameters of family guidelines. If the unit fails to provide this open environment, you will be stifled and will suffocate. You must be given the opportunity to be the unique person you were created to be. You must be allowed to change and grow.

The attitude of individualism negates the attitude of comparison. Comparing individual family members is unfair. No one wins and everyone loses when comparisons are made between family members. There are countless examples of parents comparing one child to another. Seldom are the results beneficial; usually, the results are devastating.

The results are devastating when a spouse comparison is made, particularly when income is the issue. Who makes the most? Who works the hardest? Who is the most inconvenienced? These are just a few of the questions that arise when you play the comparison game. I cannot think of one benefit as a result of comparing individuals. You are you and you cannot be compared to anyone other than yourself.

You Are In-Comparable

Along with comparing, comes competing for sake of competition. Whether it is spouse competing with spouse, parent competing with child, sibling competing with sibling, no one wins. There are too many families hurting because they play the competing game.

Each member must be allowed to stand on his/her own merit and develop that merit to it's fullest potential.

4. Attitude Of Changing

There is nothing constant in life except **change**. The only place you won't find change is in a vacuum, and I guarantee, you don't live in a vacuum. Because of the fact that you live in a changing world, you are forever changing. You will not be the same tomorrow as you are today. Change is a necessary and vital part to your life-journey.

From the beginning of your journey, birth, to the end of your journey, death, you will be in a state of change. You will experience change in all six areas of your life. Your body will change; your thoughts and attitudes change; your environment and surroundings change; your beliefs change; your relationships change; your job, career and finances change. Everything changes.

To achieve family balance within the unit, each member must change and grow. Sometimes, it is difficult to accept change. There are times when you may not agree with the changes other family members are making or they may not agree with the changes you are making. This is to be expected because each family member is unique and making individual choices. It is a challenge for the family unit to always understand the changes that any one member may choose to make.

Resisting change will not deter it. To choose to accept that change is one major road on your life's journey, may be one of the most demanding and challenging choices of your entire journey. Your attitude toward change will determine how you use it as a friend or an enemy.

Make Change Your Friend, Not Your Enemy

When you find yourself resisting change, examine the fears you may have attached to the change. To prefer your comfort zones to unchartered waters is a human quality. Many times you are uncomfortable when your comfort zones are disturbed. However, disturb them you must. In order to enjoy family balance, you must develop a positive attitude concerning the inevitable process of change.

To help you develop a positive attitude about wanted or unwanted changes, consider these systems:

1. Identify the change as specifically as possible.

2. Ask questions about the change.

3. Determine the results of the change.

4. You have the right to agree or disagree and to state your position.

5. Look for the benefits in the change.

6. Let go of the fear and all negative feelings connected to the change.

When you are choosing change, give consideration to the feelings of other family members. When other family members are choosing change, give them the consideration that you would like for them to give you.

5. Attitude Of Togetherness

The balanced family will develop the attitude of togetherness. Togetherness indicates a healthy exchange between family members. Happy, productive, successful families spend time together. They arrange to get together for fun. They plan special occasions to share time and laughter with each other.

The Family That Laughs And Plays Together
Stays Together

Strong families are committed to each other. They know they can depend on each other in the good times, as well as, in the bad times. Balanced families support one another and the unit takes priority over individuals when necessary.

Togetherness means you build each other as individuals. Each member of the family contributes to the positive feelings of other members. They habitually relate to each other on strengths, rather than on weaknesses or on tearing each other down.

SignPost:

You Never Step-Up
By Stepping-On

Togetherness also indicates that the balanced family rallies together during times of personal problems or crises. Members realize just how much they mean to each other.

Togetherness is essential for you to enjoy a balanced family and a more beautiful lifestyle.

The five attitudes of a balanced family are:

1. Attitude Of Unconditional Love
2. Attitude Of Goal-Setting
3. Attitude Of Individualism
4. Attitude Of Changing
5. Attitude Of Togetherness

Family Balance Includes Attitudes

C - Communication
A - Attitudes
R - Reinforcement
E -

Reinforcement

Family reinforcement indicates that there is a cohesiveness within the unit. It shows that there is support, understanding, empathy, recognition, appreciation and praise for individuals. Reinforcement is a two-sided coin: unit reinforcement and individual reinforcement.

Family unit reinforcement confirms the position of the family unit. In good times and in bad times, the family prevails. This is particularly needed in times of severe crisis, i.e.: divorce, sickness, death. Anything that seems to threaten the strength of the unit will ultimately threaten the strength of the individual. Effective reinforcement between all members of the family is extremely important in order to maintain the unit.

Individual reinforcement from other family members confirms individual importance. When you make a choice that affects you or the family unit, you want the love and support of your family. Even in times when others don't support your choice, you seek their support of you as an important part of the family. Even when you make choices with which your family disagrees, you can still look to your family to offer support to you as an individual. It is not necessary to support any given action, reaction or response as much as it is necessary to support the person.

Reinforcement is something you need as you grow and change and become a self-motivated student of life. You need to know that others are with you, are there for you and **care** about you. You need encouragement, kindness, uplifting. It is the responsibility of each family member to learn to provide reinforcement for others.

Spouses must learn to reinforce each other as they change, as they grow, as they improve themselves. Children in the family need the reinforcement of both parents and siblings. Without reinforcement, you question your worth, your value, your ability to make proper choices, etc.

With the reinforcement that comes from the family, you learn to feel good about who you are, what you are doing and where you are going. With positive reinforcement, you grow into a happy, healthy, and balanced individual.

You can also grow into a happy, healthy, balanced individual without the positive support of a family, but it is definitely more difficult and more of a challenge for you. There are thousands of examples of people who have "made it" without a family unit. However, seldom does anyone "make it" without some form of reinforcement from others. It is an innate need for the human mind, heart and spirit to be encouraged from outside sources. When people do not have a positive family support system, they look elsewhere to find one. On the positive side, they look for friends, people at work or church, etc.

On the negative side, people find gangs, cults, or groups that will offer them reinforcement. You will find and get reinforcement: the question is: Where?

To enrich the reinforcement in your family, consider the following systems:

1. Always listen to all sides before you make a judgment.

2. Express your possible dislike of a given situation.

3. Ask questions to learn how the other person may feel.

4. Do your best to put yourself in the other person's place.

5. Never close a door on a relationship that could develop into a closer one.

6. Let the family member know that you love him/her regardless, and that no matter what the outcome of a specific choice, your love will not diminish.

7. Keep the lines of communication open.

8. Build the worth of the individual and emphasize his/her good qualities.

Family Balance Means Reinforcement

C - Communication
A - Attitudes
R - Reinforcement
E - Extra Effort

Extra Effort

There is no area of life that requires **more** extra effort than the family area. To enjoy family balance, it will require the extra effort of every member of the unit. There is no such thing as an **easy** productive relationship. Every worthwhile relationship is built upon certain strong foundations. One of these foundations is extra effort.

Extra effort means that you are willing to go the extra mile. You will choose to do what someone else might not do in order to make the family a fully functioning unit.

When you are in balance, you accept your responsibility to do your part, to carry your share of the load, to contribute in a positive and productive way for the betterment of the family. In every group, including the family, there is always one or two leaders. There is always someone who takes the initiative. If you are to promote family balance, you may need to be that person.

Haven't you heard people say: "Well, I wrote them last. If they want to hear from me, they can write me."

Others will say: "I went to see them last. If they want to see me, they know where I live."

Inside the family unit, you may find discrepancies in who wants to do certain things, and in who doesn't want to do certain things. If the goal of the family is to make it a fully functioning unit, then each member does whatever it takes to reach that goal. I understand not wanting to do certain things. Cleaning the toilet is not particularly my favorite hobby; I choose to do it because is contributes to the family goal.

As you travel the family road of your life-journey, you will be called upon to go the extra mile. This is a system that invades every road of your life-journey. You will also be called upon to go the extra mile at work, with your friends, and most certainly, with your family.

In order to reach family balance, each and every member must contribute to the extra-effort system. It cannot just be left up to one or two individuals. Each individual has a part to play in the success or lack of success of the family unit.

Family Balance Means EXTRA EFFORT

In this discussion, I have only scratched the surface of all the systems that can be employed to achieve family balance. One entire book is being planned to deal with this issue in a more in-depth perspective. I hope I have stirred within you the desire to want to increase your family balance. I believe if you practice and enhance these systems, you will be a more balanced contributor to a most vital institution we call the family.

RECAP FOR "FAMILY BALANCE"

Family Balance is: "CARE"

> C - Communication
> A - Attitudes
> R - Reinforcement
> E - Extra Effort

SignPosts For Your Life-Journey

1. The Message is Not The Message Sent;
   The Message Is The Message Received

2. Your Face Is Your Billboard;
   Check Your Billboard

3. Don't Worry That Your Children Never Listen To You;
   Worry That They Always Watch You

4. Never Say: "I'm Sorry"

5. Never Say: "I'll Try"

6. Eliminate "But" From Your Communication

7. It's Not **What** You Say That Hurts Or Heals;
   It's **How** You Say It

8. Relationships Are Built, Not Born

9. Everything Is A Matter Of Choice;
   Choice Equals Results

10. To Touch Is To Live

11. A Hug A Day Keeps Emptiness Away

PERSONAL SELF-INVENTORY

1. List three major problems that I see in my family structure:

    1. _____

    2. _____

    3. _____

2. Do I set aside a certain time each week for a family meeting where we can discuss the family as a whole and the members individually?

    _____

    If so, when? _____

3. Do I forget and forgive my family members for mistakes?

    _____

4. Do I hold grudges and bring up past mistakes? _____

5. Can I love unconditionally? _____

6. How good are my listening skills? _____

    _____

7. List two things I can do to improve my listening skills:

    1. _____

    2. _____

    3. _____

8. Do I judge my family members harshly? _____

9. Do my family members know that I appreciate them? _____

10. List two ways I show my appreciation:

    1. _____

    2. _____

11. Am I expressive with my feelings? _____

12. List two ways I could improve my expressiveness:

    1. _____

    2. _____

13. What kind of attitudes do I have toward my family? _____

    _____

14. Do I criticize more than I compliment my family? _____

15. Name one compliment I have given today to a family member:

    1. _____

16. Do I give the extra effort when it is needed to make constructive things happen? _____

    Example: _____

17. Describe the way I feel about the part I play in the family unit:

    _____

    _____

    _____

DR. ZONNYA'S FIRST AID

1. Set aside a specific time each week for a family get-together. Everyone must attend and contribute.

2. In the family get-together, discuss each member's goals, accomplishments and failures, and then discuss the family as a unit.

3. Plan at least <u>four</u> mealtimes together each week. Choose positive and challenging topics for discussion. Never quarrel or argue at the table.

4. Establish guidelines for the entire family. Adults, as well as children, need to have guidelines within the family structure.

5. Each month, each member can choose to read one self-improvement book. At the end of each month, discuss the book(s). This will give the family a common ground on which to be expressive.

6. Plan one recreational activity each week.

AFFIRMATIONS

An affirmation is a positive statement that expresses a specific belief concerning you and the state of the affairs of your life. It begins with "I" or "My" and always will serve to reinforce all that is unique, special and distinctive about you. Use it often throughout the day. It inspire, encourage and motivate you as you commit yourself to balanced living for a more beautiful lifestyle.

I, _____, believe that

love begins with me, that I can give love, accept love, and share love,

and do love.

I, _____, assume my

responsibility for achieving effective communication with my family.

I, _____, accept

myself as a changing person and allow the others in my family the

right to change.

"Your children are not your children.
They are the sons and daughters of life's longing for itself.
They come through you, but not from you, and
though they are with you yet, they belong not to you.
You may give them your love, but not your thoughts, for
they have their own thoughts. You may house their bodies,
but not their souls, for their souls dwell in the house of
tomorrow, which you cannot visit, not even in your dreams.
You may strive to be like them, but seek not to make them like
you, for life goes not backward nor tarries with yesterday."
—Kahill Gibran, "The Prophet"

Chapter 12

IT'S UP TO YOU

"Love not just what you are;
Love what you can become."
—Miguel De Cervantes

Although we have arrived at the conclusion of this specific discussion on systems to help you achieve balance in your life, we have only begun to explore the alternatives that exist for getting off your yo-yo and living a more fulfilling life. Each and every day should serve to bring you closer to the kind of lifestyle you want to enjoy. It will not be easy. It will be worth the time, effort and commitment that you will give.

If there is just one phrase that I could choose to describe how you will travel your life-journey, it would be: "It's Up To You." A volatile choice must be made on your part as to what you want out of life and what price you are willing to pay to achieve it. There is always a price. The balanced life is not free, but it is reasonable. "It's Up To You" how you will experience your life-journey.

There are two questions that you must ask yourself every day, as you travel the many roads of your life-journey. First: What do I want? Second: What am I willing to do to get it?

When you were created, you were given all that you need to create for yourself a beautiful lifestyle. If you do not enjoy the more,

253

better, greater of life, you must look inside yourself to discover what the problem is, how it evolved, and what you can do to solve the problem.

Balanced living is an alternative system to assist you in getting off your yo-yo. I have seen countless hundreds and thousands of people put these systems into practice and create for themselves a more beautiful lifestyle. It can be done and you can do it. "It's Up To You."

Whatever you are today, wherever you are today, whoever you are today, you are a product of your choices in each of the six areas of life. The greatest power you have is the power to choose. Consciously or unconsciously, you decide your individual fate in life. Certainly there are situations that you face that you cannot control, but you can always control how you choose to respond to them. Once you can accept this system, you can then begin to make dramatic visible differences in your life. You will experience more balanced living and less yo-yo living.

Everybody wants to be happy, healthy, have good marriages, make lots of money, etc., but no one ever gets anywhere in life by wishing. It takes a basic philosophy, a basic principle, a basic foundation to build on, and a system to employ. Add to that faith and work and you can begin to fulfill the desires of your heart and get off your yo-yo.

Thoreau's marvelous line from *WALDEN* says: "Oh God, to reach the point of death only to find that you have never lived at all." What an indictment to the human spirit and potential. For me, the greatest thing we have is the opportunity to fully live life, not just get through life. Life is the quality which distinguishes a vital and functioning balanced person from a dead one. Life is only in the hands of the one who possesses it. If you ever leave your own individual living to someone else, you will never live! You must assume your own unique position on the roads of your life-journey. There will be no one else who will travel the life-journey like you. You will chart your own course, design your own road maps and choose how you will travel the journey.

Because you are in charge of your life and the choices you make, you are always able to create for yourself the kind of life you desire. You have the power. You can do it. "It's Up To You." Nikos Kazantzakis, the famous artist says it this way: "You have your brush, you have your colors, you paint paradise, then in you go."

You literally can paint the kind of life you want to experience. You can paint your life a heaven or you can paint your life a hell. You can paint your life in balance or you can choose to paint a yo-yo life for your entire life-journey. The good news is that you do have the power to create for yourself a balanced lifestyle.

My purpose, in sharing these thoughts and ideas with you, has been to reinforce knowledge you already have, to encourage you to apply the knowledge and to offer you refreshing insights into how you can live life to its fullest. What you have experienced in the pages of this book are thoughts and ideas that serve to encourage you and inspire you to get off your yo-yo and go for the beautiful lifestyle that is your birthright.

One of the systems I teach in my seminars is that your mind is filled with light-bulbs. Some of them are burning brightly, some dimly and some aren't burning at all because they have never been turned on. New or reinforced thoughts and ideas serve as a switch for you to flip for more light in your life. The more light you have, the more clearly you can travel the roads of your life-journey. With more light, you will be able to see what is ahead. You will be able to make choices and changes that will make your journey more enjoyable. An interesting note about light is that it was the first part of creation. There needed to be light to proceed. So it is with your life. You need light to proceed and you will only make productive choices and changes as you have the light to create them.

The perceptive writer, Flannery O'Connor, affirmed a basic truth: "There may never be anything new to say, but there is always a new way to say it. And since, in art, the way to saying a thing becomes a part of what is said, every work of art is unique and requires fresh attention."

I sincerely hope that I have provided you with just **one** refreshing thought, idea or system that you can use on your most exciting and challenging journey called "life." I trust the Signposts added light to your many roads and thereby have given you even greater power to make the choices and changes to get off your yo-yo. Balanced living is available to you and it guarantees you a more beautiful lifestyle. Remember: **IT'S UP TO YOU!**

AFFIRMATIONS

An affirmation is a positive statement that expresses a specific belief concerning you and the state of the affairs of your life. It begins with "I" or "My" and always will serve to reinforce all that is unique, special and distinctive about you. Use it often throughout the day. It will inspire, encourage and motivate you as you commit yourself to balanced living for a more beautiful lifestyle.

I, _____, accept

balanced living as a system to approach life on a daily basis, to help

me enjoy a more beautiful lifestyle and get off my yo-yo.

I, _____, choose

this day to make it my best and most fulfilling day. This is it! It's up

to me!

I, _____, know that

life must be lived and that I must live it. I also know that my life

cannot be lived successfully unless I make choices for the results I

want in my life.

"The great purpose of life is to live it."
—Oliver Wendell Homes

A NOTE FROM THE AUTHOR

For the past fifteen years, I have been sharing my message of inspiration, motivation, information and humor with thousands of audiences. I address the Fortune 500 corporations, national, state and regional conventions, Chambers of Commerce and businesses of all sizes and kinds. I share my message in churches, with youth groups and in public seminars all across the country.

I have literally seen hundreds and thousands of lives benefitted from the messages I present. I am confident that you would receive great benefits and results from being a part of my audience. I invite you to share a unique experience with me. You will never be the same after our time together.

In addition to speaking, I also share my many messages on audio cassette and on video cassette. I have many that you will be interested in adding to your library.

For information about my speaking schedule, about how to order materials or about scheduling me to speak for you and your group, please write or call:

Dr. Zonnya
P.O. Box 612900
Dallas, TX 75261
1-888-725-9103

WEIGHT LOSS DIET PLAN

2 BOOKS IN 1: KETO DIET FOR BEGINNERS, AUTOPHAGY

FRANCES SPRITZLER

CONTENTS

KETO DIET FOR BEGINNERS

AUTOPHAGY

KETO DIET

FOR BEGINNERS

A Guide to Lose Weight and Feel Amazing
Simple Low Carb Recipes (2019 Edition)

Frances Spritzler

INTRODUCTION

Congratulations on purchasing *Keto Diet for Beginners* and thank you for doing so! We hope this book will provide you the answers you are looking for regarding the keto diet.

If you have purchased this book, you have probably heard about this diet that has become very popular in recent years. People have been raving about how it helps them lose weight and prevent risk factors of diseases like diabetes or heart disease. The keto diet has become popular for that exact reason - it works! With extensive scientific research done on this method of dieting, studies show this low-carb method can be the most effective way to lose weight and see other improved signs of health that could increase your life span.

The keto diet does require some education before getting started because it is a very precise diet that requires following a certain macronutrient count. Your daily intake should be composed of 75% high-quality fats, 20% protein, and around 5% carbohydrates.

The science behind the diet details how carbohydrates are linked to increased risk of obesity, diabetes, and heart disease. The body tends to use a high intake of carbs to produce glucose molecules for energy. With keto, you are changing the makeup of what you eat to rely on fat instead. That means the body harnesses energy through a process called ketosis which uses ketone molecules composed of fat. This means you're burning excess weight and losing weight and giving yourself a more rich and sustainable source of energy. Studies show this can give you a boost of physical energy as well as more clear mental aptitude.

This book aims to give a great beginner's guide to keto and the information you need about making this the diet for you. From learning about how the diet works, the benefits and disadvantages, and the possible side effects, you are able to discern exactly what the scientific research states about keto and how it could be beneficial to you. Before starting, it's important you speak to your doctor to ensure that keto would be right for you. Whatever your goal may be regarding the keto diet - losing weight, maintaining stable blood sugar levels, stabilizing hormone levels, decreasing your cholesterol or blood pressure - your doctor can confirm whether keto will work for you.

With our tips for success, you will be able to take those first steps to begin the keto diet and know what side effects to look for and how to tackle the keto flu. By staying focused, meal planning, and avoiding stress, you can have great success in implementing keto into your life. Not only that, we are including a 14-day keto meal plan with recipes for breakfast, lunch, and dinner! By knowing exactly what keto ingredients you should shop for, you have an array of delicious keto recipes to make! With extra recipes for breakfast, lunch, and even dessert, you can feel confident that you will enjoy your meals while still sticking to a keto diet.

We hope this book will give you a thorough understanding of the keto diet. This diet has become so popular because of the millions it has helped, and we would love to see you gain the same health benefits! Whether you're hoping to lose weight or follow the road to better health, keto can get you there and our book can help!

There are plenty of books on this subject on the market, thanks again for choosing this one!

HOW THE KETOGENIC DIET WORKS

IF YOU'RE BRAND NEW TO THE KETO DIET, TAKING SOME TIME
to educate yourself on its properties and the science behind it is a
great way to begin. The keto diet's aim is to guide the body away
from creating glucose molecules from the carbohydrates you
consume and use a pathway called ketosis instead. This pathway
can only occur low in carbohydrates which is why the diet aims to
minimize your carb intake. It focuses on a diet rich in healthy fats
and proteins so that your body goes through ketosis to produce
ketones instead. These ketones are made from fat molecules your
body has stored away and it gives you a richer source of energy.

A standard keto diet has a macronutrients breakdown that is high
in fat, a moderate amount of protein, and low in carbohydrates. If
you're not already familiar, "macronutrients" is the term given to
the components of your diet that your energy and fuel comes from.
For a keto diet, the macro breakdown would be:

75% fat

20% protein

5% carbohydrates

*U*sually, carbohydrates make up the majority of what we eat in a day - nearly 60 to 70%! With following the keto diet, you're recommended to stay around 20 to 30 grams. That means net grams of carbohydrates after you subtract the fiber from the total carbohydrates per serving. For example, if you are eating something that has 18 grams of carbohydrates with 4 grams of fiber, your net would be 18 - 4 = 14 net grams of carbs. As a beginner of keto, it's very important to track your macro intake and especially your net carbs to ensure you are staying at the allowed proportions. That's where you'll see the most optimal weight loss and health benefits. Some athletes can tweak the keto diet to allow for a greater carbohydrate intake to help them have the energy for their training sessions, but the standard keto diet's aim is a very minimal carb intake.

When you are following keto and minimizing your carbohydrate intake so drastically, your body is not able to synthesize glucose molecules like it normally would have. It follows a different metabolic pathway called "ketosis," and the liver converts the high-quality fatty acids you are consuming into "ketone" molecules. This form of energy is considered a lot more efficient because it contains more energy per molecule compared to glucose which is a very "quick" form of energy that can often leave you drained. It's by creating and burning these ketone molecules that your body can lose weight. It produces these ketones from the fat it has stored to replenish your energy supply, instead of like before when you would have consistently been eating carbohydrates throughout the day to make simple sugar glucose molecules.

One of the main problems with synthesizing glucose is that it stays in the bloodstream and raises your blood sugar levels. This can be very dangerous for pre-diabetic or diabetic patients who have trouble with their insulin production. Insulin is an essential hormone created by the pancreas and is used to transport glucose to cells throughout the body. If you eat something high in carbohydrates, like bread or starches, your glucose levels will rise and your pancreas will secrete extra insulin to transport it throughout the body. When this continues to happen, the body can become insulin resistant which means it makes more than enough insulin, but the insulin cannot perform its transport duties efficiently. This is very risky for diabetes patients which can cause very high blood sugar and insulin levels leading to an array of serious symptoms and conditions.

If you're not diabetic or considered pre-diabetic, consuming too many carbohydrates can still be unhealthy for you because of the harmful effect they have on the body. Too much glucose synthesized by the body can increase your risk for diabetes, obesity, and other diseases. When the body has an excess intake of carbohydrates, it actually stores it as fat. That means you're putting on weight and continuing to consume carbs in an unhealthy cycle. With the keto diet, people have noticed that once they cut carbs from their diet, they have noticed the excess weight falling off. Not only that, if you are consuming too many carbohydrates throughout the day, you can feel the side effects of your blood sugar level being unstable. Symptoms like headaches, mood swings, irritability, and fatigue will creep up on you despite the extra calories you're consuming.

Some critics of the keto diet will say that you are unnaturally pushing your body towards a state of ketosis as an extreme method to lose weight. But human nature tells us that is not true! The body was created to have multiple pathways of harnessing energy in case there was every any scarcity in resources. Our ancestors in the past did not live in a society like today where food is in such abundance. They had periods of "feast and famine," where they had to adjust and change their eating habits depending on what was available. And when that happened, their body adjusted with them. It's all about how you train your body to work for you. When the body notices a decrease in carbohydrates, it naturally sends out receptors to initiate a different pathway, or in this case, ketosis. This is the same response the body would have if you were trying to quit smoking or stop consuming sugar. Your body becomes dependent on a substance, but you have the power to change how it responds. With keto, you're trying to break the body's dependence on carbohydrates because you are looking at improving your health. By motivating yourself and reminding yourself of your goals, you can follow keto and gain success!

KETO DIET BENEFITS & DISADVANTAGES

THE KETO DIET HAS BECOME SO POPULAR IN RECENT YEARS because of the success people have noticed. Not only have they managed to lose weight, but scientific studies show that the keto diet can help you improve your health in many others. As when starting any new diet or exercise routine, there may seem to be some disadvantages so we will go over those for the keto diet as well. But most people agree that the benefits outweigh the adjustment period!

Benefits

Losing weight! For most people, this is the first and foremost benefit of switching to keto! Their previous diet method may have stalled for them or they were starting to notice weight creeping back on. With keto, studies have shown that people have been able to follow this diet and relay fewer hunger pangs and suppressed appetite while losing weight at the same time! You are minimizing your carbohydrate intake which means less blood sugar spikes. Often, those fluctuations in blood sugar levels are what make you feel more hungry and prone to snacking in between meals. Instead, by guiding the body towards ketosis, you are eating a more fulfilling diet of fat and protein and harnessing energy from ketone molecules instead of glucose. Studies show that low carb diets are very effective in reducing visceral fat (the type of fat you commonly see around the abdomen that increases as you become overweight and obese). This reduces your risk of obesity and improves your health in the long run.

Decreases the risk of Type 2 diabetes. As we mentioned in the previous chapter, the problem with carbohydrates is how unstable they make blood sugar levels. This can be very dangerous for people who have diabetes or are considered pre-diabetic due to unstable blood sugar levels or family history. Keto is a great option because of the minimal intake of carbohydrates it requires. Instead, you are harnessing the majority of your calories from fat or protein which will not cause blood sugar spikes and ultimately put less pressure on the pancreas to secrete insulin. Many studies have found that diabetes patients who followed the keto diet lost more weight and ultimately reduced their fasting glucose levels. This is great news for patients who have unstable blood sugar levels or are hoping to avoid or reduce their diabetes medication intake.

Improve cardiovascular risk symptoms to overall lower your chances of having heart disease. Most people assume that following keto that is so high in fat content has to increase your risk of coronary heart disease or heart attack. But the research proves otherwise! Research shows that switching to keto can lower your blood pressure, increase your HDL good cholesterol, and reduce your triglyceride fatty acid levels. That's because the fat you are consuming on keto are healthy and high-quality fats so they tend to reverse many unhealthy symptoms of heart disease. They boost your "good" HDL cholesterol numbers and decrease your "bad" LDL cholesterol numbers. It also decreases the level of triglyceride fatty acids in the bloodstream. A high level of these can lead to stroke, heart attack, or premature death. And what are high levels of fatty acids linked to? High consumption of carbohydrates. With the keto diet, you are drastically cutting your intake of carbohydrates to improve fatty acid levels and improve other risk factors. A 2018 study on the keto diet found that it can improve as many as 22 out of 26 risk factors for cardiovascular heart disease! These factors can be very important to some people, especially those who have a history of heart disease in their family.

Increases the body's energy levels. We compared briefly about the difference between the glucose molecules synthesized from a high carbohydrates intake versus ketones produced on the keto diet. Ketones are made by the liver and use fat molecules you already have stored. This makes them much more energy-rich and a lasting source of fuel compared to glucose, a simple sugar molecule. These ketones can give you a burst of energy physically as well as mentally allow you to have greater focus, clarity, and attention to detail.

Decreases inflammation in the body. Inflammation on its own is a natural response by the body's immune system, but when it becomes uncontrollable, it can lead to an array of health problems, some severe, some minor. The many health concerns include acne, autoimmune conditions, arthritis, psoriasis, irritable bowel syndrome, and even acne and eczema. Often, removing sugars and carbohydrates from your diet can help patients of these diseases avoid flare-ups - and the good news is keto does just that! A 2008 research study found that keto decreased a blood marker linked to high inflammation in the body by nearly 40%. This is great news for people who may suffer from an inflammatory disease and are willing to change their diet to hopefully see improvement.

Increases your mental functioning level. Like we elaborated earlier, the energy-rich ketones can boost the body's physical and mental levels of alertness. Research has shown that keto is a much better energy source for the brain than simple sugar glucose molecules are. With nearly 75% of your diet coming from healthy fats, the brain's neural cells and mitochondria have a better source of energy to be able to function at the highest level. Some studies have tested patients on the keto diet and found they had higher cognitive functioning, better memory recall, and were less susceptible to memory loss. The keto diet can even decrease the occurrence of migraines which can be very detrimental to patients.

Decreases risk of diseases like Alzheimer's, Parkinson's, and epilepsy. The keto diet was actually created in the 1920s as a way to combat epilepsy in children. From there, research has found that keto can improve your cognitive functioning level and protect brain cells from injury or damage. This is very good to reduce the risk of neurodegenerative disease which begins in the brain due to neural cells mutating and functioning with damaged parts or lower than peak optimal functioning. Studies have found that following keto can improve the mental functioning of patients who suffer from diseases like Alzheimer's or Parkinson's. These neurodegenerative diseases sadly have no cure, but the keto diet could improve symptoms as they progress. Researchers believe that is due to cutting out carbs from your diet which reduces the occurrence of blood sugar spikes that the body's neural cells have to continually adjust to.

Can regulate hormones in women who have PCOS (polycystic ovary syndrome) and PMS (pre-menstrual syndrome). Women who have PCOS suffer from infertility which can be very heartbreaking for young couples trying to start a family. There is no cure for this condition, but it is believed that it is related to many similar diabetic symptoms like obesity and high insulin levels. This causes the body to produce more sex hormones which can lead to infertility. The keto diet has become a popular method to try and regulate insulin and hormone levels and could increase a woman's chances of getting pregnant.

Disadvantages

Your body will have an adjustment period. It depends from person to person on how many days that will be, but when you start any new diet or exercise routine, your body has to adjust to the new normal. With the keto diet, you are drastically cutting your carbohydrates intake, so the body has to adjust to that. We will talk more about it in the next chapter but it's often dubbed the "keto flu." You may feel slow, weak, fatigued, and like you are not thinking as quick or fast as you used to. It just means your body is adjusting to keto and once this adjustment period is done, you will see the weight loss results you anticipated.

If you are an athlete, you may need more carbohydrates. If you still want to try keto as an athlete, it's important you talk to your nutritionist or trainer to see how the diet can be tweaked for you. Most athletes require a greater intake of carbs than the keto diet requires which means they may have to up their intake in order to assure they have the energy for their training sessions. High endurance sports (like rugby or soccer) and heavy weightlifting do require a greater intake of carbohydrates. If you're an athlete wanting to follow keto and gain the health benefits, it's important you first talk to your trainer before making any changes to your diet.

You have to carefully count your daily macros! For beginners, this can be tough, and even people already on keto can become lazy about this. People are often used to eating what they want without worrying about just how many grams of protein or carbs it contains. With keto, you have to be meticulous about counting your intake to ensure you are maintaining the necessary keto breakdown (75% fat, 20% protein, ~5% carbs). The closer you stick to this, the better results you will see regarding weight loss and other health benefits. If your weight loss has stalled or you're not feeling as energetic as you hoped, it could be because your macros are off. Find a free calorie counting app that and be sure you look at the ingredients of everything you're eating and cooking.

POSSIBLE SIDE EFFECTS & THE KETO FLU

When you're switching to keto, your body is making the adjustment from having a diet that consists mostly of carbohydrates to a mere ~5%! That can be a tough adjustment so it's only natural that your body needs a little bit of time before it fully immerses itself in keto. Your body has to now go through the process of ketosis which means you may notice some new side effects along the way. By looking for these physical signs, you can get an idea of how your body is progressing.

Here are some of the signs and how you can adjust to them.

- Bad breath: Don't worry - this will be temporary! As your body goes through ketosis and produces ketones, the ketone molecules contain acetone which is known for having a very distinct fruity smell. When it mixes with saliva, it can become very strong and give off the odor of bad breath. It's a sign that your body is now burning fats for fuel. Most people say this goes away in a week or two as your body completely adjusts to ketosis.

Solutions: chew sugar-free gum to mask the smell, have good oral hygiene, and drink lots of water to ensure your mouth has enough saliva

- Feeling lightheaded or drowsy: In the beginning stages of ketosis, you are going to be losing excess water weight through urination where the body excretes minerals from the body. Because of this, you might feel fatigued, dizzy, or lightheaded as your body adjusts. It's only natural that your body will feel slow and sluggish as you adjust to this change in your diet.

Solutions: add extra salt to your food to keep your electrolytes balanced, ask your doctor about adding a magnesium supplement to your diet, eat foods high in potassium like avocados, dairy, and poultry

- Hypoglycemia (low blood sugar): This is very common for someone starting keto because you are reducing your carbohydrate intake which is what causes blood sugar spikes! Your body will definitely notice the lack of carbs and go into a low blood sugar mode where you feel tired, hungry, or very slow and drained. It will take a couple of days to adjust.

Solutions: have a keto-friendly snack between meals to keep your blood sugar up, start your keto diet slowly by cutting back on carbs instead of going right to 5% to give your body a learning curve

- Digestive issues: Constipation or diarrhea may occur considering you are changing what your diet consists of so much. You are suddenly going to high fat and moderate amount of protein which can lead to constipation as your body adjusts. Or some people's bodies experience diarrhea instead due to the low-carb intake and high-fat content.

Solutions: stay hydrated and drink enough water, ensure you are eating fibrous vegetables in your meals, add a fiber supplement powder to your drinks or food, cut back on dairy if you are still experiencing digestive issues

- Increased urination: As we mentioned above, your body will be urinating more as you go through ketosis because it is getting rid of water weight you have accumulated. But this also means it is excreting minerals like sodium, potassium, and magnesium which are necessary to keep your body in an electrolyte balance. No matter what, you should continue to drink more than enough water when on ketosis to prevent dehydration from occurring. Even if it means extra bathroom trips!
- Muscle cramps: As your body excretes excess water weight and minerals, you can feel muscle cramps as your muscles adjust to the new electrolyte balance. They are most common in larger muscles like your legs.

Solutions: continue to stay hydrated, add a little more salt to your food to counteract the mineral loss, ask your doctor about adding a magnesium supplement

The Keto Flu

All these common side effects of keto are often lumped together and called "the keto flu" by keto experts and trainers. That's because the combination of these symptoms can really mimic how you feel when you have the flu. Usually, these will occur in the first few days that you begin keto because your body is recognizing the drastic cut in carbohydrates you have implemented. Symptoms would include things like poor focus, stomach pain, dizziness, fatigue, vomiting, nausea, drowsiness, headaches, difficulty sleeping, and irritability.

Symptoms can depend entirely from person to person. Many people believe it's due to the body cutting back on carbohydrates and going into a "withdrawal" mode. If you're worried about the symptoms, it can be a good idea to begin slowly by cutting back on carbs instead of going "cold turkey". But even then, symptoms can depend on your genetics, water intake, individual health, and physical fitness level. Some people might get the keto flu very severely, while others may just notice a sluggishness for a few days before they recover.

It can feel disappointing when you're so excited about keto about seeing the weight drop off. But you have to remind yourself that this a temporary adjustment that your body is going through. Just like you'd have difficulty adjusting to a new diet or aches and pains after a new workout. Following some of our tips, you can fight the severity of your symptoms and hopefully allow your body to adjust even faster. The "flu" will pass, and you'll soon feel the benefits of keto!

Stay hydrated. This is very key no matter what diet you follow, but especially important on the keto diet. Some people's digestive systems have a tough time adjusting to the change in diet with such a high fat intake and low carbs. When you begin keto, your body first begins shedding water weight through urination. That means your glycogen levels are decreasing as water and minerals leave the body and you may feel symptoms like dizziness, drowsiness, and fatigue. To combat this, you should be drinking more than enough water to stay hydrated. Most health institutions recommend anywhere from 10 to 11 glasses a day for women and up to 13 glasses for men. If you are physically active or live in a dry climate, you should drink more to compensate for the moisture you lose in sweat. Even if it means more bathroom trips, drinking enough water will help you stay hydrated as your body goes through the keto flu.

Add extra salt and electrolytes to your diet. Due to losing minerals from urination, the body is losing vital elements like sodium, potassium, and magnesium which are the key to maintaining an electrolyte balance. If your electrolyte levels become too low, you can feel symptoms like dehydration such as muscle cramps, nausea, and fatigue. This will only exacerbate your keto flu symptoms! To ensure you have enough electrolyte intake, increase your intake of iodized salt in the seasoning of your food. Also, try and enjoy foods that are full of minerals such as avocado and quinoa that contain magnesium, and mushrooms, spinach, and broccoli that are high in potassium.

Avoid high endurance exercises. If you're feeling the symptoms of keto flu, you should avoid high-intensity workouts that could cause injury to you in your condition. Trying to complete an intense workout when you are already feeling tired, dizzy, or having muscle cramps is not a good idea and will handicap your performance. If you take part in high endurance workouts, heavy weightlifting, or Cross Fit, you should abstain while you are feeling affected by the keto flu. Once you feel better, you can resume these workouts, but you don't want to push your body too hard.

Count your macros. When you first begin keto, it's very important you are keeping daily track of your macronutrient intake to see the exact breakdown of what you are eating. Your symptoms may be prolonged if you aren't sticking close enough to the keto formula of 75% fat, 20% protein, and ~5% carbs. If you're eating too many carbs, your body will continue to make glucose and not go through ketosis. If you're not eating enough fat, then your body doesn't have enough fat to go through ketosis. It's very important you know your exact intake to look at the numbers in case your symptoms don't subside in a few days.

Add some clean carbs to your diet. If you feel like you're still battling the keto flu, you can try adding some "clean" carbs to your diet to increase your carb intake. This might help to ease your symptoms and give your body a little more time to adjust. This would be things like vegetables or berries like blueberries or straw-berries. Other fruits may tend to be too high in natural sugars, so you should avoid those. This could help you feel better when battling these keto flu symptoms, so you can get through your day. But remember, you will eventually have to minimize those carbs to around 5% of your daily macro count if you want to truly be on keto. That's what the research shows the most potential for weight loss and gaining other health benefits.

Ensure you are getting a good night's rest. Some people experience difficulty sleeping when on the keto diet so it's impor-tant you try and have a good night's sleep to help you recharge your body for the next day. This will help to give you energy and combat the sluggishness and tiredness you are feeling due to the keto flu. Avoid caffeine before bedtime and try to limit your screen time so you feel sleepy. Allow yourself to relax before bed and enjoy activities like breathing exercises, meditation, or prayer that give you a sense of calm. A melatonin or magnesium supplement may help you fall asleep faster.

ULTIMATE KETO DIET SHOPPING LIST

WHEN IT COMES TO STARTING A NEW DIET, YOU WANT TO BE clear about what foods you can and cannot eat to avoid confusion. If you know exactly which items should be on your shopping list, you can feel more confident making keto-friendly recipes and know exactly which ingredients you should no longer be using.

ere's a helpful guide of what you should and should not be eating on keto.

oods to Eat

eat: With a diet requiring 20% daily protein intake, meat is going to be the main source that will give you the vitamins, minerals, and energy you need.

Remember, you don't want it to be equivalent to your fat intake which should be about 75%, but it is a necessary fuel needed in your meals. You don't want to have too much because that just turns into extra weight gain and slow your body's journey to ketosis. Try to choose fattier cuts so that it also counts as some fat being consumed at the same time. You should also try to buy organic or grass-fed meat to reduce any risk of ingesting growth hormones or pesticides from the animal. The higher quality food you're eating, the better the keto results you will achieve. Avoid cold cut or processed meats like a sausage that are high in carbs.

- chicken, turkey, goat meat and lamb meat, beef, steak, bacon, ham, pork

Seafood & Fish: This is another great source of protein that is also high in omega 3 fatty acids. Recent research has found that these are fatty acids that keep your heart healthy and increase your good cholesterol numbers, improve your vision and brain health, and decrease your blood pressure. Seafood includes such a vast category - mussels, shrimp, lobster, clams, etc. And there are many different varieties of fish you can try from your local grocery or fish store. Try and incorporate seafood into your meals a few times a week to gain the health benefits it provides.

Dairy: Dairy is also an integral part of the keto diet but something you should be careful about. That's because most dairy products are full of carbs and protein at the same time so you don't want to throw your daily macros out of balance. That could knock your body out of ketosis! You also want to try and choose full-fat dairy products and buy organic to ensure you feel full longer and are adding to your fat intake. Some of the most common dairy products you'll use on keto include butter, cheeses, and ghee for frying or cooking your foods. You want to avoid evaporated or condensed milk though which are very high in sugars.

- heavy cream, half n half, cheeses like swiss, feta, parmesan, Colby, mozzarella, cheddar, cream cheese, sour cream, ricotta cheese, Greek yogurt, eggs

*E*ggs: These are a great snack and source protein that you'll want to incorporate into your diet on keto. Whether it's a quickly boiled egg with lunch or dinner, or scrambled eggs or egg keto muffins for breakfast, this is a great way to up your protein intake and gain healthy fats. Try and buy free-range eggs so you have less risk of ingesting hormones.

*V*egetables: The keto diet does allow you to have a variety of vegetables, but you have to be aware of the carbohydrate intake you're consuming as well. The lower you maintain your carbs, the more likely your body will stay in ketosis. You should try and avoid starchy vegetables that tend to grow underground like yams, beans, potatoes, sweet potatoes, and corn, as they tend to be higher in carbs. Instead, leafy green vegetables are very keto-friendly and a great base for salads or a side for a protein dish. They are very nutritious but still low in carbs.

- lettuce, celery, asparagus, spinach, cauliflower, broccoli, kale, Brussel sprouts, carrots, onions

*F*ruit: Fruits tend to be a little trickier on keto because they are packed with natural sugars and carbohydrates. The important thing is being aware of what fruit you're eating and how much of it. For example, 1 banana can have up to 25 net grams of carbohydrates! You don't want to eat too much fruit in a day which will ruin your daily macro count and increase your carbohydrate intake. Some fruits which tend to be less sweet are lower in carbohydrates so you want to stick to those. Blackberries are less sweet than blueberries or strawberries, and clementines are less sweet than oranges. Olives are also a fruit that is a great source of fat and low in carbs - they're the perfect addition for a salad.

- avocado, clementine, blackberries, raspberries, kiwi, cantaloupe, lemon, grapes, apples, peaches

*R*aw Nuts & Seeds: These can be a very healthy keto-friendly snack and a great way to boost your intake of protein and fats. You do want to avoid snacking as much as you can on keto, but in the adjustment phase, you may feel cravings for carbs so these are a great alternative. Nuts are high in protein too, so you want to assure you're not having too much because that will skew with your daily macro count. Also, be sure you're not having chocolate covered nuts or salty nuts - those are extra unhealthy calories you don't need!

- Cashews, pistachios, almonds, pine nuts, hazelnuts,

*D*rinks: We've reiterated many times how important staying hydrated is on the keto diet. It will help with your digestion, fight off dehydration, and keep your body functioning at an optimal level. Most keto researchers recommend nearly a gallon of water a day on keto! The keto diet naturally has a diuretic effect on the body so it's important you are replenishing those fluids. Try and limit your caffeine intake though because research shows it could stall your weight loss. Also, remember not to use sugar in your drinks though you can use heavy cream in your tea or coffee.

- water, keto-friendly coffee (no sugar or high carb creamers), black or green tea, coconut or almond milk, hard liquor (tends to be lower in calories than beer or wine)

*F*oods to Avoid

*S*ugars: These definitely need to be off your grocery list and you want to be sure you're not adding them to your coffee or tea either! "Sugar" refers to a whole category of items such as soda, candy, cookies, baked goods and sweets, and fruit drinks. Even things that are labeled as "diet-friendly" or "sugar-free" should be avoided because the artificial components will still cause blood sugar spikes just like glucose would. There are some keto-friendly artificial sweeteners you can use for your recipes, smoothies, or making keto desserts, but be sure you've done your research!

Sugary Fruits: As we mentioned, fruits can be a tricky arena on keto because they tend to contain natural sugars and carbs. You can include low carb fruit in your day, but be sure you are reading the label and including it in your macro count. If you have too much fruit, that can make up your entire carb count for the day!

Root (starch) Vegetables: These root vegetables are packed with nutrients because they grow underground in the soil, but the high amount of starches has the body processing them like natural sugars. You should avoid things like potatoes, yams, beets, and turnips. Instead, you should be filling your diet with leafy green vegetables which tend to be lower in carbs.

Breads & Whole Grains: Even though whole grain products are healthier for you than refined grain products, with keto, you want to stay away from these carbohydrates. All they will do is increase your blood sugar level and push you out of ketosis! Things like pasta, lentils, beans, bread, rice, corn, and cereal should be avoided so that you can keep your carbohydrates low.

. . .

*T*rans Fats: Trans fats are linked to a higher risk of cardiovascular disease and should be avoided. Some oils are unhealthy like canola or sunflower, and you should try to use avocado oil, ghee, or grass-fed butter instead when you are cooking or sautéing your foods. This will give you a bump in your daily fat content too. Margarine is another unhealthy substitute for butter that should be avoided. Instead, use butter or ghee.

*L*ow-Fat Foods: It sounds silly considering you're on a diet and your first thought would be eating low fat but with keto, it's the complete opposite! You want to reach for foods that are higher in fat content like Greek yogurt or full-fat cheese. This will help you maintain your daily 75% fat macro count to ensure you are staying in ketosis.

TIPS FOR KETOGENIC SUCCESS

How to Get Started on Keto

If you're looking to get started, here are some tips we can give you on how to begin.

- Clean out your kitchen. The best way to start is to be aware of your carbohydrate and sugar intake so you know exactly what you should not be having on keto. If you don't want to throw out the items or can't donate them, at least slowly finish them so you can know not to buy again and that you will be removing these items from your grocery list. That includes things like pasta, soda, bread, candy, and snacks.
- Get used to eating more vegetables and protein. These are a very important part of keto and what will give you most of your energy. As you're researching keto, you will come to know how meat is important and which vegetables you should be eating more of. Get used to

having those in your diet now before you make the switch
to keto. Get familiar with fish and seafood if you haven't
eaten it much before.

- Put together a keto-friendly grocery list. We've dedicated
an entire chapter of what items you can and cannot eat so
it's a great way for you to see exactly what you should be
buying for your keto meals. Be sure you have a diverse
array of protein, vegetables, some fruits, dairy, and fats
that will consist of your keto diet.

- Have a food scale and measuring cups. This might seem
like silly advice, but if you are going to be sticking to keto
recipes, you need to have the correct portion sizes, not
"eyeballing" portions. Be sure you have measuring cups
and a food scale so you can properly make your recipes
when you meal plan.

- Count your calories. Remember, those hidden carbs
count. Carbs - Fiber = Net Carbs. You have to keep track
of your carbs throughout the day to assure you are
sticking as close to the keto formula as possible. That's
what will enable the most weight loss and give you a
chance at gaining the most health benefits.

- Meal plan. This is a great idea especially if you work
throughout the week. To avoid temptation, meal prep one
day a week so you know exactly what you will be having
for lunch and dinner. This will make you more confident
in following keto. Find meals that you would like to try
and that fit your expertise in the kitchen.

- Don't stress! The more stressed you are, the harder it will
be for your body to maintain ketosis. Instead, be
confident about what you've learned about keto and how
you are looking forward to losing weight and gaining
other health benefits. See it as a positive change that you

can be in control of as you are armed with new knowledge on how to succeed. Be motivated, stay relaxed, and get a good night's sleep to give yourself the energy you need.

Maintaining Ketosis

After you're on keto, it can be tough to maintain it and fit it into your individual busy lifestyle. You might feel discouraged by the keto flu symptoms if you haven't yet been noticing the surge of energy that ketosis brings. Maybe you're feeling overwhelmed by what you should and should not eat. Here are some of our tips on how to maintain your keto diet successfully!

Stay hydrated. This is something we have repeated many times because it is that important on keto no matter how long you've been on it. It can be easy to get lazy about drinking enough water because you feel you've been on keto long enough now or you're not feeling any side effects, but it's important you stay hydrated for your body to avoid dehydration. Especially if you are physically active, you should be drinking even more! Carry a water bottle with you and be sure you are filling it often throughout the day. There are even apps that can track your water intake or water bottles you can write on with a dry erase marker.

Keep track of your macros. There are many free apps you can download that have calorie trackers and will keep a chart of your daily macros you're consuming, but it's still important you are aware of your daily intake. Remember, it's all about keeping carbs low and fats high. You want to know how to calculate your net carbs: Total Carbohydrates - Dietary Fiber = Net Carbs. So when you have a snack, it's important you're aware of this number because it can add up fast! By inputting all your information for meals and snacks throughout the day, you will have a log to back on to see your progress on keto, and even in case you are stalled on losing weight. It could be because your carb number has gotten a little too high, or maybe your protein has increased. It's important to keep that keto balanced if you truly want to be on the keto diet.

Be aware of your protein and fat intake to make sure you're not eating too much. Remember, it's 75% fat and 20% protein. If you are eating too much protein then that means the body is converting those protein amino acids into glucose which will kick your body out of ketosis! Remember, we don't want glucose production - we want the body to use the ketones it has stored. Spread out your daily protein over 2 or 3 meals and ensure you're not eating too much at once. If you're not losing weight, then it could be because you're having too much protein. Same goes with too much fat. It's 75% fat you should be staying at. If you consume too much, then you're just gaining weight!! The idea is to still remain calorie deficit, so by having a 70-75% break-down of fat will keep you full for longer.

Be sure you have enough salt in your diet to maintain a balance of electrolytes. With the keto diet having a diuretic effect, you will be urinating more which has you lose vitamins and minerals. High carbohydrate diets actually cause our kidneys to retain more sodium, so when we switch to low carb, the kidneys secrete all that extra sodium. If your electrolyte levels become too low, you could feel symptoms like muscle cramps, fatigue, and dizziness. To counteract this, be sure you're consuming enough salt in your meals and add an extra pinch just to ensure you are staying in balance. Himalayan salt is a great alternative, too. Veggies that are high in sodium like cucumber and celery are also important to include in your diet.

Think about trying intermittent fasting. This is a technique that breaks your day into "eating" and "fasting" hours. It can be as easy as 12-hour divisions so you are eating for 12 continuous hours, then fasting for 12. There are many numerous health benefits of intermittent fasting, and it's been shown to be a great way to lose weight. For people who tend to snack throughout the day, it's a great way to ensure they are cutting back on those calories and helping them stay calorie deficit to lose weight. If you're interested, research more into it!

Try and exercise if you're feeling up to it. The adjustment to keto flu can make you feel sluggish and unable to exercise, but incorporating exercise into your keto diet is a great way to accelerate your weight loss. It keeps your heart healthy, your muscles agile, and will help you sleep better, too. Burning those excess calories is a way to lose more weight! With keto, you want to avoid high-intensity exercise or sports that do not allow for breaks since your body is no longer using glucose as its source of energy. But performing low-intensity activities like jogging, walking, cycling, yoga, Pilates, and dance is a great way to get your heart pumping and keep you active. You can even maintain a weightlifting routine as long as you are not using too much weight which might put a strain on your muscles.

Stay relaxed and avoid stressful factors in your life. Chronic stress will affect your body's ability to burn fat and stay in ketosis which will ruin all your weight loss goals. Stress will cause your body to secrete cortisol, the stress hormone, which ends up driving up your blood sugar levels, cause mood swings, false hunger pangs, and weight gain. That can make it a lot harder for you to maintain your keto diet if you end up craving carbs even more and are gaining weight. To try and maintain your keto diet, it's important you avoid stress and try and stay as relaxed and positive about your new lifestyle. Try yoga, a massage, or meditation. Maybe breathing exercises or prayer, or a nighttime relaxation routine that will help you feel calm and allow you to cope with stress.

Improve the quality of your sleep. If you are not getting enough restful sleep at night while you're on keto, your body will continue to secrete stress hormones which can elevate your blood sugar levels. At least 7 to 9 hours of sleep is recommended for healthy adults. If you are physically active, you should try and rest more! This will help you feel physically and mentally alert. Try and have a nightly bedtime routine which gets you relaxed and helps your body wind down. Avoid screens, keep your bedroom cool and dark without disruptions, and avoid caffeine in the evenings so it will not disrupt your sleep cycle. If you have a relaxing exercise you like to perform, like guided meditation or breathing, prayer, or yoga, this a great time to relax and empty your mind. Over the counter melatonin can also help you have more restful sleep if necessary.

KETO BREAKFAST RECIPES

Avocado Eggs with Bacon

2 servings total

142 calories per serving

Fat (g): 13

Protein (g): 5

Carbs (g): 3

Fiber (g): 2

ngredients:

- Bacon (1 slice)
- Hard-boiled Egg (1)
- Avocado (.25)
- Butter (1 teaspoon)

- Olive Oil (1 teaspoon)

*D*irections: Preheat your oven to 350 degrees F. Be sure your egg is hard-boiled and cut into half and remove the yolks to a separate bowl. Add avocado, olive oil, and salt and pepper. Then fry your bacon in the butter in a frying pan on the stove. Crumble the pieces and add to your avocado and egg yolk mixture then spoon that back into your egg whites.

Cheese Omelet

2 servings total

873 calories per serving

Fat (g): 80

Protein (g): 40

Carbs (g): 5

*I*ngredients:

- Cheddar Cheese (7 ounces, grated)
- Eggs (3)
- Butter (2 tablespoons)

*D*irections: Whisk your eggs in a bowl and mix with about half of your grated cheese. Season with some salt and black pepper. In a small pan, melt your butter and then add the egg mixture. Let the eggs cook and then add the remaining cheese and fold over so it melts.

Keto Bacon, Eggs, and Avocado

2 servings total

1045 calories per serving

Fat (g): 100

Protein (g): 27

Carbs (g): 24

Fiber (g): 16

ngredients:

- Eggs (4)
- Avocado (1, sliced)
- Butter (2 tablespoons)
- Bacon Slices (4)
- Walnuts (1 tablespoon, chopped)
- Bell Pepper (.25, sliced)

*D*irections: First, fry your bacon in butter on the stove until crispy. Then fry your eggs in the same bacon fat. Arrange your eggs, avocado slices, bacon, and bell pepper on a plate and garnish with chopped walnuts. Add a pinch of salt and black pepper.

KETO LUNCH RECIPES

MUSHROOM BACON SKILLET

2 servings total

204 calories per serving

Fat (g): 8.5

Carbs (g): 8.2

Fiber (g): 0.4

Protein (g): 14

ngredients:

- Thyme (2 sprigs)
- Minced Garlic (1 teaspoon)
- Salt (.5 teaspoon)
- Mushrooms (2 cups, halved)

- Pork Bacon (4 slices)

*D*irections: First, fry your skillet until it is crispy. Then add your mushrooms and sauté until they begin to soften and turn golden brown. Add your thyme, garlic, and salt and stir for another few minutes before removing from heat.

Keto Fried Chicken

4 servings total

461 calories per serving

Fat (g): 27

Carbs (g): 7

Fiber (g): 3

Protein (g): 33

ngredients:

- Chicken Thighs (8)
- Dried Italian Herbs, Salt, Black Pepper (1 teaspoon each)
- Butter (1 tablespoon, melted)
- Sunflower Seeds (1 cup)
- Sesame Seeds (.5 cup)

*D*irections: First, preheat your oven to 425 degrees F. Grind your seeds and seasonings in a blender until they are a fine texture. Then add the seasoned mix to a bowl and dip each chicken thigh in it and shake off excess crumbs. Drizzle the melted butter on the chicken thighs. Bake for about 30 minutes but be sure to turn the chicken over halfway through.

Cauliflower Bake

4 servings total

492 calories per serving

Fat (g): 45

Carbs (g): 5.8

Protein (g): 14

Fiber (g): 1.5

ngredients:

- Cauliflower Head (1, cut into florets)
- Cream Cheese (2 ounces)
- Cheddar Cheese (1.25 cup, shredded)
- Bacon (6 slices, cooked and crumbled)
- Heavy Cream (1 cup)
- Butter (2 tablespoons)
- Green Onion (.25 cup, chopped)
- Salt & Black Pepper (1 teaspoon each)

*D*irections: Preheat your oven to 350 degrees F. First, blanch your cauliflower florets following the instructions on the bag and set it aside. In a large pot, melt your cream cheese, butter, heavy cream, salt, and pepper and about 1 cup of the cheddar cheese. In a baking dish, add the cauliflower, cheese sauce, and almost all of the crumbled bacon and green onions. Stir well and garnish with the rest of the bacon, cheese, and green onions. Bake for 30 minutes until the cheese is golden.

Parmesan Chicken Tenders

4 servings total

400 calories per serving

Fat (g): 24

Protein (g): 42

Carbs (g): 8

Fiber (g): 5

ngredients:

- Almond Flour (.75 cup)
- Egg (1)
- Chicken Breasts (2)
- Parmesan Cheese (.75 cup, grated)

*D*irections: Set your oven to 400 degrees F. Combine your cheese and almond flour in a dish. In another separate dish, beat your egg. Cut your chicken breasts into strips. You want to dip each strip in the egg and then in the flour mixture at least twice so it is coated well. Place on a lined baking sheet. You can bake for 14 to 18 minutes until golden and crisp.

Baked Fish Sticks

4 servings total

276 calories per serving

Fat (g): 11.4

Protein (g): 38

Carbs (g): 6

Fiber (g): 4

ngredients:

- Egg (1)
- Water (1 teaspoon)
- Pork Rinds (1 bag)
- Coconut Flour (2 tablespoons)
- Cod Fillets (~12 ounces)

*D*irections: First, you should preheat your oven to 400 degrees F. Until then, cut your fish into strips and sprinkle with your spices and seasoning. Pulse your pork rinds in a food processor until they are fine, or just mash up in a plastic bag. Mix with the almond flour. Whisk the egg and the water together. Dip the fish in the egg mixture and then the flour and pork rind mixture until the fish is well-coated. Place on a lined baking sheet and bake for 12 to 15 minutes until golden brown.

Roasted Tomato Soup

4 servings total

225 calories per serving

Fat (g): 20

Protein (g): 6.8

Carbs (g): 9

Fiber (g): 4.3

ngredients:

- Olive Oil (.25 cup)
- Chicken Broth (4 cups)
- Heavy Cream (.5 cup)
- Salt & Black Pepper (1 teaspoon)
- Garlic Cloves (3-4)
- Tomatoes (1 pound)

*D*irections: First, preheat your oven to 400 degrees F. Core your tomatoes and place on a lined baking sheet with your garlic. Now, you can season those with your salt, pepper, and olive oil. Let them roast for about 20 to 30 minutes until soft and then once cool, blend in a blender with half the chicken broth. Strain that mixture into a saucepan and then add the heavy cream and rest of the chicken broth and simmer for 10 to 15 minutes. Adjust seasoning as needed.

Steak Stir Fry

2 servings total

287 calories per serving

Protein (g): 38.9

Fat (g): 11

Carbs (g): 12

Fiber (g): 6

ngredients:

- Onion (1, sliced)
- Red Pepper (1, sliced)
- Minced Garlic (1 teaspoon)
- Ginger (1 teaspoon, grated)
- Soy Sauce (1 tablespoon)
- Salt & Black Pepper (1 teaspoon)
- Beef Broth (1 cup)
- Mushrooms (8 ounces, sliced)

- Beef Sirloin (.5 pound, thinly sliced)
- Olive Oil (2 teaspoons)

*D*irections: First, add your olive oil to a large saucepan. You want to begin by cooking your beef, garlic, and grated ginger. Mix all the seasonings and spices with the beef and cook until your meat is brown. Add the onion, pepper, and mushrooms to the skillet and stir fry. Cook for a few minutes until golden brown then pour in the soy sauce and beef broth. Add back in the beef and combine everything.

Roasted Brussels Sprouts & Bacon

2 servings total

Fat (g): 21

Protein (g): 15

Carbs (g): 4

Fiber (g): 1

ngredients:

- Butter (2 tablespoons, melted)
- Salt & Black Pepper (1 teaspoon each)
- Bacon (8 strips)
- Brussels Sprouts (.5 pound)
- Olive Oil (1 teaspoon)

*D*irections: Preheat your oven to 375 degrees F first. Cut off the ends of your Brussels sprout and cut in half or quarters as you prefer. Toss with the olive oil, salt, and black pepper. Spread out on a lined baking sheet and bake for about 30 minutes, being sure to give the tray a toss a few times so it's roasted evenly. Then you can fry your bacon on the stove in the butter and crumble the pieces once cooked. Once Brussels sprouts cooked, add them to a bowl and garnish with the bacon.

Keto Egg Salad

2 servings total

563 calories per serving

Fat (g): 51

Protein (g): 20

Carbs (g): 7

Fiber (g): 5

ngredients:

- Avocado (1)
- Hard-boiled Eggs (6)
- Mayonnaise (.3 cup)
- Mustard (1 teaspoon)
- Lemon Juice (1 teaspoon)
- Fresh or Dried Herbs (1 teaspoon)

*D*irections: Have your eggs hard-boiled, peeled, and chopped into small pieces. You can season with some salt and black pepper for flavor. Mash your avocado and then in a bowl, mix your eggs, avocado, mustard, mayo, lemon juice, and any fresh herbs.

KETO DESSERT RECIPES

PEANUT BUTTER MILKSHAKE

1 serving total

245 calories per serving

Carbs (g): 13

Fiber (g): 4

Protein (g); 36

Fat (g): 6

*I*ngredients:

- a handful of ice
- Cottage cheese (.5 cup)
- Almond milk (.5 cup)
- Peanut butter (2 tablespoons)

- Sugar Substitute of Your Choice (1 tablespoon)
- Vanilla Extract (1 teaspoon)

 irections: Combine all your ingredients and blend until smooth.

Blueberry Muffins

6 servings total

135 calories per serving

Fat (g): 12

Carbs (g): 5

Fiber (g): 1.4

Protein (g): 4.3

 ngredients:

- Lemon (zest and juice from it)
- Blueberries (.5 cup)
- Coconut Flour (.25 cup)
- Butter (melted, .25 cup)
- Sugar Substitute of Your Choice (2 tablespoons)
- Eggs (4)
- Vanilla Extract (.5 teaspoon)
- Baking Powder (.5 teaspoon)

irections: Preheat your oven to 350 degrees F. Combine the coconut flour, baking powder, lemon zest and juice, butter, vanilla, and sweetener together in a bowl. Mix in your eggs one at a time and then taste to be sure you've used enough sweetener. Grease 6 muffin spots in a tin and then add the batter evenly to each one. You can bake from 13 to 17 minutes until lightly golden brown.

Keto Chocolate Peanut Butter Cups

12 servings total

145 calories per serving

Fat (g): 13

Carbs (g): 8

Fiber (g): 3.2

Protein (g): 3

ngredients:

- Dark Chocolate (sugar-free, 6 ounces)
- Cocoa Butter (1 tablespoon)

eanut Butter filling:

- Peanut Butter (.5 cup)
- Butter (2 tablespoons)

- Vanilla Extract (.5 teaspoon)
- Sugar Substitute of Your Choice (.25 cup)

*D*irections: Grease your muffin tin where you will set the peanut butter cups. In the microwave, melt the chocolate and mix with the cocoa butter until smooth. Pour about half the chocolate into the muffin liners and then refrigerate 15 to 20 minutes until it hardens. Then melt your peanut butter and butter and mix with the vanilla and substitute sugar. Divide that into each muffin tin and then harden in the fridge for another 10 to 15 minutes. Then add the rest of the chocolate on top and refrigerate until frozen solid.

Chocolate Fudge

8 servings total

145 calories per serving

Fat (g): 12

Carbs (g): 4

Fiber (g): 2

*I*ngredients:

- Dark Chocolate (sugar-free, 4 ounces)
- Coconut Butter (.75 cup)
- Vanilla Extract (1 teaspoon)
- Sugar Substitute of Your Choice (.5 teaspoon)

*D*irections: In the microwave, first melt your chocolate and coconut butter. Combine with the sweetener and vanilla extract and then pour into a lined baking sheet. Refrigerate until the mixture has hardened and cut into 8 pieces.

Raspberry Chocolate Bark

10 servings total

89 calories per serving

Fat (g): 8

Carbs (g): 3.2

Fiber (g): 1.5

ngredients:

- Raw Nuts (.25 cup, unsalted)
- Raspberries (.5 cup)
- Coconut Butter (.5 cup)
- Cocoa Powder (unsweetened, 1 tablespoon)
- Almond Butter (.25 cup)
- Sugar Substitute of Your Choice (1 tablespoon)

*D*irections: Chop your nuts until they are roughly bite-size pieces. In a bowl, mix together your almond butter, coconut butter, sweetener, and cocoa powder and spread onto a lined baking sheet. Microwave your raspberries to ensure they are soft and juicy and then add to the chocolate as a topping along with the raw nuts. Refrigerate until the tray hardens. Cut into 10 pieces.

Coconut Cookies

8 servings total

148 calories per serving

Carbs (g): 7

Fiber (g): 6

Fat (g): 31

ngredients:

- Sugar Substitute of Your Choice (.5 cup)
- Coconut Oil (.25 cup)
- Salt (a pinch)
- Coconut Flakes (unsweetened, shredded, 3 cups)
- Vanilla Extract (2 teaspoons)

*D*irections: Combine everything in a food processor and pulse well. Then form ball shapes and decorate with toppings like dark chocolate chips or additional raw nuts. Let them harden at room temperature.

Keto Chocolate Chip Cookies

12 servings total

163 calories per serving

Fat (g): 17

Protein (g): 4

Carbs (g): 3

ngredients:

- Egg (1)
- Salt (a pinch)
- Butter (.5 cup)
- Dark Chocolate Chips (sugar-free, .5 cup)
- Vanilla Extract (1 teaspoon)
- Egg (1)
- Sugar Substitute of Your Choice (.75 cup)
- Almond Flour (1.5 cups)

Directions: Preheat your oven to 355 degrees F. Melt your butter in the microwave and combine it with the egg, vanilla, and sweetener. Then add the salt, baking powder, and almond flour and ensure the batter is smooth. Gently fold in the chocolate chips. Make 12 evenly-sized cookie balls and place on a lined baking tray. Bake until the edges turn brown, anywhere from 8 to 15 minutes.

14-DAY KETOGENIC DIET MEAL PLAN

To get you started, here is a 14-day sample keto meal plan that provides you recipes for breakfast, lunch, and dinner!

WEEK 1: MONDAY

BREAKFAST

Bacon and Eggs

2 servings total

287 calories per serving

Fat (g): 22

Protein (g): 15

Carbs (g): 1

· · ·

ngredients:

- Eggs (4)
- Bacon Slices (4)

*D*irections: In a small skillet, add your bacon and fry until golden and crispy. Set aside and then fry your eggs in the bacon fat as you prefer them (scrambled or sunny side).

*L*UNCH

*L*amb Kebabs

2 servings total

314 calories per serving

Protein (g): 20

Carbs (g): 0

Fat (g): 23

*I*ngredients:

- Ground Lamb (.5 pound)
- Parsley (.5 bunch, chopped)
- Salt& Black Pepper (1 teaspoon)
- Paprika (1 teaspoon)
- Lemon Juice (1 teaspoon)

irections: Set your oven to 300 degrees F. Combine all the ingredients and blend together in a food processor or with your hands to ensure everything is well combined. Make round 2″ meatballs or form kebabs on wooden skewer sticks. Bake for 20-30 minutes until cooked through. Garnish with parsley.

INNER

ork Chops in Pesto

2 servings total

853 calories per serving

Fat (g): 70

Protein (g): 53

Carbs (g): 2

Fiber (g): 0

. . .

ngredients:

- Red Pesto (4 tablespoons)
- Butter (2 tablespoons)
- Pork Chops (2)
- Mayonnaise (.25 cup)

irections: Combine half your pesto and the mayonnaise to make a rub and rub on your pork chops. Fry in the butter until golden brown and cooked. Add the rest of the pesto as a topping.

WEEK 1: TUESDAY

𝓑REAKFAST

𝓜ushroom Omelet

1 serving total

492 calories per serving

Fat (g): 38

Protein (g): 30

Carbs (g): 6

Fiber (g): 2

. . .

*I*ngredients:

- Eggs (3)
- Butter or Ghee (1 tablespoon)
- Mushrooms (3-4, sliced)
- Onion (2 teaspoons, diced)
- Shredded Cheese (2 tablespoons)

*D*irections: Crack your eggs into a bowl and season with salt and pepper. In a skillet, melt your butter and add the egg mixture and let it cook. Then add your onions, cheese, and mushrooms and flip and cook the egg to the other side.

*L*UNCH

Shrimp and Zucchini Noodles

4 servings total

228 calories per serving

Fat (g): 16

Protein (g): 17

Carbs (g): 9

Fiber (g): 2

ngredients:

- Butter (2 tablespoons)
- Vegetable Stock (.25 cup)
- Parmesan Cheese (grated, 3 tablespoons)
- Peeled Shrimp (1 pound)
- Zucchini Noodles (1 pound, pre-packaged)
- Lemon Juice (1 tablespoon)
- Salt, Black Pepper, Red Chili Flakes (.5 teaspoon each)
- Minced Garlic (1 teaspoon)

irections: First, melt your butter in a large skillet and fry your garlic and shrimp together. Season with your spices and cook the shrimp through. Add the vegetable stock, lemon juice, and zucchini noodles and cook until tender. Garnish with the cheese.

INNER

Oven-Baked Chicken

2 servings total

993 calories per serving

Protein (g): 59

Fat (g): 83

Carbs (g): 1

 ngredients:

- Chicken (whole bird, ~1.5 pounds)
- Butter (3 ounces)
- Minced Garlic (1 teaspoon)
- Salt & Black Pepper (1 teaspoon)

*D*irections: First, preheat your oven to 400 degrees F. Melt the butter and add your salt, pepper, and minced garlic to it. Then rub that marinade into the chicken. Bake on the lower rack for from 1 to 2 hours until the internal chicken temperature reaches 180 degrees F.

WEEK 1: WEDNESDAY

*B*REAKFAST

**reakfast Egg and Avocado Burrito**

1 serving total

528 calories per serving

Fat (g): 42

Protein (g): 21

Carbs (g): 11

 ngredients:

- Eggs (2)
- Bacon (2 slices)
- Olive Oil (1 tablespoon)
- Cherry Tomatoes (4-5, sliced)
- Avocado (.5, diced)
- Lettuce Leaf (1)

*D*irections: In a saucepan, first add your olive oil and then cook your eggs until scrambled well. Set aside and then cook your bacon. On your lettuce leaf, add your tomato, bacon, avocado chunks, and cooked egg to eat like a lettuce burrito.

*L*UNCH
Greek Salad

2 servings total

581 calories per serving

Fat (g): 51

Protein (g): 17

Carbs (g): 20

Fiber (g): 5

ngredients:

- Tomatoes (3, chopped)
- Olive Oil (3 tablespoons)
- Green Pepper (.5, finely diced)
- Red Onion (.5, chopped)
- Cucumber (.5, diced)
- Feta Cheese (crumbled, .25 cup)
- Black Olives (8-10)
- Red Wine Vinegar (.5 tablespoon)

irections: Make sure your veggies are cut into bite-size pieces and then top with feta cheese and olives. Combine the olive oil and vinegar and drizzle as a dressing.

INNER

Brazilian Steak

4 servings total

428 calories per serving

Fat (g): 31

Carbs (g): 1

Protein (g): 31

ngredients:

- Minced Garlic (2 teaspoons)
- Fresh Parsley (1 tablespoon, chopped)
- Olive Oil (2 tablespoons)
- Butter (4 tablespoons)
- Salt & Black Pepper (1 teaspoon)

irections: Pat your steak dry and season with half the minced garlic, salt, and pepper. Then heat your oil in a dish and brown your steak on both sides. Set aside. In another skillet, melt your butter and add the garlic and mix until lightly golden. Serve this over the steak as a dressing. Garnish with parsley.

WEEK 1: THURSDAY

REAKFAST

reen Smoothie
1 serving total

229 calories per serving

Fat (g): 22

Carbs (g): 5

Protein (g): 1

Fiber (g): 1

ngredients:

- Almond Milk (.5 cup)
- Mint Leaves (8-10)
- Coconut Milk (full-fat, .5 cup)
- A handful of ice
- Fresh Parsley (1 tablespoon, chopped

*D*irections: Combine all your ingredients and blend until smooth.

*L*UNCH

eta Cheese Stuffed Bell Peppers

2 servings total

642 calories per serving

Fat (g): 54

Protein (g): 29

Carbs (g): 14

Fiber (g): 3

ngredients:

- Bell Peppers (2)
- Hot Sauce (low carb, 1 teaspoon)
- Eggs (2)
- Feta Cheese (11 ounces, crumbled)
- Green Olives (10, sliced)

irections: First, preheat your oven to 400 degrees F. Prepare your bell peppers by first cutting them in half and removing the seeds. Mix all the other ingredients in a bowl to make a frothy egg mixture. Stuff the peppers with the filling and then allow them to bake from 20 to 25 minutes until the tops are golden brown.

INNER

Chicken Leg with Veggies

2 servings total

642 calories per serving

Fat (g): 37

Protein (g): 60

Carbs (g): 10

Fiber (g): 4

*I*ngredients:

- Chicken Legs (2)
- Butter (melted, 1 tablespoon)
- Paprika (1 teaspoon)
- Zucchini (.5 cup, diced)
- Broccoli (.25 cup)
- Baby Carrots (8-10)
- Cherry Tomatoes (6-8, halved)
- Cumin Powder (1 teaspoon)
- Salt & Black Pepper (1 teaspoon each)

*D*irections: First, preheat your oven to 400 degrees F. Massage your chicken with spices and add to a lined baking tray. Spread out your veggies on the tray and drizzle with the melted butter. Bake for 40 to 50 minutes until chicken is brown.

WEEK 1: FRIDAY

. . .

REAKFAST

ow Carb Blueberry Smoothie

1 serving total

411 calories per serving

Fat (g): 43

Protein (g): 4

Carbs (g): 11

Fiber (g): 1

Ingredients:

- a handful of ice
- Vanilla Extract (.5 teaspoon)
- Blueberries (.25 cup)
- Coconut Milk (.75 cup, full-fat)
- Lemon Juice (1 teaspoon)

Directions: In a blender, combine all your ingredients until smooth.

. . .

*L*UNCH

*T*una Salad with Hardboiled Eggs

2 servings total

403 calories per serving

Protein (g): 20

Carbs (g): 7

Fiber (g): 2

*I*ngredients:

- Lettuce (1 cup, torn)
- Onion (.5, chopped)
- Sour Cream (2 tablespoons, full fat)
- Lemon Juice (1 tablespoon)
- Tomato (.5, diced)
- Tuna (1 can, drained)
- Mayonnaise (2 tablespoons)
- Hard-boiled Eggs (4)
- Olive Oil (1 tablespoon)

 irections: Have your eggs hard-boiled and ready or boil them in boiling water. Peel and slice and set aside. Then in a salad bowl, combine your tuna with lemon juice and mayonnaise and season with salt and black pepper. Tear your lettuce into the bowl and add the tomato, onions, and sour cream. Mix everything together and add the olive oil as a dressing.

INNER

 **round Beef Plate**

2 servings total

903 calories per serving

Fat (g); 79

Protein (g); 47

Carbs (g): 6

Fiber (g): 1

ngredients:

- Ground Beef (.75 pound)
- Bell Pepper (.5, diced)
- Cucumber (.5, diced)
- Butter (2 tablespoons)
- Olive Oil (2 tablespoons)

- Lettuce (.25 cup, torn)
- Cheddar Cheese (.25 cup, shredded)

irections: In a frying pan, add the butter and then brown your ground beef in it. Season with salt and black pepper. Once cooked, remove from the heat and combine your chopped veggies and cheese. Drizzle with olive oil.

WEEK 1: SATURDAY

REAKFAST

**o Bread Breakfast Sandwich**

2 servings total

331 calories per serving

Fat (g): 30

Protein (g): 20

Carbs (g): 2

ngredients:

- Cheese (2-3 slices)
- Smoked Ham (2-3 slices)
- Eggs (4)

73

- Butter (2 tablespoons)

irections: In a skillet, melt the butter and add one egg at a time and cook it. This will be the "base" of your sandwich. Then add the cheese and ham and another egg will be the top "bread". You can add this back to the pan if you want to melt the cheese.

*L*UNCH

*L*ow Carb Taco Salad

2 servings total

242 calories per serving

Protein (g): 22

Fat (g): 14

Carbs (g): 7

Fiber (g): 2.1

ngredients:

- Avocado (.5, diced)
- Parsley (.5 bunch, chopped

- Lettuce (1 cup, torn)
- Ground Beef (.25 pound)
- Red Onion (.5, chopped)
- Sour Cream (2 tablespoons, full fat)
- Shredded Cheese (3 tablespoons)
- Tomato (1, chopped)
- Garlic Powder, Salt, Paprika, Cumin Powder (.5 teaspoon each)

*D*irections: Combine all your spices first in a small bowl so they are well mixed. Then in a skillet, brown your ground beef and add it to a bowl with the taco seasoning you have prepared. Add the rest of your chopped vegetables, shredded cheese, and sour cream. Garnish with cilantro.

*D*INNER

arlic Scallops
2 servings total

372 calories per serving

Carbs (g): 8

Fiber (g): 1

Protein (g): 25

Fat (g): 18

. . .

ngredients:

- Scallops (1 pound)
- Minced Garlic (3 teaspoons)
- Fresh Parsley (2 tablespoons, chopped)
- Salt, Red Chili Flakes, Black Pepper (1 teaspoon each)
- Butter (.25 cup, melted)
- Lemon Juice (2 tablespoons)

irections: In a large skillet, add a little of the melted butter and cook your scallops with the spices. Make sure they are cooked through with a nice sear and then add the rest of the butter, the garlic, and lemon juice. Garnish with fresh parsley.

WEEK 1: SUNDAY

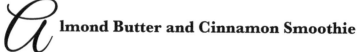REAKFAST

$\mathcal{A}$lmond Butter and Cinnamon Smoothie

1 serving total

318 calories per serving

Fat (g): 27

Protein (g): 19

Carbs (g): 10

Fiber (g): 5

ngredients:

- Sugar Substitute of Your Choice (10-12 drops)
- Almond Milk (1 cup)
- Almond Butter (2 tablespoons)
- Almond Extract (.25 teaspoon)
- Salt (a pinch)
- Ground Cinnamon (.5 teaspoon)
- a handful of ice

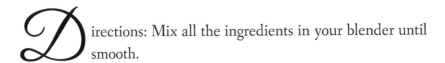irections: Mix all the ingredients in your blender until smooth.

UNCH

almon and Green Beans

1 serving total

391 calories per serving

Protein (g): 33

Carbs (g): 9

Fiber (g): 3

ngredients:

- Olive Oil (3 tablespoons)
- Green Beans (1 cup, cooked)
- Minced Garlic (2 teaspoons)
- Salmon Fillet (1)
- Lemon Juice (1 tablespoon)
- Fresh Rosemary (1 tablespoon, or 2 tablespoon dried herbs)

irections: First, season your fish with salt, black pepper, and a little olive oil. Then cook it in some olive oil in a skillet. Add the lemon juice. Add your green beans to the pan and then season with the herbs and minced garlic.

INNER

Cauliflower Pizza

1 serving total

1017 calories per serving

Protein (g): 68

Fat (g): 74

Carbs (g): 23

Fiber (g): 7

ngredients:

- Shredded Cheese (4 ounces)
- Salt (a pinch)
- Eggs (2)
- Cauliflower (5 ounces, grated)

oppings:

- Bell Pepper (.25, sliced)
- Onion (.25, sliced)
- Dried Herbs (1 tablespoon)
- Olives (8-10)
- Shredded Cheese (2 ounces)
- Mozzarella Cheese (2 ounces)
- Tomato Sauce (4 tablespoons)

*D*irections: First, preheat your oven to 350 degrees F. Be sure your cauliflower is grated and then mix it with the salt, eggs, and the cheese until well combined. Spread this mixture onto a lined baking sheet to make a circle about 11 inches big. Before adding your toppings, bake for around 15 minutes until lightly golden brown. Then bake again with the toppings until the cheese is melted.

WEEK 2: MONDAY

REAKFAST

eto Pancakes

2 servings total

382 calories per serving

Fat (g): 33

Protein (g): 15

Carbs (g): 13

Ingredients:

- Sugar Substitute of Your Choice (5-8 drops)
- Almond Flour (.5 cup)
- Coconut Flour (2 tablespoons)
- Salt, Cinnamon, Vanilla Extract, Baking Powder (.5 teaspoon each)
- Eggs (3)
- Butter (1 tablespoon)
- Heavy Cream (2 tablespoons)

*D*irections: Combine the sweetener, salt, baking powder, cinnamon, coconut flour, and almond flour in a bowl. Add in your butter, cream, eggs, and vanilla extract until the batter is thick. In a pan, add your pancakes and cook until bubbles form at the edges. Flip and cook the other side. This will make 2 pancakes.

*L*UNCH

*K*eto Deli Plate

2 servings total

221 calories per serving

Protein (g): 40

Fat (g): 60

Carbs (g): 11

Fiber (g): 3

*I*ngredients:

- Olive Oil (3 tablespoons)
- Mozzarella Cheese (7 ounces)
- Minced Garlic (2 tablespoons)

- Tomatoes (2, sliced)
- Olives (10)
- Prosciutto (7 ounces, sliced)

irections: On a plate, create your deli platter by laying out your meat, tomatoes, olives, and cheese. Drizzle with the garlic and olive oil and sprinkle salt and black pepper.

DINNER

Keto Chili

3 servings total

353 calories per serving

Fat (g): 22

Protein (g): 34

Carbs (g): 7

ngredients:

- Butter (1 tablespoon)
- Carrots (1 cup, chopped)
- Cumin Powder, Black Pepper, Paprika, Garlic Powder, Salt (1 teaspoon)

- Chipotle Powder (1 teaspoon)
- Ground Beef (1 pound)
- Beef Broth (1 cup)
- Celery (2 stalks, chopped)
- Tomato Sauce (1 can ∼15 ounces)

*D*irections: In a large pot, allow your butter to melt then sauté your vegetables until soft. Add your beef and spices and mix well and brown your meat. Add the tomato sauce and the beef broth and let the mixture simmer 20 to 25 minutes until the liquid reduces.

WEEK 2: TUESDAY

*B*REAKFAST

 **estern Ham Omelet**

2 servings total

662 calories per serving

Fat (G): 56

Protein (g): 35

Carbs (g): 6

Fiber (g): 1

. . .

*I*ngredients:

- Eggs (3)
- Shredded Cheese (.25 cup)
- Bell Pepper (.25, chopped)
- Heavy Cream (1 tablespoon)
- Onion (.5, chopped)
- Butter (1 tablespoon)
- Deli Ham (5-8 pieces, sliced)

*D*irections: In a bowl, combine together your eggs, half the cheese, and cream and whisk well. You can season with salt and black pepper. In a skillet, begin by melting your butter. Sauté your onions, ham, and peppers until they are soft. Add your eggs and cook until the omelet is firm. Garnish with the leftover cheese and fold the omelet to allow the cheese to melt.

*L*UNCH

*K*eto Cheese and Salami Plate

2 servings total

1012 calories per serving

Carbs (g): 13

Fiber (g): 10

Fat (g): 102

Protein (g): 32

 ngredients:

- Avocado (1, sliced)
- Macadamia Nuts (.5 cup)
- Salami (.5 cup)
- Lettuce (.25 cup, torn)
- Brie Cheese (.5 ounce)
- Olive Oil (2 tablespoons)

 irections: Arrange your cheese, lettuce, nuts, avocado, and salami on a plate and drizzle with olive oil to serve.

 INNER

Shrimp Avocado Salad with Feta

2 servings total

411 calories per serving

Fat (g): 33

Carbs (g): 12

Fiber (g): 6

Protein (g): 21

ngredients:

- Shrimp (8 ounces, peeled)
- Avocado (1, diced)
- Tomato (1, diced)
- Olive Oil (1 tablespoon)
- Butter (2 tablespoons, melted)
- Fresh Parsley (3 tablespoons, chopped)
- Feta Cheese (.25 cup, crumbled)
- Lemon Juice (1 tablespoon)

Directions: Mix together the shrimp with the melted butter and then cook it in a skillet. Set aside. Combine the other ingredients except for the olive oil in a large bowl along with the shrimp. Drizzle the olive oil and add your black pepper and salt.

WEEK 2: WEDNESDAY

BREAKFAST

eto Almond Butter Mocha
2 servings total

114 calories per serving

Fat (g): 7

Carbs (g): 11

Protein (g): 2

*I*ngredients:

Almond Milk (1.5 cups)

Espresso Powder (2 tablespoons)

Sugar Substitute of Your Choice (1 teaspoon)

Vanilla Extract (.5 teaspoon)

Cocoa Powder (1 tablespoon, unsweetened)

Almond Butter (1 tablespoon)

*D*irections: Mix almond butter, the espresso and cocoa powder, vanilla extract, stevia sugar powder, and almond milk in a blender until thick.

*L*UNCH

*A*vocado, Chicken, and Cucumber Salad

2 servings total

523 calories per serving

Fat (g): 37

Protein (g): 40

Carbs (g): 10

Fiber (g): 5

ngredients:

- Avocado (.5, diced)
- Tomatoes (2, chopped)
- Rotisserie Chicken (1.5 cups, shredded)
- Cucumber (.5, chopped)
- Olive Oil (1 tablespoon)
- Red Onion (.25 cup, chopped)
- Lemon or Lime Juice (1 tablespoon)

irections: Mix together your cucumber, tomatoes, avocado, chicken, and onion in a bowl and season with a pinch of salt and black pepper. Drizzle the olive oil and lemon juice until well combined.

INNER

. . .

Pesto Chicken with Veggies

2 servings total

411 calories per serving

Fat (g): 32

Carbs (g): 12

Fiber (g): 4

Protein (g): 22

Ingredients:

- Butter (2 tablespoons)
- Asparagus (.5 pound, halved)
- Tomato (1, diced)
- Chicken Thighs (.5 pound)
- Salt, Paprika, Black Pepper (1 teaspoon)
- Pesto Sauce (3 tablespoons)
- Olive Oil (1 tablespoon)

Directions: In a skillet, melt your butter and add your chicken thighs. Season with your spices and then add your tomatoes. Remove the chicken if it is cooked and then add your asparagus and pesto. Add the chicken back to the skillet and drizzle with olive oil.

WEEK 2: THURSDAY

. . .

 REAKFAST

 pinach and Feta Egg Scramble

2 servings total

341 calories per serving

Fat (g): 29

Protein (g): 16

Carbs (g): 4

Fiber (g): 1

 ngredients:

- Feta Cheese (.25 cup, crumbled)
- Minced Garlic (.5 teaspoon)
- Feta Cheese (.25 cup, crumbled)
- Fresh Baby Spinach Leaves (8-10)
- Butter (1 tablespoon)
- Heavy Cream (2 tablespoons)
- Eggs (4)

*D*irections: In a bowl, mix together your eggs and cream. In a skillet, melt your butter then add the spinach and garlic until the spinach is wilted. Season with salt and black pepper. Add your eggs and cook to your liking. Garnish with feta cheese.

 UNCH

 **aesar Salad**

1 serving total

207 calories per serving

Carbs (g): 8

Protein (g): 9

Fiber (g): 2.1

 ngredients:

- Hard-boiled Egg (1)
- Lettuce Leaves (4-5)
- Broccoli (.25 cup)
- Tomato (1, chopped)
- Cucumber (.5, chopped)
- Low Carb Salad Dressing (1 tablespoon)

 irections: Tear your lettuce into a bowl and add the tomato, broccoli, and cucumber. Add the dressing and hard-boiled egg.

INNER

arlic Baked Salmon

3 servings total

273 calories per serving

Fat (G): 14

Carbs (g): 2

Fiber (g): 0.2

Protein (g): 31

Ingredients:

- Minced Garlic (1 teaspoon)
- Lemon Juice (2 tablespoons)
- Salt, Paprika, Black Pepper (1 teaspoon)
- Lemon Juice (2 tablespoons)
- Butter (2 tablespoons)
- Salmon (∼1 pound cut into 3 fillets)

*D*irections: Preheat your oven to 375 degrees F. First, let your butter melt in a skillet and add the garlic. Turn off the heat before the garlic burns. Use a brush to spread this marinade to the fillets of salmon and then season with the spices. Cover the fish with foil so the sauce does not leak and then bake for 12 to 16 minutes until the fish is firm.

WEEK 2: FRIDAY

*B*REAKFAST

 aspberry Avocado Smoothie

1 serving total

212 calories per serving

Fat (g): 20

Carbs (g): 13

Fiber (g): 8

Protein (g): 3

ngredients:

- Avocado (.5, peeled)
- Raspberries (.25 cup)

- Lemon Juice (2 tablespoons)
- a handful of ice
- Sugar Substitute of Your Choice (5-8 drops)
- Water (.5 cup)

irections: Mix all the ingredients in your blender until smooth.

UNCH

 eto Pizza

3 servings total

124 calories per serving

Carbs (g): 4

Fat (g): 8

Protein (g): 11

Fiber (g): 1

ngredients:

- Pepperoni Slices (8-10)
- Pizza Seasoning (1 teaspoon)

- Low Carb Pizza Sauce (.5 cup)
- Bell Peppers (.25 cup, chopped)
- Mozzarella Cheese (1 cup)
- Onion (2 tablespoons, chopped)
- Tomatoes (.25 cup, sliced)

*D*irections: Set your oven to 400 degrees F. Spread out your cheese on a lined baking sheet so there are no holes anywhere. Add the pizza seasoning and bake for 6 to 8 minutes golden brown. Then add the other ingredients as your pizza topping and bake for another 5 to 8 minutes until golden brown.

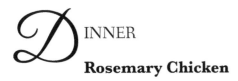

*D*INNER

Rosemary Chicken

1 serving total

481 calories per serving

Fat (g): 32

Protein (g): 30

Carbs (g): 7

Fiber (g): 2.4

• • •

ngredients:

- Broccoli (.5 cup)
- Fresh Rosemary (1 teaspoon)
- Chicken Breast (1)
- Butter (2 tablespoons, melted)
- Olive Oil, Salt, Paprika, Black Pepper (1 teaspoon each)

irections: Combine the melted butter with the salt and black pepper and rub this on the chicken. In a large skillet, add the olive oil and then cook the chicken with the rosemary for 4 to 8 minutes until golden brown. Add the broccoli to the pan and cook until soft.

WEEK 2: SATURDAY

REAKFAST

ow **Carb Blueberry Pancakes**

2 servings

469 calories per serving

Fat (g): 44

Protein (g): 15

Carbs (g): 21

Fiber (g): 14

ngredients:

- Eggs (3)
- Baking Powder (1 teaspoon)
- Cream Cheese (2 ounces)
- Almond Flour (.3 cup)
- Salt (a pinch)
- Fresh Blueberries (1 ounce)
- Butter (1 tablespoon, melted)
- Oat Fiber (.3 cup)

*D*irections: In a bowl, combine your eggs, melted butter, and softened cream cheese. Combine the rest of the ingredients except blueberries separately and then mix with the eggs until you have a smooth batter. In a small pan, add about a .5 cup batter per pancake and let it cook before topping with blueberries. Then flip and fry some more before done.

*L*UNCH

. . .

vocado Egg Salad

3 servings total

169 calories per serving

Fat (g): 12

Carbs (g): 6

Fiber (g): 3

Protein (g): 9

 ngredients:

- Lemon or Lime Juice (1 tablespoon)
- Hard-boiled Eggs (3)
- Fresh Parsley (1 tablespoon, chopped)
- Red Onion (.25, chopped)
- Avocado (1, diced)
- Salt & Black Pepper (.5 teaspoon each)

irections: Make sure your eggs are hard-boiled and then peel and chop them into bite-size pieces. Mix with the avocado so the avocado becomes creamy and smooth. Add the parsley, salt, pepper, onion, and lemon juice. Serve immediately.

. . .

DINNER

Turkey Chili

2 servings total

382 calories per serving

Fat (g): 30

Carbs (g): 9

Protein (g): 16

Ingredients:

- Butter (2 tablespoons)
- Minced Garlic (2 teaspoons)
- Paprika, Salt, Black Pepper (1 teaspoon)
- Ground Turkey (1 pound)
- Coconut Milk (2 cups)
- Onion (.5, diced)
- Diced Tomatoes (1 can ~6 ounces)

Directions: In a large pot, add your butter and then the minced garlic. Brown your ground turkey and add the spices, tomatoes, and onion. Add your coconut milk and reduce the heat for 10 to 15 minutes for the chili to thicken.

WEEK 2: SUNDAY

REAKFAST

eto Caprese Omelet

2 servings total

532 calories per serving

Fat (g): 43

Protein (g): 33

Carbs (g): 5

Fiber (g): 1

*I*ngredients:

- Eggs (6)
- Cherry Tomatoes (6-8, halved)
- Mozzarella Cheese (.25 cup, grated)
- Butter (1 tablespoon)
- Fresh Basil (1 tablespoon, chopped)

*D*irections: In a bowl, add your eggs and season with salt, black pepper, and basil. In a large frying pan, add your butter and then lightly sauté your tomatoes. Add the egg batter and let it firm before garnishing with cheese. Let the egg mixture simmer until the omelet is set and cheese is melted.

UNCH

ucchini Pizza

2 servings total

381 calories per serving

Fat (g): 27

Carbs (g): 13

Protein (g): 33

*I*ngredients:

- Bell Pepper (.25, chopped)
- Tomato Sauce (.5 can)
- Zucchinis (2)
- Fresh Basil (1 teaspoon, chopped)
- Mozzarella Cheese (.75 cup)
- Onion (.5, chopped)
- Mushrooms (4-5, sliced)
- Chili Flakes (a pinch)

*D*irections: Preheat your oven to 400 degrees F. Cut your zucchini in half and remove the flesh. Add the tomato sauce to each zucchini "boat" and then top it with the fresh basil, onion, bell pepper, and your mushroom toppings. Set on a lined baking tray and bake for 12 to 15 minutes until the cheese becomes golden brown. Sprinkle with the red chili flakes for some heat.

*D*INNER

*K*eto Cabbage Soup

4 servings total

263 calories per serving

Fat (g): 18

Carbs (g): 6

Fiber (g): 2

Protein (g): 17

*I*ngredients:

- Ground Beef (1 pound)
- Butter (1 tablespoon)
- Water (2 cups)
- Head of Cabbage (.5, chopped)

- Minced Garlic (1 teaspoon)
- Onion (.5, diced)
- Cumin Powder, Salt, Black Pepper (1 teaspoon)
- Diced Tomatoes (1 can ~8 ounces)

*D*irections: First, add your butter to a large skillet and brown your ground beef. Then add the onion. Transfer this mixture to a large pot and add the water and the other ingredients along with your seasoning. Reduce the heat and let it simmer for 30 to 40 minutes until the soup becomes thick.

CONCLUSION

Thank you for making it to the end of the *Keto Diet for Beginners*. We hope this book was informative and able to provide you with the information you were seeking regarding the keto diet. This diet has become very popular in recent years but it can seem overwhelming to beginners. We hope we were able to clear any misinformation and give you a very thorough understanding of the diet and exactly how it works. In fact, it has become a widely researched topic in scientific communities because of the array of results it produces! You not only lose stubborn weight you haven't been able to get rid of, but also can improve so many other aspects of your health and even prevent diseases like obesity, neurodegenerative diseases, diabetes, and heart disease.

Once you understand the daily macronutrient count of keto, you can see why it is so important for the body to stay at that breakdown in order to facilitate the process of ketosis. With 75% fat, 20% protein, and around 5% carbohydrate intake, you are able to guide the body away from producing glucose and harness energy through fat-rich ketones instead. That gives you more physical energy, better cognitive functioning, and lets you lose weight at the same time!

Whatever your goal is regarding keto, we are here to help you succeed! With our detailed introduction to the diet, possible side effects, and tips for success, we want you to be aware of how your body will adjust and how you can ease that adjustment process. Things like staying hydrated, getting enough sleep, incorporating light exercise into your routine, and counting your macros is a great way to ensure you are able to continue making progress on keto. With our chapter on a keto-friendly shopping list, you will know exactly what ingredients you should be buying, and which ones you should be avoiding. We urge you to be aware of your caloric intake and track your macros using an app to assure you are staying in ketosis. Not only that, being aware of your net carbohydrate intake is the key so your body is not inadvertently consuming too many carbs and going back to the old ways of producing glucose.

With our 14-day meal plan, you have delicious recipes to make for breakfast, lunch, and dinner. Meal prepping is a great way to ensure you have keto-friendly meals prepared and that you are not tempted to break your diet and reach for the fast food! Not only that, we provide you keto-friendly desserts! That way you can satisfy your sweet tooth with some delicious sugar-free dark chocolate recipes while still remaining in ketosis. As long as you are aware of your caloric intake, you can maintain your state of ketosis and avoid gaining weight.

If you feel keto is right for you, be sure you contact your doctor to assure you are healthy enough to start this diet and do not have other underlying health concerns. We have included tips to guide you on your journey, how to tackle the keto flu, a shopping list of foods, as well as dozens of recipes to get you started!

If you've found this book helpful toward your keto journey, we'd appreciate a review!

AUTOPHAGY

Body's Natural Intelligence for Anti-Aging
and Healing – Intermittent Fasting for
Weight Loss & Self-Cleansing

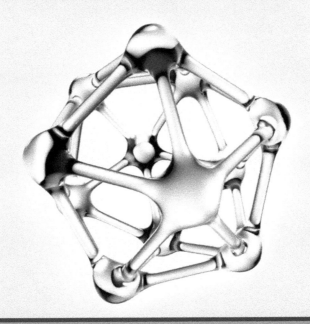

Frances Spritzler

INTRODUCTION

Thank you for purchasing *Autophagy: Body's Natural Intelligence for Anti-Aging and Healing – Intermittent Fasting for Weight Loss & Self-Cleansing*, and congratulations on doing so!

As you begin your journey into understanding this biological and natural process in your body, you will learn some very interesting things about how your body works. When you first learn about what autophagy is, it may sound a little gross, scary, unreal, or strange. Yes, the definition of the name is a little "off," but what it does for your body certainly is not! As you work from chapter to chapter of this book you will find information and advice pulled from various publications and scientific journals. You will learn what the process is, how it works in your body, what the current research reveals, and how you can use it to truly "cleanse" your body.

Using this healthy and natural process, you can help support your general health, boost your immune and metabolic systems, get glowing skin, and lose weight. You can also choose the method for doing this that works for your life! No need to give up all the foods and activities in your life that you enjoy! Instead, small tweaks here and there can make all the difference in how you live your life for years to come. It may sound "simple" or "too good to be true." This is because it is simple to explain, but the mental willpower and determination you need to make these tweaks will make the difference between just reading about how you can take control of your health and weight, and actually embracing it. Once you are done reading this book, hopefully, you are ready to get going!

There are plenty of books on this subject on the market, thanks again for choosing this one! Every effort was made to ensure it is full of as much useful information as possible. Please enjoy!

WHAT IS AUTOPHAGY?

THE WORD "AUTOPHAGY" IS DERIVED FROM THE ANCIENT
Greek word, meaning "hollow" or "self-devouring." It may sound
ominous, but it is a natural process in your body to help you regulate the various cellular components you need and do not need for
proper functioning. It is descriptive of the process of regulation,
and how your body breaks down cells if they are dysfunctional or
unnecessary. Those parts that are removed are then recycled or
properly disposed of so you can have a healthy body. It is an
orderly process or degradation and dissolution.

There are three primary types of autophagy, which occur
in your body: chaperone-mediated autophagy, or
CMA; microautophagy, and; macroautophagy. Each type has a
unique role and purpose in your body. When you are sick or have
a disease, your body's response to this stress, which is your body's
natural survival instinct, is a response that adapts to the problem at
hand. Because of its adaptability, it will either show up and help

kill or destroy cells or break them apart to try to restore them. At times, the process can appear to support the morbidity of the affected cells. In cases where your body becomes extremely starved, the natural autophagy process will breakdown parts of cells to help the cell survive on less energy, leading to the best chance of survival. They remove the "unnecessary" components at the moment to help the cells keep up their energy levels.

*I*n 1963, when Dr. Christian de Duve discovered the function of the body's lysosomes, he coined the name, "autophagy." Later, in the 1990s, researchers studying yeast found autophagic-like properties, which lead to the discovery of the process. A Nobel Peace Prize in Physiology or Medicine was awarded in 2016 to Yoshinori Ohsumi, a Japanese researcher who was prominent in the 1990s autophagy deduction. Prior to all of this, in 1962, Keith Porter and a student first observed the process of autophagy at Rockefeller Institute. They identified the lysosome quantity was increased in rat's livers after glucagon was introduced. They observed how some moved to the center of the cells but had a severe flaw in their interpretation—they did not consider the organelles that already existed and the formation of the lysosome. Their name, "autolysis" was coined after Christian de Duve and Alex Novikoff's work, but it was not accurate. This is why de Duve was credited with the discovery in 1963. Christian de Duve began his work after being introduced to a study published in early 1963 by Hruban, Spargo and their colleagues. Their publication described "focal cytoplasm degradation." This observation and study were based off a German study from 1955 studying injuries. Their observations launched de Duve's own inquiry, which ultimately leads to his coining of the process as "autophagy." Not making the same conclusion as Porter and his student, de Duve observed that the function of the lysosome was influenced by the glucagon, but it was a major part of the cellular degradation in the liver of the subjects. During this study, de Duve and his student Russell Deter explained that lysosomes were the reasons for the autophagy caused by glucagon. This is the first moment that lysosomes were described as the center for intracellular autophagy.

*A*fter Ohsumi received his award for his work with autophagy, the field grew dynamically throughout the 21st century. Several studies were conducted on the subject, shedding light on new tools for scientists to learn about human's response to disease and their general health. In 1999, Beth Levine and her group of researchers made an incredible discovery that altered the course of autophagy and researchers ever since. Levine and her group identified a strong connection between autophagy and cancer. Even today, the main research topic of autophagy relates to cancer. Another common theme in research is the relationship between immune defense and neurodegeneration. In 2003, the first Gordon Research Conference in Waterville focused on autophagy. Later, in 2005, Daniel Klionsky published a scientific journal focused on autophagy, titled "Autophagy." In 2007, the first Keystone Symposia and Conference held in Monterey was dedicated to autophagy. Research continues to unfold new and interesting applications of understanding about autophagy and its role in the human body.

The Process of Autophagy

All three types of autophagy are facilitated by genes related to autophagy and related enzymes. Because of the size of macroautophagy, it is further divided into "selective" and "bulk" macroautophagy. "Selective" refers to organelle autophagy. This includes ribophagy, coprophagy, pexophagy, lipophagy, and mitophagy. The main type of autophagy in a person's body is Macroautophagy. The primary purpose is to remove damaged organelles from cells or proteins that are not in use. The process works like this: the phagophore selects the items that need to be removed and it surrounds them. This creates an autophagosome, or a double membrane, surrounding the selected organelle or protein. The autophagosome then makes its way through the cell's cytoplasm until it reaches a lysosome. When it finds one, and the two bind together. The autophagosome enters into the lysosome and begins to degrade because of the lysosomal hydrolase.

Other times, the autophagy is more direct, which is known as Microautophagy. The cytoplasm material is engulfed directly into the lysosome. The lysosomal membrane folds inward or is a cellular protrusion called "invagination." A more complex process than the other two is the CMA, or "chaperone-mediated autophagy." The pathway is very specific and involves recognition by a hsc70-containing complex. Basically, this means that when hsc70 complex is present, a protein must have a site that will recognize it. This recognition allows the complex to bind to it, creating CMA-substrate/chaperone complex. This complex then is able to bind to a protein bound for the membrane of the lysosome through the CMA receptor of the protein. This allows the complex to enter the cell. Once inside, the protein unfolds and is sent through the membrane with the help of the hsc70 chaperone. This process is significantly different, mainly because of the translocation of the protein material in a singular manner. It is also an extremely selective process, only allowing very specific material to cross over the barrier of the lysosome.

$\mathcal{T}$wo processes related to Macroautophagy include lipophagy and mitophagy. Lipophagy occurs in both fungus and animals. Autophagy can degrade lipids. In plants, this process is not identifiable yet. Lipid Droplets, or LDs, are the target. These little spheres are the center of most triacylglycerols, or TAGs, and are also a single layer of protein for a membrane and phospholipids. This process was observed and defined in 2009 during a study on mice. The other process, mitophagy, is a result of autophagy. When autophagy does its "job," mitochondria can experience selective degradation. This is most commonly observed when the mitochondria are stressed or damaged, making it defective. This process encourages mitochondrial turnover and also stops the dysfunctional mitochondria from piling up. If too much-damaged mitochondria accumulate the cell can begin to degrade. Even if there are healthy mitochondria present alongside dysfunctional mitochondria, the process is still applied to all present in the cell.

The Function of Autophagy

There are several functions of autophagy, including Xenophanes, nutrient starvation, infection, programmed cell death, and repair mechanisms. Autophagy is present in a variety of cellular functions for a variety of reasons. Below is a brief synopsis of these functions and how autophagy is involved.

Xenophagy

When an infectious particle enters the body, there is degradation caused by autophagy. This is a term most often applied and found in microbiology. In addition to breaking down an infected particle, this almost-mechanical process of autophagy in your cells is critical to helping your immune system. For example, if your body is attached by an intracellular pathogen such as the bacterium that causes tuberculosis, Mycobacterium tuberculosis, the mechanics and mechanisms that choose what mitochondria to degrade are also responsible for degrading this pathogen.

Nutrient Starvation

Autophagy is present at high levels in yeasts when there is nutrient starvation. This is necessary because the unnecessary proteins are degraded and recycled amino acids are used to synthesize the protein to keep your body alive. An example of this process being present is when an animal severs its ties with its trans-placental food supply after birth. Often in a body that is rich in nutrients form mutant cells of yeast that stop the autophagy process, but when those nutrients deplete, so do these mutant cells. When a body enters into starvation, this process is necessary to help keep the body alive as long as possible. It has been shown in studies with mice and is essential for vacuoles protein degradation when starving.

Infection

Your body has intracellular "danger" receptors, such as Galectin-8, which roam your body looking for trouble. When these receptors sense something is attacking the body, like vesicular stomatitis virus, they begin autophagy on the intracellular pathogens. Galectin-8, for example, binds to the critical vacuole and calls for an autophagy adaptor, like NDP52. This then begins the development of an autophagosome and the degradation of the bacteria.

Programmed Cellular Death

PCD, or "programmed cellular death," is related to the look of the autophagosome and relies on the protein in autophagy. This often is associated with a specific process, which is now called "autophagic PCD." There is still debate, much like the "chicken and the egg," about whether cell death caused this process or if this process caused the death of the cell. The process could be an attempt to repair the cell, or an attempt to stop cellular death, or it could be the reason the cell is dying. To this day, there are no histochemical or morphological studies that show the cause in the relationship between the death of the cell and the activity of autophagy in it. What was previously the favored opinion, that autophagy was actually causing the cells to die, has fallen in popularity as more evidence leans towards the possibility of the process trying to save the cell. For example, some arguments present insect metamorphosis as an example of a form of PCD that shows how the cells can be saved instead of killed. It is a distinct cellular change that no other example has shown. After a viral infection, the degree, and type of stress that signals for regulation can determine the chances of a cell of survival or death. These recent studies still need more research to show this relationship; however, the biochemical and pharmacological results are promising.

Repair Mechanism

The reason you age is that your body stops removing damaged cells, but rather allows them to accumulate in your body. This is why you begin to get wrinkles and your muscles begin to breakdown. Degeneration of autophagy is credited as one of the reasons for this cellular accumulation. This is because a working autophagic process breaks down the dysfunctional proteins, cell membranes, and organelles. If your body decides to no longer use this process, you begin to start aging. When there are lysosomal damage autophagy receptors, like by "directors" Galectin-8 and

Galectin-3, and autophagy is present. When this is triggered, galectins often call for help from other receptors like NDP52 and TRIM16. This also directly impacts AMPK and mTOR activity in your body. AMPK and mTOR, on the other hand, activate and also inhibit autophagy respectively in your body.

HOW AUTOPHAGY WORKS

A PHAGAPHORE IS THE "HALLMARK" OF THE AUTOPHAGY process. It is a double-membrane structure that moves around. Unlike secretory transport vesicles that separate from an organelle carrying "cargo" inside already, the phagophore picks up its load while it is assembling. The sequential expansion allows the phagophore to take on a little load or a large load. There is a lot of flexibility in how much they can carry. When it expands to load in something, it separates the cytoplasmic parts, including other, complete organelles, lipids, and proteins. As soon as it is loaded, it closes and turns into an autophagosome. Once matured into the autophagosome, the cargo remains contained in the lumen. Through-membrane fusion the autophagosome delivers its load to the lytic compartments. In plants and fungi, this is vacuole and in metazoans it is lysosomes. Once there, the cargo is degraded and recycled.

· · ·

*J*t is possible to see autophagy broadly categorized into two categories—nonselective and selective. It is categorized by what is being picked up or "eaten." When studied more extensively, it is broken down further into macroautophagy, microautophagy, and CMA, or chaperone-mediated Autophagy, as described in the previous chapter. In order for the cells in your body to be in balance or in homeostasis, autophagy must be present and functioning properly. In addition, autophagy is necessary for cellular survival when your body is stressed, such as when it is nutrient deficient. The process of autophagy is upregulated. This means that the degradation and sequestering of parts of the cell are determined by the severity of the situation. Once it arrives and assesses the "damage," the process returns macromolecules into the cytosol. This is essential to the metabolic reaction of the cell and generates power and energy.

*T*he process of autophagy is precisely orchestrated and tightly regulated. The pathological and physiological role it plays in your body is essential, as evidenced by its support in the health of your cells both when your body is under stress, like starvation or infection, and while healthy. It has been found that this process is also critical during the development of mammals. It is a vital modulator of a number of disorders and diseases as well. The role of the pathway is better understood when you understand autophagy's involvement in both human development and diseases. The implication of this knowledge can be used to more effectively treat disease as well as support general health. While it is now understood how the process works from a general function and morphology, the pathway is intricate and the exact steps in the process are still being discovered.

Autophagy Mechanisms

Large molecules are broken down in cells through multiple catabolic pathways. One of the most notable pathways is the collaboration of ubiquitin, a small protein, with an additional cellular protein. After, this typically leads to more ubiquitin molecules to create a chain of polyubiquitin. This releases amino acids, using proteasome to mark the protein for degradation. Other, similar mechanisms for degradation exist with additional biological polymers. For example, this process exists for lipids and carbohydrates as well.

There are two reasons why autophagy is unique: first, it is able to select what and how much cargo it wants to carry, and, second, it is very flexible. It can encourage degradation for a substantial variety and number of substrates, allowing cells to rapidly and effectively recycle the materials used in basic cellular building. This is especially important in the face of nutrient deficiency. In addition, the pathway of autophagy is the single one able to degrade an entire organelle. It can do this in a targeted manner or at random. The complicated setting for eukaryotic cells is balanced by this crucial process.

The process is very regulated, only releasing and increased when necessary. It is also tightly monitored so it can respond in a timely fashion. The TOR complex 1, or a cell's main metabolic sensor, is highly aware of how much amino acids and growth factors are present. It prevents autophagy when there is an abundance of these in the cell. When there are not enough of these present in the cell, the TOR complex 1 is turned "off," and autophagy is allowed to increase. While this is happening, additional molecular regulators keep an eye on cells for the levels of various nutrients, like glucose, or ATP energy. When the receptors sense that these items are low, they trigger autophagy.

*O*nce autophagy begins, multiple proteins related to autophagy, called Atg, come together to create the phagophore and the next steps of autophagy. In the 1990s, the ATG genes of yeast were discovered. This discovery altered the course of autophagy research and the understanding of the process forever. Prior to this discovery, autophagy was just a generic description of the process. After this, science understood that the process is a major mechanism occurring at the molecular level. Autophagy's primary mechanism was further defined in a study using Saccharomyces cerevisiae, budding yeast that is genetically tractable. After this, more research in other organisms has followed. This spiral of discovery showed the world the conservative evolution in the function and nature of the machinery in autophagy in all living forms—from humans to yeast.

*S*cientists are fairly clear about the process of autophagy, but the puzzle is far from being completed. There are still many missing pieces to the overall picture of autophagy. For example, it still remains to be established by autophagosome's membrane donor. In addition, scientists still cannot determine precisely how regulations of the expansion of the phagophore are accomplished. It is not understood how frequent autophagosome is generated. Additional questions come up when scientists look at the various types of autophagy and its selectivity as well as the mystery of the triggering and regulation process. Human disease, healthy development and growth, and development of embryos have all been linked to the autophagy process; hence, uncovering more information about the process is vital for human homeostasis.

When Autophagy Goes Wrong

Cancer, neurodegenerative disorders, and infectious disease are pathologies all linked to the deregulation of the autophagy process. As more research is produced, it is becoming more evident that the relationship between disease and autophagy is vital to creating more effective therapies and interventions for some of the worst human diseases impacting our society today.

Yasuko Rikihisa of the College of Veterinary Medicine at Virginia Tech, first reported the induction of autophagy in 1984. The study produced showed that when incubated mammalian cells were infected with a tick-borne illness, rickettsiae, the cells triggered autophagosomes to be formed. Unfortunately, the understanding of this process on eukaryotic cells has just begun. Part of this process has shown to limit inflammation. Inflammation is critical to helping the body heal from infection or disease, but extended inflammation can cause tissue damage and other diseases. These preliminary findings suggest that in addition to monitoring the elimination of pathogens, it can also prevent unnecessary tissue degradation by limiting the presence of inflammation at the site.

. . .

*a*t the Weill Cornell Medical College, J. Magarian Blander discovered that autophagy is vital to the stress response pathway of a cell when there is an infection present. The autophagy process is necessary for triggering the immune response after the stress is found in an infected cell. But at the Jan Lunemann's lab at the University of Zurich, it was discovered that it was not always helpful to modulate the immune system through autophagy. The process of autophagy may actually aggravate diseases like multiple sclerosis, or MS, which is an autoimmune disease impacting the central nervous system. Nerve degeneration and autoimmune disease is still an uncertain area for autophagy.

*I*t is clear, however, that one of the main roles of autophagy is protection against several neurodegenerative disorders, like Parkinson's Disease and Huntington's Disease. One of the main culprits that lead to Huntington's disease—the mutant HTT, an aggregation-prone protein—is degraded through autophagy, according to the research published by David Rubinsztein and his colleagues at the Cambridge Institute for Medical Research. With regard to Parkinson's disease, reduction of mitophagy is a primary reason for pathogenesis. This is not surprising and the understanding that homeostasis of mitophagy is necessary for healthy neurological functioning.

*C*ancer is also connected to autophagy. The Levine Group discovered in 1999 that mice with only one autophagy-related gene, Becn-1, had more tumors. Research has shown that autophagy is critical in preventing tumor creation and also in stopping malignancy in present tumors. The generation and progression of tumors have several factors that respond to this dual role autophagy plays in the process. Tumors are prevented because autophagy suppresses the known stressors that cause tumor growth, such as mitochondrial dysfunction, metabolic disruption, and genomic instability. But once a tumor is created, the "playing field" changes dramatically. Growth and proliferation of a cell with a tumor have more metabolic demands than a healthy cell. But because of cancer, the vasculature cannot supply it with the necessary nutrients. This means the cell relies on upregulating autophagy to meet its growing needs. This means that inhibiting autophagy can actually help "starve" cancer cells. The challenge scientists face with this knowledge is the balance necessary for tumor starvation without also causing neurodegeneration and increasing the likelihood of infection. Because the process is not straightforward and autophagy is still being revealed, it is important the therapies using autophagy for cancer treatment are approached with extreme care.

The study of autophagy is still underway and a popular field for exploration. It is exciting is for science to explore because of the many benefits it provides to our bodies. It plays a critical role in our health and wellbeing. While some crucial and beneficial mechanics have been revealed over the last several decades, understanding of autophagy is still in its early stages. Things related to the initiation, progression, and regulation have provided the present understanding of autophagy, but there are still many questions that scientists are looking to answer. In fact, many would say there are still more questions than answers, especially regarding proteins related to autophagy. Therapeutic intervention, in particular, is looking into the role autophagy plays in the process of pathophysiology. It is interesting to recognize that a person's instinctual need to eat to stay alive extends beyond the need to consume food, but it includes the need to eat oneself, at least, on a cellular level.

THE BENEFITS OF AUTOPHAGY

It may sound a bit ominous to say that you are eating yourself, but the reality is that your cells are doing this all the time inside of you. And the purpose is to help repair or remove damaged cells so you can live a healthy and balanced life. Some even claim that this process is the secret to a long life, even the "fountain of youth," if you will. When you need to save energy, fight away an infection, or heal damage, your body begins the autophagy process. This chapter outlines 12 of the most common and beneficial reasons you want autophagy in your life and working right.

1. It can help save your life.

This may sound a little dramatic, but it is true. This biological response has one primary purpose—to save you. Anytime something compromises your life at a cellular level, autophagy is triggered to stop it. This includes when your body is extremely stressed, you are invaded by infection, or when you are starving. The process seeks to minimize any damage and repair as much as possible. You can use this known and natural process in collaboration with other ancient healing techniques, like intermittent fasting where your body relies on fat for fuel and not glucose. This combination activates autophagy to help stave off infections, lower inflammation, and heal the damage caused by inflammation and infection. Glucose is an intruder and known invader. Inflammation is known to inhibit your immune system from functioning properly in the locations being inflamed. Because of autophagy, humans and almost all living beings have and still can use autophagy to conserve their energy and repair problems, especially in times where energy is not readily available. It is also a vital piece of the body's immune system and your ability to fight disease and reduce the risk of developing cancer.

2. It can help you live a longer and more full life.

hile the research is still being conducted in the area of this benefit, preliminary findings show that there are anti-aging benefits to autophagy as well. It may sound "too good to be true," but the benefits do not just stop at skin-level. Your cellular health is improved with a fast-acting and efficient autophagy response in your body. Cells do not simply bring in nutrients all the time; sometimes they degrade and remove parts that no longer work for them. They self-heal by recycling damage or removing toxins from their entity. As your body heals itself, the cells begin to function more efficiently. While they may be older cells, they have new energy and begin acting more like a newer cell. This can be used to explain why some people look much younger than their chronological age. Their biology suggests that they are much younger. The fewer toxins your body has to fight back, and how efficient your body is at healing itself, the younger your cells, and your overall body look.

3. It helps your metabolism function more efficiently.

*Y*our cells generate energy from mitochondria. They are the components that burn fat and create ATP or your body's currency for energy. Autophagy removes or helps replace parts of a cell, such as the mitochondria. As the mitochondria create energy, it leaves behind a lot of toxic build up. This can lead to cellular damage. Autophagy is a proactive process to help break the residue early to prevent the preventable "wear and tear" on your cells. In addition, the process of autophagy on other parts of the cell encourages the rest of the cell to work properly as well. It means that when it works more efficiently your cells create protein as well as burn off fuel. The healthier your cells are, the better you are at burning fuel sources. This means you have a more efficient and effective body.

4. It lowers your risk of developing a neurodegenerative disease.

*T*he proteins that are in your brain and around it begin to stop working correctly. They are not folded correctly and end up resulting in disease in your brain. This is a long time process, but the malfunction begins at a much earlier age. When your body is functioning properly, autophagy removes the proteins that are not working right. This means that these defective proteins do not have the ability to accumulate and build up, leading to these diseases. For example, Parkinson's disease requires autophagy to remove the a-synuclein and Alzheimer's disease requires it to remove amyloid. Both are malfunctioning proteins. When you have constantly high blood sugar, your body cannot remove the "clutter" that builds up around your brain. This is why many medical professionals recognize the connection between diabetes and dementia. Autophagy cannot activate when you have a lot of glucose, allowing this build up to occur. Stabilize blood sugar and you can clear more dysfunction, supporting your brain health.

5. It can help stabilize inflammation.

Not all inflammation is bad. Your body needs to send fluid and swelling to places that are damaged or infected to help isolate the damage before it can be cleared up. The problem lies when inflammation becomes a chronic condition. This starts to wreak havoc on your tissues and body. It leads to a host of illnesses and diseases. When your body is functioning properly, and autophagy can do its job, it creates the "just right" situation of inflammation in your body. It supports the triggering response for inflammation—either encouraging the inflammation or squashing it. For example, when there are invaders and inflammation is necessary, autophagy helps pass along the message that inflammation is necessary. In fact, it is autophagy that alerts your immune system that it needs to attack and just how it needs to do it. On the other hand, autophagy is also responsible for telling your immune system to lower your inflammation. Antigens are the proteins that are released to your immune system to trigger inflammation. When your cells do not need the inflammation, autophagy removes those signals.

6. It helps fight off infectious diseases.

*A*s mentioned previously, your immune system is recruited when autophagy calls for it. Viruses or microbes that reside in cells, such as HIV or Mycobacterium, can also be directly removed through autophagy. This is because it is a flexible and adaptive process that can take on small and large loads to support the health of your cells. In addition, when you suffer from an infection, it leaves behind various levels and kinds of toxins in your body. Autophagy removes these toxins. This is particularly helpful to you with food-borne illnesses.

7. It helps your muscles perform better.

*M*uscles need to be repaired after you work them out. The process of "building" muscle is actually an attack on the muscle, inflaming it and creating little micro-tears. This inflammation and tearing need to be healed. In addition, during exercise, you need more energy. Your body responds at a cellular level by triggering autophagy. It first begins by lowering the amount of energy necessary to work that targeted muscle. It then removes the damaged parts and helps bring homeostasis to your energy with the intention of preventing further damage to the area.

8. It helps prevent cancerous cells from forming.

· · ·

*T*he best way to treat a disease is to prevent the disease. This is especially true for cancer. Pro-cancer responses in your body, such as the response to damaged DNA, unstable genomes, and chronic inflammation, are suppressed with autophagy. In a study on mice that were genetically engineered to have a lower-functioning autophagy process, they experienced a significantly higher rate of cancer development than those with an average autophagy process. Once cancer develops, it can use the autophagy process to gather more fuel for its rapid growth and also "hide" from your immune system. More research on this relationship between cancer and autophagy is being conducted and necessary to make significant breakthroughs in more effective therapeutic options for those at risk and suffering from cancer. Additionally, it is still hazy how much damage chemotherapy-affected non-cancerous cells have on the process and activation of autophagy. More research is being conducted and necessary to identify if the damage of chemotherapy on cancer cells—by killing them directly—is better for you and your overall health than the ability of your own cells to handle the invasion. For example, if you could trigger autophagy to attack and treat those affected cells, is that a better treatment option than introducing chemotherapy? The results of this research could be revolutionary for cancer treatment in the future.

9. It can help your digestion and digestive health.

*Y*our gastrointestinal tract's cells in the lining are always working. Actually, if you are very curious, you can examine your feces and see that the majority of your excrement is actually made up of your own cells! When your

GI tract triggers autophagy, those cells are restored, repaired, and cleared out of toxins that they do not need. They also alert your immune system to turn on or off as needed. Chronic inflammation in your bowel is a common illness to battle. This is typically in response to a chronic trigger for your immune system to work in your GI tract. Having this constantly working ends up over-whelming your bowels, which means you need to be able to support this always-working system by giving it a chance to rest, repair, and renew. For example, giving your bowel an extended break from digesting food so it can properly trigger autophagy and heal itself is a great benefit you can encourage during intermittent fasting or fasting periods.

10. It can help clear and support the health of your skin.

*Y*our skin is the largest organ in your body and it is the one that also interfaces with the world around you. This means it is directly and immediately impacted by things like physical damage when something touches it, changes to the humidity levels, cold or hot temperatures, light, air pollution, and chemicals. Skin takes on a lot of damage and needs constant repair from the top of your head to the bottoms of your feet. When skin cells have accumulated toxins or damage, they stay where they are and they age. Your skin cells are constantly being replaced without autophagy, but the process of autophagy is necessary for helping heal and repair your existing ones. This helps the skin stay young and "glow." Because of the skin cell's interaction with exterior influence, there is a greater opportunity for them to collect bacteria that can lead to serious damage to your body. The best way to support your skin cells is to take care of your skin from the inside and out. The more you support your autophagy process, the better your skin will look and feel.

11. It helps you maintain or achieve a healthy weight.

*T*here are several reasons your autophagy process supports a healthy weight. Here is a quick list of a few of those reasons;

- Autophagy protects your protein but burns your fat for fuel. If you are fasting for an extended period of time, you will lose mass from protein loss, but shorter fasts trigger autophagy to burn your fat stores for energy and protect your protein levels. This means you will settle into healthier weight for your body type.
- Autophagy stops unnecessary and chronic inflammation. Chronic inflammation triggers your body to store energy because of the increase in insulin. As you lower your insulin levels through autophagy, the less inflammation you have, allowing your weight to find a healthy balance.
- Autophagy lowers the toxin levels present in your cells. If you can get the toxins out of your body, the fewer fat cells you need to store the "baggage."
- Autophagy helps your metabolism be more efficient. It encourages this efficiency by healing cellular parts that create and "package" proteins and create energy. This is very helpful when your cells switch from burning glucose for energy instead of fat.

12. It minimizes the deaths of your cells.

. . .

here is a term often confused with autophagy, apoptosis. Autophagy is about self-consumption of cells, while apoptosis is cellular death. Unlike autophagy, cellular death is messy and leaves behind garbage that needs to be cleaned up. Your body triggers inflammation to go to the site and get it back to working order. If you can prevent your cells from dying this messy death by encouraging repair or clean removal, the less effort your body requires to clean up and create new cells. In addition, you will minimize unnecessary inflammation by self-eating instead of destroying. Reducing the number of cellular deaths allows that energy to be reallocated to help create new cells that have a higher turnover, like your GI tract or your skin. Not all cells require constant replacement, so the more you can repair the existing ones, the more you allow your body to spend its energy elsewhere, the better your health will be.

HOW TO ACTIVATE AUTOPHAGY

You may be onboard with the idea of having your cells eat each other, but are probably now wondering how you would go about doing it. Or more accurately, how you would trigger your body to kick start this process for you. The good news is that autophagy is a response to stress. This means that when you stress your body in certain ways, the process is triggered. But not all stress will do the trick. When you add a little bit extra stress to your body, the self-consumption process is elevated. This added stress can be uncomfortable at the moment, but the idea is that this little bit of extra stress can lead to incredible, long-term joy. Adding more stress in a controlled manner can result in amazing benefits to your body. There are three primary ways to induce your autophagy process; exercise, fasting, and decrease your carbohydrate intake significantly.

Exercise

. . .

*Y*ou have probably heard for a long time now that diet and exercise are the keys to a long and healthy life. This is no different, and the science to back up this is here for you in the first and second chapters. Exercise stresses your body at the moment. This is why people have pains after a hard workout, grunt when it is challenging, and sweat. Working out your muscles is actually damaging them, as introduced in the previous chapter. When your muscles work hard, they get little tears in them that need to be repaired. Your body responds to these tears quickly, and while repairing the damage you just did, the body makes the muscle stronger so it can resist any future "damage" you might inflict upon it. You may not think of exercising as a way to clean out your cellular build up or toxins, but its one of the most common and popular ways to renew your cells. This helps explain why you feel so fresh and rejuvenated after a good, hard workout.

*I*n one study on mice with highlighted autophagosomes, the researchers found that after they ran on a treadmill for 30 minutes their autophagy process was dramatically increased. An autophagosome is a resulting structure in the autophagy process. It forms around the damaged or toxic part of the cell and removes it to be disposed of, leaving behind the healthy parts of the cell. The increase in exercise provided evidence that these became more efficient and frequent than when the mice for less active. And it did not just increase the rate of autophagy while exercising! The increased rate of self-consumption continued for 80 minutes after stopping exercise. While there are no concrete studies or information regarding how much or how often a human should exercise to increase autophagy, it is clear the relationship exists in humans as well. Dr. Daniel Klionsky, a University of Michigan cellular biologist, explains that it is hard to determine the level of exercise a human must undergo to trigger their autophagy process, but there are so many clear benefits to exercise that no matter what you do, it will help support your body on some level. The best assumption to make in this case is to engage in more intense exercise regimens a few times a week for the best results. This is for general health benefits, but will also be the best amount of controlled stress on your body to trigger your autophagy.

Fasting

*C*leanses that introduce any form of food or drink besides water into the body will actually prevent the trigger of autophagy, not allowing the body to effectively cleanse itself of toxins, as desired on a cleanse. Instead, simply skipping a meal or two or three can be the best stress on the body that triggers autophagy, offering a true cleanse. Your body will probably not like it at the moment, but the benefits will be something it will enjoy for a long time. Research has shown, over and over again, that engaging in an occasional fast can help you lower risks of various illnesses like heart disease and diabetes. The reason for these benefits that medical professionals and scientists claim is because of autophagy.

*T*here are several studies that have been published that specifically look at fasting, autophagy, and brain health. It is clear there is a distinct connection between lowering the risk of developing a neurodegenerative disease, like Parkinson's disease or Alzheimer's disease, when you engage in short-term fasts. Other studies reveal that intermittent fasts help support proper brain function, brain structure, and neuroplasticity. This is what helps your brain learn new information easier. While this information is exciting, it is not completely clear if autophagy is the reason and most of these studies are conducted on animals. While the benefits are promising, they are not always applicable to human subjects.

*T*here are a variety of adaptations for intermittent fasting, and it is something that can fit into almost anyone's life because of this. You can choose to abstain from eating food anywhere between 12 to 36 hours in a stretch, always drinking a lot of water during the fast. You can also engage in moderate to light physical activity during this time to help your body upregulate the results, but it is not typically advisable to engage in intense workouts during a fasting period. In addition, you can choose to fast only during certain times of the year, a certain day of the month, or one or more days a week.

Decrease Your Intake of Carbohydrates

*F*asting on a regular basis can be a challenge for many people, especially if you are used to constantly eating. In addition, this is contradictory to a lot of popular advice available now, encouraging people to eat little meals consistently throughout the day to boost metabolism. What research has shown, however, is that eating constantly does not keep your metabolism and hunger "satisfied," but rather creates a constant "hunger" hormone that keeps you wanting to eat and eat. Instead, when you fast, you learn the difference between true hunger and a triggered response at the time you normally eat a meal. You break your body of these habits and encourage it to focus on your cellular repair and fat-fuel burning instead. If you are having trouble getting into an intermittent fasting schedule, you can mimic the benefits in another way by decreasing your intake of carbohydrates.

*T*his similar process is called ketosis. A lot of people who work out regularly or are looking to improve their long-term health and well-being have been turning to this type of eating regimen. The concept aims to significantly reduce the carbs that are consumed so your body must use the fat for fuel instead of injected glucose from the conversion of the carbs. When your body enters into ketosis, it mirrors a lot of the same changes to your metabolism that autophagy offers. You get to enjoy the benefits of fasting without having to complete fast. In addition to the similar benefits to your metabolism, ketosis has been shown to help you maintain healthy body weight, protect your muscle mass, prevent and fight tumors, lower your risk of type-2 diabetes, minimize the risk of neurological diseases, and treat some brain disorders, like epilepsy. For example, in one recent study, more than 50% of the children with epilepsy that followed this diet experienced more than half the frequency of seizures than their peers not following the diet.

*I*n addition to removing a lot of the carbs, you increase your intake of healthy fat. Most of your calories, up to 70%, come from fat on the Keto diet. This means eating a lot of meat, avocado, peanut butter, to name a few. Protein is up to 30% of your daily caloric intake. If you have room for carbs, you need to keep them to less than 50 grams every day. This is an extreme diet that many people ease into over time. If you can, being with a mix of fat/protein/carbs with your carb intake not exceeding 30% of your daily caloric intake and work back from there. Some find this regimen of eating more challenging than fasting, so it is wise to look into and try out what method works best for you in triggering your autophagy response.

*I*f you are still looking at these three primary methods for triggering autophagy and wondering if there are other, easier ways, you will be discouraged to find that there are none. There will be a lot of money when researchers find a way to trigger autophagy or mimic it in a synthetic form like a pill, and it is being researched and considered now, but this is a long way off. Until the process is better understood, it is not possible to chemically induce the process in a human body. It is also unwise to turn to synthetic and chemical methods to avoid dieting and exercise for your well-being. It is also important to note that there are anti-epilepsy drugs being developed to mirror the state of ketosis in the body. If those become available, it is probable that people will begin taking them to mimic autophagy in the body instead of approaching it through traditional diet and exercise methods.

*K*eep in mind that the process of ketosis in the body is complex, as the process of autophagy. The idea that a single pill can mimic this entire, intricate and complex process is unrealistic. The stress required to enter ketosis, for example, may be an integral part of the process. This means you will need to still exert effort and energy to get the pill to work, in any form. It is also likely that the pill will only encourage one or two of the benefits of ketosis for a person suffering from epilepsy, and not target any other benefits of ketosis. Yes, the three methods of activating autophagy and ketosis listed above all require effort and it is important to also remember that you do not need to do each of them every day to get the results and benefits. Just a couple of hours a week or month can do the trick for supporting your cellular health.

Finally, there are plenty of published research available to show the indication of the various benefits of autophagy as well as how to activate it in a healthy way. The little bit of short-term and controlled stress can lead to controlled and systematic self-destruction so you can end up living a longer, healthier life. It is an ancient survival process that is designed to help the body in times of stress, like when your ancestors had to go days between meals that they hunted to feed themselves and their family. Starvation and physical exertion have the ability to kill you, but over millions of years, human bodies have evolved to turn those "bad" situations into something that can actually help you.

EXTENDED WATER FASTING

If you want to greatly improve your health and life, you can turn to this ancient strategy for healing and health; water fasting. Keep in mind; however, this process requires practice, patience, and strategy. You do not want to begin this fasting method without prior planning and research. You need to understand what the results can be, what it does to your body, and what can happen if you are not carefully monitoring your progress.

The first thing you need to know is why you should consider fasting. There are many different benefits to fasting. For starters, it is the absolute best method for controlling your insulin and glucose levels. Even better than medicine! One of the best measures for a healthy, long, and meaningful life is your glucose levels. If you can keep these controlled, you can expect to live a healthy, long life. You want your body to run on its own energy source, fat cells, not on spikes of insulin and glucose. If you keep these levels low and stable, your body will keep using its own fuel for energy. Also, fasting helps to keep testosterone levels even. When you eat, your testosterone levels lower, which is what triggers an increase in insulin and glucose. This, in turn, increases inflammation and ultimately aging of your cells. When you establish a lasting habit, your body changes its relationship with food. You recognize that you do not "need" food all the time to stay active and healthy. Your body discovers, or rather re-discover, that it is able to maintain a healthy level of glucose and fuel itself with its fat stores.

Another benefit of fasting is autophagy itself. When autophagy increases, so do a host of health benefits in your body, as described in the previous chapter. This response to fasting can lead to amazing and "miraculous" changes to your body, like improved skin appearance and texture, shrinking cancer, and cured diseases, among others. One researcher found that engaging in a water-only fast for four days can help reset your immune system. Some people need a longer fast, especially in the beginning, while others can do it for only a day or two to experience the benefits. It is best to work with a medical professional and closely observe your body during this time to make sure it is reaching its optimal reset. As you age, your blood begins to accumulate a lot of T-cells. Each one is programmed to fight a certain microbe. But the problem is that these T-cells have been programmed, and you do not have enough "student" T-cells that can learn to adapt to new problems. This compromises your immune system. When you fast, however, you give your body time to remove the unnecessary cells and rebuild your immune system with the "student" T-cells.

The third benefit of extended water fasting is epigenetics. This means the process of changing the "bad" genes into "good" ones, encouraging the "good" genes to do more, and turning off "bad" ones that cannot or will not convert. Anytime you fast, your genes start to shift back to their natural, beginning state. They are changed into healthier versions of themselves and also positively impact your dietary choices. This can occur during a single day fast or during extended fasts, but the more frequent you fast and support the natural and healthy state of your genes, the better benefits you can experience.

The final benefit of extended water fasting includes hormone sensitivity. You can really experience the shift in your hormones when you fast. One particular hormone that you can notice a change in is your growth hormone. During a fasting period, you are not creating more hormones, but rather, becoming more sensitive and aware of the ones you have. Any hormone connected to your health and healing is dramatically increased during fasting periods.

In addition to being clear about what you can experience when you fast, it is clear about why you want to fast. It is important to be clear about why you want to trigger autophagy. For some people, it is to lose weight but for others, it is to support their health. Take a moment to be honest about your intentions with autophagy and fasting, so that as you begin your process, you know how to monitor your progress and success accurately. For example, if your goal is to support your general health and minimize the risk for cancer and other diseases, tracking your weight is not the best gauge for success. If you are looking to find and maintain a healthy weight, monitoring your hormones may not be the best use of your time. Your "why" can be deeper as well. Many people turn to autophagy and fasting to prolong their life so they can be a meaningful part of their family for a longer period of time. Others do it to control a disease that they have been diagnosed with. And still, others fast for religious reasons.

The task of extended water fasting is a challenge. It is best to begin the preparation for this type of autophagy trigger by mentally preparing for the timeframe. There will be a time when it feels like your body and your mind are aligning to beg you for food. It is stressed and operating in uncharted territory. You are breaking long-held habits and patterns, which is stressful. But remember, when you hit day three and you are longing for a big meal, that this stress and it leads to amazing benefits later. You need to mentally prepare ahead of time for this temptation and challenge. How will you plan on overcoming these urges in a healthy manner? This temptation and desire will occur for a day or two and then you can expect to have a shift in perception. Your mindset changes and your mental acuity are returned. You are no longer obsessed with food but are rather turned away by the idea of it. At this point, your body has realized that it is operating better now without the glucose-fueled energy it was used to before. Prepare yourself to get through the "tough times" so you can get to this state.

While you are on your extended water fast, it is advisable to prepare for changes to your mental alertness. Before starting, you may have some "brain fog." You could experience trouble concentrating and remembering things. When you are fasting, your alertness may be enhanced. You feel more focused and engaged. You have a better memory. It is like the fog is lifted. Prepare to experience a dip in this process. However, as you enter into the phase where your body and mind are asking for food, your mental acuity could be limited. You may find yourself constantly distracted, having trouble focusing on anything other than food, and being forgetful. This is your body adjusting. Once you leave this phase, you will return to this clear and focused mental awareness that you experienced before. It can seem like a dramatic swing each time, but when you experience the clarity, you will know what stage you are dealing with.

It is also important to consider the weight loss you will experience rapidly. When you fast you can expect to drop large amounts of weight quickly. You are also experiencing a removal of toxins that have been stored for a long time in your body, particularly deep in your tissues. The good news is that your body will not drop into unhealthy territory right away. In fact, it will drop down rapidly to a healthy weight balance and sit there. If you find you drop weight and then it stagnates for a while at a certain number, chances are that weight is where you need to be for your body's homeostasis. As you continue to fast, you will see fluctuations in your weight still, but not as dramatic once you reach your balance. This is in part because your body instinctively knows that it needs to remove the affected tissue and dysfunctional DNA but leave the healthy muscle alone. When you do this, medical professionals are in awe about how your body will eat a tumor while fasting. Endometriosis, a reproductive issue involving scar tissue, is also consumed while fasting and as autophagy is increased. Other benefits you can experience include cleared congestion and better breathing patterns.

It is also possible for others to experience weight gain. As you heal your gut, your body can then begin to build muscle like it was not able to do previously. As you increase hormones like your growth hormone, estrogen, and testosterone, you can expect your body to absorb food better. This can lead to weight gain for those that need it in order to reach a more balanced, healthy weight. Bodybuilders use this fasting then feasting method to help them rapidly gain weight in muscle mass.

You can track your levels during a fast to make sure things are progressing as they should. For example, you should be able to see that your glucose levels are dropping down low and that ketones are rising. Ketones are necessary for you to enter into ketosis, a benefit described in the previous chapter. Glucose needs to be minimal in your body so that your cells switch to using fat as a fuel source instead. You can track your levels with blood, urine, or saliva testing kits. Ketones should remain anywhere from 0.5 mmol/L and 5.0 mmol/L so your body is functioning properly in ketosis. Some people can operate at a healthy level with ketones as high as 7.0 mmol/L; however, you do not want them to rise about 8.0 mmol/L. For glucose, you want your numbers in the 60s if your ketones are above 3.0 mmol/L. This "sweet spot" is what most people believe and see as the best place for bad cell removal and repair. If you can get to this balance between ketones and glucose you can be sure that your body is functioning optimally.

During your extended water fast, make time for rest. You may experience a dip in energy, especially in the beginning days, but you will probably still feel a good amount of energy. Be careful not to overexert yourself during this time, though. Exercise on extended water fast will do more harm than good right now. Your stores of protein are healing and exercise can damage this process. Minor to moderate activity is ok, but try to avoid anything too aggressive. Give your body the time it needs to restore itself by taking it easy during this time.

The concept is simple, do not eat anything, and drink plain water only. Maybe sprinkle a little sea salt for something different, but try not to introduce in anything that can kick in your metabolism. But while it is simple to grasp, applying it and sticking to it is not. Like preparing for the "hard days," when your body and mind are asking for a big, greasy meal, you need to remember that most of this is a mental game. You have habits and neuropathways that have been ingrained for a long time that you are altering. It is not wrong, but it does take control. Bringing in a support team to help keep you motivated can do wonders when your mind is struggling. Maybe this is a significant other who is cheering on you, or a "partner in crime," who is doing it along with you. It can be your healthcare professional or any person who will help you stay on the course. You need to make the commitment, stick to it, rely on your support system, and be clear about your purpose. And if you fail, just give it another try. Every little step you make towards supporting your health is beneficial, so just keep going!

INTERMITTENT FASTING

THERE ARE SEVERAL STUDIES ON THE BENEFITS AND EFFECTS of intermittent fasting on the body. There are several different "kinds" of intermittent fasting, but one of the most common is fasting from 12 to 36 hours one or more days during the week. The process of autophagy is vital to the homeostasis of living organisms at a cellular level, and it has been found in various living entities including humans, bugs, animals, fungi, plants, and yeast. It helps the body defend itself against neurological diseases, infections, and malignancies. There are many trials looking to capitalize on the benefits of autophagy and the defense against these harmful illnesses that are affecting millions. Instead of turning to medicines and chemicals, many researchers are encouraging people to look towards a short-term restriction of food instead. This is also called intermittent fasting.

. . .

*T*he regulation and process of autophagy involve events at a molecular level and the studies in tissue and yeast culture have added to the contemporary understanding of how it works in your body. Unfortunately, it is hard to see the process in tissues and organs that are intact, particularly the brain. It is not hard to see because of the lack of vivo mammalian models. For example, a study on a mouse provided excellent identification and evidence of the autophagy process through its production of autophagosomes and the associated protein. This study, in particular, is most often referenced marker for mammalian cells and the autophagy process. There have also been many studies on mice regarding intermittent fasting and the restrictions in vivo. Many researchers and scientists agree that autophagy is triggered during intermittent fasting and it affects many tissues and organs in the body. What is not known are its effects on the brain. Scans after two days of intermittent fasting showed no indication of autophagy in the brain. This seems to indicate that the brain is somehow more metabolically "privileged." It also indicates that a more serious stressor, such as a direct brain injury or trauma, is required to stimulate autophagy in this particular organ.

*F*urther studies on this relationship have shown that this is not the case. One particular study on mice shows that intermittent fasting does have an effect on the autophagy process in the brain. Their approach revealed that at a certain resolution autophagosomes are increased and categorized in detail. In addition to this approach, the study published in 2010 in the scientific journal, *Autophagy*, titled "Short-term fasting induces profound neuronal autophagy," it used another method that is a bit more standard, the TEM, or transmission electron microscopy. This traditional method definitively exposed that there was a significant increase in autophagosomes in the brains of mice that were following an intermittent fasting diet. This is unlike previous conclusions, but this study clearly and definitively proves that restricting food through short-term diets, or intermittent fasting, can trigger a rapid and profound response in autophagy in the body and in the brain.

For many millions of years and across many cultures, intermittent fasting is practiced for cultural and spiritual reasons. In recent years, science has begun to explore the relationship between a person's health and intermittent fasting and have concluded there are numerous benefits to this diet plan. This "proof" may be more modern, but many cultures have long understood that there are incredible benefits when you restrict food intake for a short period of time. Prior to the study published in 2010 mentioned above, the benefits seemed to apply to your entire body, with the exception of your brain. The previous train of thought was that the brain was somehow spared the effects of short-term nutrient deprivation, including the positive benefit of autophagy. The rest of your body was able to enjoy the benefits— removed toxins, repaired cells, and refreshed immune system. While it could make sense to "spare" the brain the stress of nutrient restriction, even for a short period of time, the loss of upregulated autophagy in the brain was concerning.

Thankfully, after the study published in 2010, a contemporary understanding of intermittent fasting and autophagy has changed. Now, the scientific community understands that intermittent fasting benefits the body and the brain. There is actual evidence that there is a dramatic increase in autophagy in the brain, as well as the body when a person participates in an intermittent fasting diet plan. It is especially seen in the Purkinje and cortical neurons. This finding in 2010 led to additional studies on therapeutic applications of intermittent fasting and neurodegenerative diseases and other brain disorders. It is from this study that modern science now sees how autophagy cleanses the brain tissue and restores your brain back to the desired balance.

*D*uring the study, there were three novel conclusions and observations that are worth noting, particularly when it comes to autophagy and intermittent fasting;

1. In mammals, especially in the mice used in the study, which consumed an average diet, the researchers were able to localize and identify autophagosomes in both the Purkinje and cortical neurons.
2. In those specific neurons, when food was restricted for a short time, during the mouse's intermittent fasting period, there was a significant increase in the number of autophagosomes, which were observed alongside physical changes to the subject's characteristics as well. The results of their observations were either from the lower rate of fusion between lysosomes and autophagosomes or from the increase creation of autophagosomes. The key protein that restrains autophagy, mTOR, is reduced in the Purkinje cells of a mouse that is intermittent fasting, leading to the conclusion that the observation is from the increased

production of autophagosomes. This is why the conclusion of the study explains that having more autophagosomes is from an increase in production rather than from a blockage to the maturation of the autophagosome. But it is worth noting that there is no concrete evidence of this at this time.

3. It is important to note that the changes resulting from intermittent fasting are different depending on what cell in the brain you are looking at. This is because the process of autophagy differs from one cell type to the next in your body. This is an adaptation or evidence of evolution in the body to help meet the physiological needs of the individual cells. When autophagy is blocked in studies, it is clear that the outcome of this is determined by the tissue or cell type it was not able to respond to. For instance, in a study where the autophagy to the brain was interrupted, the brain experienced a degenerative disease. Prior to this observation, it was assumed that cells that were similar would have similar responses to an increase in autophagy, but now it is shown that this is not the case in vivo. While there was an increase in autophagosomes, the distribution and size had some differences as well as similarities in both types of cells. Because there is a difference between these similar cells, and this observation challenges the previous assumptions regarding cellular response and autophagy, it is clear more research is needed in this area. It is particularly important to study this further in relation to intermittent fasting.

*T*here is significant clinical relevance to the discovery of intermittent fasting and its role in supporting the health of the body and the brain. It has been known for a long time that restricting the process of autophagy to the brain can lead to neurodegenerative diseases. The findings of this study described in this chapter suggest the reverse is true, too; that upregulating the production of autophagy can actually help prevent and treat neurodegenerative diseases. This process can actually help protect your brain. For example, in one study, it is shown that when a model is starved in vitro the neuronal cell lines begin to eliminate molecules that are toxic as well as mitochondria that are damaged from the affected neuron. In another study on tissue cultures, the mutant proteins responsible for Huntington disease and Parkinson's disease, a-synuclein, are able to be removed using autophagy induced by intermittent fasting.

*O*n the other hand, there are some studies that indicate intermittent fasting improves your mind, not because of the lack of caloric intake, but because of the natural response that is triggered when your body begins to fast. In order for a drug to replicate the effects of intermittent fasting on the brain especially, it must first be able to pass through the blood-brain barrier. Once it reaches the brain intact, it then needs to stimulate the upregulation of the autophagy in the brain. And even if the drug is capable of the first two processes, scientists need to also make sure that the process and the chemicals are harmless to the subject. The medical world is years away from accomplishing something like that. Instead, intermittent fasting is a simple, inexpensive, healthy, and reliable method for supporting the health of your body and your brain. It is an excellent alternative to taking a drug to regulate and heal your body. This is why intermittent fasting is such an attractive process for cleansing and healing your body and brain. Keep in mind, as mentioned in extended water fasting, watching your body's response is necessary. If you chronically starve your body, it can lead to autophagy inhibition instead of upregulation. This could lead to neuronal damage, rather than protection, and defeat the purpose of the practice.

One of the best things you can do, when you determine to try this method for your mental and physical health and protection, is to find a healthcare professional that can support and monitor you along the way. The effects of a short-term, intermittent fast are not as significant as the extended water fast suggested in the previous chapter, but it will still lead to stress on your body and challenges. Again, most of the challenge is mental, meaning you need to gather a good support team to encourage your progress, and you also need to prepare for your success. Begin by coming up with your purpose for intermittent fasting. Perhaps it is to support your mental clarity and protection, as the focus of this chapter describes, or maybe it is to lose weight or support your general health. Being clear about your purpose will allow you to turn back to it when you want to reach for something to eat during a fasting period. In addition, you will want to have a plan in place when those tempting times happen. There will be times when you are supposed to be fasting but you are tempted to break your fast. Determine how you will respond to these situations.

Finally, involve your support system in your goals. Maybe recruit a friend, family member, or loved one to join you on your intermittent fasting schedule. Have people support you and keep you on track. This group will be your strength when you are stressed and challenged. Once you find a schedule and break your old habits, these will not be as critical, but in the beginning, they can make the difference between successfully completing a fasting period and not. And, as mentioned before, if you do not make it through a fasting period, do not be too hard on yourself. Any step to support your health is good, so just keep going!

THE FASTING-MIMICKING DIET

YOUR LONG-TERM HEALTH CAN BE IMPROVED, IT IS FULL OF nutrients, and it is scientifically supported. As an alternative to the two other dieting methods mentioned in the previous chapters, this diet allows you to still eat food but enjoy the benefits of fasting. If you do not think you could take on a full fast, this is something worth trying and exploring, especially in the beginning. It is a modified type of fast. You do not cut out food completely, but you do eat a small amount that still produces the results of a fast on your body. This is something you can do a few times a week to get the best results. You can also follow this type of diet for five consecutive days to also get the most out of your efforts. The food you consume needs to have a good combination of calories, protein, and carbs, and be high in fat. Your caloric intake needs to be less than 40% of your normal limit. This is what encourages your body to enjoy the therapeutic benefits of fasting while still supporting your body with electrolytes and nutrients and a lot less stress.

. . .

*I*f you restrict your calories for too long or fast for too long, you can end up harming your body and counteracting your purpose. On the other hand, following a fasting-mimicking diet can be safer for longer periods of time. It can also be more effective if you follow it right.

Fasting-Mimicking Versus Fasting

*O*ne of the similarities you will find right away regarding fasting and fasting-mimicking diet is the proliferation of rumors and myths. For example, it is common to hear people claim that your muscles will deteriorate if you do this diet or fast. You may also hear claims that you will stunt your metabolism or that it is an extremely unhealthy thing to do to your body. While these facts are true for a person who is actually starving, or is cutting out, or restricting for years, it is simply not true for someone who is rationally approaching fasting or the fasting-mimicking diet. Unhealthy approaches, like actually starving yourself or severely cutting calories for months or years, can result in damage to your metabolism and are particularly dangerous for people who have other health concerns. But, especially with fasting-mimicking diets, you get all the benefits of fasting without you actually cutting out food completely. This means far less and not as severe side effects.

Benefits of Fasting-Mimicking Diet

*I*f you return to the previous chapters outlining the benefits of autophagy and the benefits of fasting in relation to autophagy, you could basically "copy and paste" them here. They are essentially the same:

- Refresh and renew your immune system
- Increased removal and recycling of damaged or dysfunctional cells or cellular parts, including cancerous and infectious particles
- An upregulated autophagy process throughout your body
- Ketosis lowers the amount of fat tissue in the body
- Less oxidative stress and C-reactive proteins in the body, most likely because of the autophagy process
- Longevity promoted through increased expression of your genes
- Improved brain development, protection, prevention, and performance through upregulated autophagy as well as more BDNF, or brain-derived neurotrophic factors. BDNF helps the brain grow new neurons and current neurons survive longer.
- Lowered glucose levels, better regenerative markers, and homeostatic stem cell levels
- Lowered risk for various diseases such as cancer, diabetes, and neurodegenerative diseases like Parkinson's and Alzheimer's.

By mirroring or "ticking" your body into thinking it is fasting, your body can trigger and stimulate these responses in your body so you can enjoy these benefits. What you are also doing is making sure that your body continually receives the nutrients it needs and craves every day.

How the Process Works

*A*s you begin your research into fasting-mimicking diet plans, it is important to start in the same manner as the other two methods listed earlier; start with your "why" or your purpose. Be clear about why you are doing this diet and what you want to get from it. If it is to lower your risk of cancer, how will you make sure you are supporting this health goal and know what you are doing is working? If you want to improve your mental focus, how will you measure this for success? Start with a purpose, develop a plan, and determine how you will know it is "working" for you. This preparation will make sure you are ready for the challenges that inevitably lie ahead.

*M*ost research on the fasting-mimicking diet suggests that five or more days are best to get your glucose levels low enough that your body enters ketosis, or begins burning fat for fuel instead of glucose. This means you want your glucose index below 1.0. For some people, especially those that have done this diet a few times, they will only need to follow it for three or four days to see the results, while others may always need to follow it for six or seven days. Do not extend this diet past seven days at a time to best support your general health. You can do this diet a couple times in a year or even once a month. The more you do it, the better your body will be at switching over into ketosis and the faster and more results you will see.

· · ·

*I*t is a good idea to measure your biomarkers to track your outcomes. You can do this with conducting labs before and after the fast or by measuring your blood glucose and ketones throughout your fasting period. Track these markers daily along with your weight to determine if the fast and caloric plan is working well for you. You may want to adjust your caloric intake up or down depending on these biomarkers. You can have a healthcare professional help you draw labs before and after your fast, or you can get at-home blood glucose and ketone test kit to monitor for yourself. An at-home bathroom scale is also helpful in this process.

*A*s you begin to prepare for your fast, prepare your environment appropriately. This means alerting your support system of what you are doing, as well as others around you that you will come in contact with during the fast. Tell them your purpose for it and why their support is helpful to you. Having someone who is doing it with you and is keeping the same schedule can be helpful as well. Also, clear out snacks and "junk food" from your house, car, and work. Remove any and all temptations, especially during your fast. Plan to get enough rest over the several days of your fast. You will probably notice a drop in energy levels as your body tries to adjust to the reduction in glucose energy supply. If you prepare for this with enough time blocked out for a good night sleep, and maybe a nap or two here and there, you will be much happier during the process. This does not mean you need to avoid daily activity or physical activity altogether. Light to moderate physical activity is good for you during this time and can actually speed up the process. Avoid strenuous actions, like long distance running or weight training, but a nice walk or yoga can be beneficial.

Some Facts To Know

*A*s you begin this diet plan, you may want to consider "easing" into it by eating foods with higher caloric content, about 50% of your total intake, and then bringing it down towards the remaining few days to between 35% and 40% of your normal caloric intake. Also, stock up on snacks and foods that are easy to grab, digest, and are satisfying in small amounts. You can look into the brand ProLon, which has developed prepackaged foods for the fasting-mimicking diet. You can get the entire kit of food designed for a five-day fasting-mimicking diet plan. They are plant-based and adjusted for a normal, healthy adult woman and man's caloric intake. One day includes meals like a tea and mixed nut bar for breakfast, kale crackers, and soup for lunch, olives for a snack, and soup for dinner. The process is meant to take the prep and stress out of the diet so you can just enjoy the benefits.

*O*f course, you do not need to buy something pre-packaged to enjoy the benefits of the fasting-mimicking diet. A ketogenic diet, which is low in carbs, is great to follow on a fasting-mimicking diet, and just requires you to space out your calories appropriately during the fasting period. It is a wise idea to plan meals for your entire fast so there is nothing to think about during the five or so days.

· · ·

A typical macro breakdown for a fasting-mimicking diet on the first day includes:

- Carbs: 34%
- Protein: 10%
- Fat: 56%

*A*fter the first day, adjust for the following macros:

- Carbs: 47%
- Protein: 9%
- Fat: 44%

*T*hese macros are different than the ketogenic diet, so adjust accordingly if you decide to follow that meal plan while restricting your calories during your fasting period.

*Y*ou are not restricted from having some conveniences during your fasting-mimicking diet, either. For example, you can have a cup of black coffee, with no sugar added, or tea. You can add coconut oil if you want, but you need to track the macros appropriately. You do not need to drink these beverages if you do not want to, and just stick to water, but they are available should you choose.

. . .

*A*lso, you may want to consider taking a supplement on your fasting days to make sure your body is getting all the required nutrients. This is especially beneficial as you learn how to balance your plate with a lower caloric limit. If you are already following a balanced and healthy diet, you may not need to supplement, but for those who need it, consider the following:

- Salt and magnesium to replenish electrolyte loss
- Liver tablets (grass-fed) to support micronutrients
- BCAA's or branch chain amino acids to prevent tissue loss, especially if you are working out heavily during your fasting days
- Powdered greens to offer a dose of micronutrients
- Algal oil or cod liver oil for omega-3

Ketosis and Fasting-mimicking Diets

*B*efore you start the ketogenic diet, it may be a good idea to start with a fasting-mimicking diet. It can help get your body into ketosis faster when you begin the ketogenic diet. In addition, focusing on ketogenic foods can help you remain in ketosis for the length of your diet. This means you will want to adjust your macros to something more like this:

- Carbs: 5-10%
- Protein: 20-25%
- Fat: 70-80%

n the ketogenic diet, the best bet is to choose something high in fat every time. This includes:

- Avocados
- Grass-fed butter
- Bone Broth
- Coconut milk
- Coconut oil

BONUS! WEIGHT LOSS AND AUTOPHAGY

So you want to lose weight? Maybe it is your primary reason for looking into autophagy, or it is an additional benefit you are excited about. Hopefully, by now, you recognize that through autophagy, one of the great benefits is that you can finally get rid of that stubborn ten (or more) pounds that seem to never leave. And you can do this alongside a healthy process that is natural and beneficial to your body. How many diet plans that promise you to lose weight can say they also help your brain function better, prevent diseases, and make your skin look younger? How many can say there is a chance you can live longer because of this plan? Not many. But when you trigger autophagy in your body, you can get all of that along with losing weight.

Now, the caveat here is that you have to have weight to lose. This only works for people who are not at their ideal weight for the age and height. This is because your autophagy process will drop you down to this ideal weight range, but no lower unless you force it, and then you lose the benefits of autophagy. Instead, you should focus on getting to that healthy weight and let your body continue to regulate your health from there. You can follow any of the methods mentioned earlier in this book to help you lose weight, but one of them that is particularly beneficial for women is intermittent fasting. But this does not mean it does not work well for men as well!

For example, in a study conducted at the University of Florida by Dr. Stephen Anton, the participants who fasted for 24 hours every other day saw notable weight loss compared to their counterparts. And these results were replicated ten times; each time those that participated in the intermittent fasting protocol saw significant weight loss. And alongside the weight loss, the study indicated several other health benefits these participants enjoyed from "switching up" their metabolism.

This switch is when your body moves from burning glucose to fat. You no longer rely on glucose and blood sugar to fuel your body and instead look to fatty acids and ketones. This is how you can get at those stubborn fat pockets that never seem to go away, no matter what diet you have tried before. When you are wanting to gain muscle and burn fat, you want to turn to your fat stores to burn off. It is the best and most natural fuel for your body. Once you begin burning your body fat, you no longer start storing it. As you run through your stores of fat, the food that does come in is burned before it can linger. This is why and how you lose weight and keep it off through autophagy. Your body is programmed to do this at its most basic, cellular level, and will thank you when you do it by being at its healthy weight, clearest skin, focused brain, and overall healthy body. You will not get as sick as often because your immune system is functioning at optimal levels. Your body is constantly targeting, repairing, removing, and regenerating cells, tissues, and organs while you fast and sleep. You are giving it the time and space to be able to do this.

Of course, this is more of a lifestyle than a temporary or "fad" diet. Triggering autophagy and entering into ketosis needs to be consistent so your body is constantly supporting your health and weight goals. In addition, once you lose the weight and drop to your healthy weight range, as you continue to burn fat and heal your body, you will be able to lose a few more pounds as you replace more fat stores with muscles and healthy tissue. You can only enjoy this benefit if you keep up the plan. This is where some plans can be too restrictive and can lead to backsliding. You can experience short-term weight loss but then fail to continue the diet and you gain back all the weight, and often more than you lost. In one statistic, it is estimated that more than 95% of women who lose weight through an extreme diet was unable to keep the weight off. The study also indicated that the health and weight of these women were worse after the diet than it was before. You do not want to be in that "boat," so make sure you choose a method for triggering the autophagy that is sustainable for you. Or choose a plan that you think you can work your way into and stay there for a length of time.

It is great to experience rapid weight loss and improved health, but you also want it to be realistic for the long-term. This may mean you start off "slow," triggering autophagy once or twice a week through a day of intermittent fasting and a day of intense exercise, or you choose a stretch of five days one month to try the fasting-mimicking diet. The goal is to start by experimenting with the different options until you decide a process that works for you and then stick with it. That is how you can enjoy the long-term results possible with an upregulated autophagy process.

Thankfully, in most instances, you can still enjoy your favorite treats and foods on your "off" days. In all three methods described in this book, none of them said you never could have a piece of cake, glass of wine, beer, or a piece of pizza again. In fact, you can enjoy those when you want, as long as it is not on a day you are fasting. Of course, your results are better if you minimize these "treats," but take a moment to think about how much easier it will be on yourself when you say, "I cannot have that donut today, but I will save it for tomorrow when I am no longer fasting." Or, "I am not going to go out to lunch today, but will take a walk outside instead. When I am done with my current triggering process I am going to make sure to treat myself to a nice dinner out."

If you want to combine the ketogenic diet with intermittent fasting, you can restrict food for 12 to 24 hours completely and then cycle in higher-levels of protein. Doing this sends your body from deprivation to intense intake, activating your autophagy process more frequently. The fasting process lowers your glucose and then the protein comes in it triggers it starting autophagy.

There is no hard and fast rule for how often you should be triggering your autophagy response for weight loss and health. This will most likely depend on you and your preferences. Some research suggests for the best results you should conduct and intermittent fast on three non-consecutive days during the week. You can rotate the days or keep them the same from week to week. This may not be feasible with your schedule or it can fit in well. If three days is too much, consider alternating it so you have a couple days one week and three days another. If you are following the fasting-mimicking diet to lose weight and trigger autophagy, aim for about five days on the diet plan about once a month. If this is too much, plan to follow the diet at least once a quarter or twice a year. Extended water fasting can be done for one to 20 days, depending on your body and needs. If you choose to follow this method, you should do so under the guidance of a professional and adjust or introduce food in when necessary.

If you want to follow the method below, it can help you lose weight and keep it off quickly. You will first begin by choosing three days out of the week that you will call your "low" days. These are designed to trigger your autophagy by stressing your cells through nutrient restriction. The remaining four days of the week are your "high" days and will begin to inhibit your autophagy response. The "low" days will include an overnight fast totaling 16 hours. For the last eight hours of the day, cut back on your protein intake significantly. Try to eat less than 25 grams of protein in this time frame. On your "high" days, enjoy. No restrictions!

The purpose of this meal plan is to increase weight loss, trigger autophagy, and support a long-term eating plan for the best results. You are activating and inhibiting autophagy constantly through this process. You need to have the "low" days with some intake after a fast because your body requires nutrients to survive. It cannot stay in a constant state of deprivation. This is what leads to starvation, the inhibition of autophagy, and eventually death. Also, restricting protein completely is not good for you either. Cutting it out altogether can lead to immune diseases and increased health risks, as well as muscle deterioration. This cyclical nature of the plan allows your body to get what it needs while also benefiting from the activated autophagy.

In addition to the minimal "low" days during the week, you get to choose when they will be! Of course, the "low" days need to remain non-consecutive, but you can select what is best for you based on your schedule. And they do not need to be the same from week to week. Also, on your "high" days, do not hold yourself back from what you want. You may notice over time that you tend to select healthier foods and are eating less, but that should come naturally and not be forced. It is this approach that helps keep this diet plan sustainable. A word of advice on choosing your "low" days is to avoid choosing a weekend for a "low." This is because most events and special treats occur on Saturday and Sunday. Consider Monday, Wednesday, and Friday as "low" days. This means every weekend you can indulge, as well as on Tuesdays and Thursdays!

To help further illustrate, here is a breakdown of what this could look like for you and your weight loss journey:

Day

Restriction

Sunday

High- No limits!

Monday

Low- fast overnight for a total of 16 hours, minimal protein intake not to exceed 25 grams for eight hours

Tuesday

High- No limits!

Wednesday

Low- fast overnight for a total of 16 hours, minimal protein intake not to exceed 25 grams for eight hours

Thursday

High- No limits!

Friday

Low- fast overnight for a total of 16 hours, minimal protein intake not to exceed 25 grams for eight hours

Saturday

High- No limits!

Make sure to customize this plan to fit your life. That is how you can best use autophagy triggering to fit into your life for a long time. Move your days and times around until you get a mix that makes sense for you. Or try another method mentioned in the book. There are plenty of options available to you for losing weight with autophagy. You just need to start triggering it!

CONCLUSION

Thank for making it through to the end of *Autophagy: Body's Natural Intelligence for Anti-Aging and Healing – Intermittent Fasting for Weight Loss & Self-Cleansing*. Let's hope it was informative and able to provide you with all of the tools you need to achieve your goals whatever they may be.

The next step on your journey, now that you have learned about what autophagy, is learn how it impacts your body in a variety of ways and determine what you are going to do with this information. Are you going to use it to help lose weight, protect your brain, reset your immune system, clear your skin, and support your general health? If so, how are you planning on doing it? There are different options presented to you in this book. You can choose what you think will work best for you and get started.

Below is a step-by-step guide for getting started:

1. Determine why you want to trigger autophagy. Is it for weight loss? Or is it to help prevent disease and illness? Be clear about your "why" and your purpose.

2. Enlist people to support you on your journey. Tell your loved ones, friends, and family about what you want to do and why. Ask them to support and encourage you as you experiment with finding a process that works for you. Maybe even find another person to embark on this journey with you!

3. Choose or develop a strategy that you think will work best in your life. Look into adding intense exercise into your week, partake in extended water fasting, intermittent fasting, fasting-mimicking or even the intermittent fasting and protein cycling plan presented in the last chapter. There are numerous combinations and options you can choose from, including type and frequency. Take a moment to look at your calendar and determine what you think will realistically fit in.

4. Clear out temptations and distractions from your kitchen, car, and work. Anything that does not fit with your strategy needs to go. Plan out some healthy meals that fit with your plan, gather up snacks that you can grab on the run, and prepare for your first trial.

5. Get started! Set a day to begin, tell your support system, and start.

Remember, you do not need to always accomplish your goals. If you do not make it through your first try, do not give up! This is just the beginning. Learn from the first attempt and adjust to better suit your situation the next time. Each time you give your plan a try, learn from what works and what does not, and adjust for next time. You are making great strides for your health, and each attempt is furthering you on this journey. Keep it up!

Finally, if you found this book useful in any way, a review on Amazon is always appreciated!